TELEVISION STUDIES
THE BASICS

Television Studies: The Basics provides a thorough overview of central debates in the field of television studies, and draws from a range of examples across the world.

Elana Levine, *University of Wisconsin-Milwaukee, USA*

Miller has pulled off the trick of writing something for both the student and the connoisseur, for combining an informed review of the field with bursts of genuine originality. In the terminology of his subject, this is a must-read TV guide.

Justin Lewis, *University of Cardiff, UK*

Television Studies: The Basics is a lively introduction to the study of a powerful medium. It examines the major theories and debates surrounding production and reception over the years and considers both the role and future of television.

Topics covered include:

* broadcasting history and technology
* institutions and ownership
* genre and content
* audiences.

Complete with global case studies, questions for discussion, and suggestions for further reading, this is an invaluable and engaging resource for those interested in how to study television.

Toby Miller is Professor of Media & Cultural Studies at the University of California, Riverside.

The Basics

TELEVISION STUDIES
THE BASICS

toby miller

Routledge
Taylor & Francis Group

LONDON AND NEW YORK

First published 2010
by Routledge
2 Park Square, Milton Park, Abingdon, Oxon OX14 4RN

Simultaneously published in the USA and Canada
by Routledge
711 Third Avenue, New York, NY 10017

Routledge is an imprint of the Taylor & Francis Group, an Informa business

© 2010 Toby Miller

Typeset in Bembo by Wearset Ltd, Boldon, Tyne and Wear

British Library Cataloguing in Publication Data
A catalogue record for this book is available from the British Library

Library of Congress Cataloging in Publication Data
Miller, Toby.
Television studies : the basics / Toby Miller.
p. cm.
Includes bibliographical references.
1. Television broadcasting. 2. Television. I. Title.
PN1992.5M55 2009
384.55′4–dc22

2009026603

ISBN13: 978-0-415-77423-9 (hbk)
ISBN13: 978-0-415-77424-6 (pbk)
ISBN13: 978-0-203-85419-8 (ebk)

CONTENTS

ACKNOWLEDGMENTS

Many thanks to Manuel Alvarado, Sarah Berry, Natalie Foster, Virginia Keeny, Linda Kim, Amanda Lucas, Rick Maxwell, Inka Salovaara Moring, Dana Polan, Kristina Riegert, Dominic Thomas, Graeme Turner, Katy Warren, and all involved in the production of this book.

INTRODUCTION
THE TELEVISUAL SUBLIME

Television. Maybe it was all a study in the art of mummification. The effect of the medium is so evanescent that those who work in its time apparatus feel the need to preserve themselves, delivering their bodies to be lacquered and trussed, sprayed with the rarest of pressurized jellies, all to one end, a release from the perilous context of time.

(Don De Lillo 1994: 136)

The discovery and use of, let us say, radium had a profound effect in medical methods. Properly used it was a boon to mankind. Improperly used it killed. In this respect, television is like radium but with one difference – radium is rare; television is exactly the opposite, for it is destined to encompass the world. With the passing of every day this genie is growing bigger and stronger.

(Richard Whittaker Hubbell 1942: 223)

In theory, democracy begs for the ear. In action, it challenges the eye.

(David Sarnoff 2004: 309)

A spectre haunts television: the Internet.

(Paul Attallah 2007: 346)

What *is* television? It stands for so many things, in so many contexts, for so many different people that the answer could cover a dozen books. A short list might include fun, boredom, public service, profit, sport, action, news, men, the United States, movies, color, disaster, routine, poisonous fumes, toxic parts, sweated manufacture, and ragpicker recycling. TV is an object produced in a factory that is distributed physically (via transportation) and virtually (via advertising). At that point it transmogrifies into a fashion statement, a privileged (or damned) piece of furniture that is there to be stared at. Audiences are the opium of television – it craves them, longing to control their time and space. When they become sick of it, their set becomes outmoded junk, full of poisons and pollutants in search of a dumping ground. In short, television has a physical existence, a history of material production and consumption, in addition to its renown as a site for making meaning. It is "an entertainment medium; a scientific phenomenon; a multifaceted industry ... a feature of modern *public* life which has a place in nearly every *private* home" (Stokes 2000: 1).

Television is very old, despite the fact that very few viewers existed until the 1950s, and, *pace* the quotation immediately above, vast numbers still don't own a set; in West Africa, for example, it remains basically an urban phenomenon (Osei-Hwere 2008: 180). In what sense, then, has TV been around so long and in so many locations? Because people have always fantasized about transmitting and receiving sounds and images across space via a box. Richard Whittaker Hubbell made the point by publishing a book in 1942 (before almost anyone possessed a TV) entitled *4000 Years of Television*. The device even has its own patron saint, Clare of Assisi, a teen runaway from the thirteenth century who became the first Franciscan nun and was canonized in 1958 for her bedridden vision of images from a midnight mass cast upon the wall. Centuries later, Pius XII declared that this was the world's first broadcast (Berger 2002; Pattenden 2008).

So television has long been part of our fantasy structure. In 1879, a *Punch* magazine cartoon imagined a husband and wife seated in front of their wide-screen set, watching mixed-doubles tennis (Settel and Laas 1969: 10). The idea was even connected to the telephone from the latter's beginnings in the 1870s, when Alexander Graham Bell envisaged sending images through his new invention (Uricchio 2008: 290). Yet we think it's novel to hear "Your television is ringing" (Standage 2006)! The word "television" was coined by the Russian academic Constantin Perskyi at the 1900 Paris International Electricity Congress. His hybrid etymology – using both Greek and Latin to name an apparatus that could bring sight from far away – nicely encapsulates the slightly illegitimate nature of TV (Lange 2003). Hugo Gernsback, editor of the first science-fiction magazine, wrote an article for *Modern Electrics* in 1909 that proposed television should be a two-way device. He envisaged it as "two mirrors" linked electrically. The complex, multi-sited development of televisual technologies in the 1920s and 1930s saw manifold conflicts of both people and methods – mad-cap and hyper-rational inventors pitched against and alongside corporations; governments and companies circling one another over who would control the coming marvel; debates over whether radio would dwarf and ultimately destroy TV; different nation-states vying to be "first" with a functioning, competitive apparatus; and scientists struggling over whether optical-mechanical or electronic-scan lines would make the best images and most reliable devices (Uricchio 2008: 297).

In the Hollywood movie *Murder By Television* (Clifford Sanforth 1935), large media companies covet the new technology, but are confounded by its inventor, Professor Houghland. He refuses to obtain a patent, because he wants to sequester television from conventional notions of property so that it can become "something more than another form of entertainment." Houghland puts on a grand demonstration, joining people across the US, then taking them live to Paris, London, and an unnamed Asian city. It's all part of a grand design to "make of this earth a paradise we've all envisioned but have never seen." But just at Houghland's moment of triumph, when TV seems set to assure "the preservation of humanity" and "make of this earth a paradise," he is killed on-screen. A doctor secretly involved with "foreign governments" (a cable to him in code is signed "J. V. S." – Soviet dictator Joseph Stalin's initials) uses the sound of a telephone ringing back in his office to radiate waves that merge with great spirals emanating from the television set to create an "interstellar frequency … a death ray." The message is clear: Houghland's invention incorporates the best and the worst of human thought and guile, and the mystery of modern life; his public-broadcasting, not-for-profit model cannot be cordoned off from capitalism; and his invention can enter the minds of spectators to control their thoughts and harm them.

As TV came close to realization, it attracted intense critical speculation. In a 1930 edition of the *Daily Worker*, a socialist newspaper, activist Samuel Brody argued that television in the US would seek to pacify audiences through "the same authentic lies" as cinema. Conversely, the Soviet Union would deploy television to "build socialism and a better world for the laboring masses" (1988: 106).

In 1935, aesthetics philosopher Rudolf Arnheim wrote a "Forecast of Television." He predicted that it would offer viewers simultaneous global experiences, from railway disasters, professorial addresses, and town meetings to boxing title-fights, dance bands, carnivals, and aerial mountain views – a spectacular montage of Athens, Broadway, and Vesuvius. TV could surpass the limitations of linguistic competence and interpretation. It might even bring global peace by showing spectators that "we are located as one among many." But this was no naive welcome. Arnheim warned that "television is a new, hard test of our wisdom." The emergent medium's easy access to knowledge would either enrich its viewers, stimulating an informed public, vibrant and active – or impoverish them, manufacturing an indolent audience, domesticated and passive (Arnheim 1969: 160–3).

Two years later, Barrett C. Kiesling said "it is with fear and trembling that the author approaches the controversial subject of television" (1937: 278), while the noted children's writer and essayist E.B. White argued in 1938 that it was "going to be the test of the modern world" (1997: 2). David Sarnoff, President of RCA, poured millions of dollars into research and development to "bring to the home a complete means of instantaneous participation in the sights and sounds of the outer world" (1942), and Adolph Bolm from the Ballets Russes welcomed television, because "to the dancer, the choreographer, and the painter it offers something unique" (1942). Hubbell praised TV's potential to "make a classroom of an entire nation" and teach the public "fine arts, surgery, or extinguishing fire bombs" (1942: 221). (Does this remind you of today's cybertarian claims about the Internet, by any chance?)

Hubbell saw the emergence of television as "a story of time and space annihilated, telescoped into the pulse beat of an electron." It had the potential to "create or consume entire nations" (1942: 9). White thought the new "peephole of science" would transport us "beyond the range of our vision," to reveal "either a new and unbearable disturbance of our general peace or a saving radiance in the sky: We shall stand or fall by television – of that I am quite sure" (1997: 2). Sarnoff hoped for "the greatest opportunity ever given us for creating close ties of understanding among the peoples of the world" (2004: 310). At the same time, he warned that TV's location "in the intimate background of one's home" made it "a far more powerful force than anything we have yet known," with the capacity to transmit "propaganda intended to arouse racial animosities, religious hatreds, and destructive class struggles" (1942). By 1949, the notion of a joyously interactive system of electric two-way mirrors was reimagined as a system of centralized surveillance and domination in George Orwell's *1984* (1977). Pope Pius XII issued an encyclical letter in 1957 admiring television's capacity to communicate "the news, thoughts and usages of every nation" as "food for the mind especially during the hours of recreation." TV offered the Vatican a means of uniting "the worldwide flock with its Supreme Pastor." But unless it was "subjected to the sweet yoke of Christ," the new technology might be a "source of countless evils," by enslaving viewers' minds.

These hopes and concerns have never really gone away. The first international multi-sited television program, 1967's *Our World*, reached 400 million people across thirty-one countries, most famously debuting The Beatles' "All You Need is Love," a stinging critique of US and Soviet imperialism. But even here, there were limitations to the utopia, because First, Second, and Third World political–economic differences restricted participation in the broadcast (Bignell and Fickers 2008a: 28; Parks 2005). On the other side of the ledger, right up to the 1970s, apartheid South Africa prohibited TV on the grounds that it would dilute the Afrikaner way of life, indoctrinate viewers into Marxism, and encourage liberation for blacks (Boateng 2008: 194–5). This utopic/dystopic oscillation is comically captured in Glen David Gold's novel *Carter Beats the Devil* (2001), where a young magician must battle Satan for control of television and preserve its eccentric inventor, Philo T. Farnsworth (who in real life had the invention wrested from him for corporate capitalism by RCA's Vladimir Zworykin).

This diabolical struggle often shames viewers as well as critics. Consider this Ivy League professor recalling New Haven follies of 1953:

In those days a Yale faculty member who owned a television set lived dangerously. In the midst of an academic community, he lived in sin. Nevertheless, in an act of defiance, we put our television set in the living room instead of the basement or the garage where most of the faculty kept theirs, and we weathered the disapprobation of colleagues who did not own or would not admit to owning this fascinating but forbidden instrument.

(Silber 1968: 113)

Half-a-century later, Argentina's *Ciudad* says: "Demonizar la television es parte de la lógica del medio" ["Demonizing television is part of the logic of the medium"] (Iribarren 2005).

Why has this essentially domestic entertainment device caused so much anxiety? Perhaps because it was the first technology to stream images and sounds into domestic as well as public space, TV has received the greatest attention (largely critical) of any cultural medium: in the eloquent words of its first great scholar, Dallas Smythe, television channels an immense "flow of representations of the human condition" (1954: 143). Most programs are dedicated to entertainment, and that focus, along with the ease of use and the double pull of vision and sound, have long produced embarrassment and even shame – for producers as well as viewers. The Director-General of the BBC at the time the new medium was becoming popular, William Haley, refused to have a set in his own home, and instructed TV executives to ensure viewers did not watch it much. This ambivalence was shared across the Atlantic: it is rumored that Jack Warner insisted that television sets never be part of Warner Bros. movies' *mises-en-scène* (though TV became a profitable home for washed-up movies, washed-up stars, and recovering and non-recovering studio alcoholics) (Airey 2004; Attallah 2007: 326; Becker 2008). Consider this exchange in Alfred Hitchcock's *Dial M for Murder* (1954):

TONY: You write for the radio, don't you?
MARK: No, television; for my sins.

US producer David Susskind confided to 1950s readers of *Life* magazine that he was "mad at TV because I really love it and it's lousy. It's a very beautiful woman who looks abominable" (quoted in

Schramm *et al*. 1961: 3). This sexist metaphor exemplifies the seemingly ineradicable binary opposition of televisual uplift versus televisual degradation. Such dreams and concerns about TV have never receded. Fifty years later, Fox Entertainment president and former NBC executive Kevin Reilly said: "NBC is like the crazy ex-wife I can't get away from" (quoted in Friedman 2009b).

And women were central to corporate calculations about TV from the very first, because they were expected to spend more time in the home than other potential viewers. In the early days of tuning sets, it was thought they would be unable to cope with the technical challenges of reception. Then there was the question of the unpaid labor they were doing in the home – how could that crucial economic and social service continue while they fell captive to commercials? The US strategy, which became orthodoxy elsewhere, was to drop plans for reconstructing the cinema in the home. Earlier assumptions about television repeating the immersive world of movies – lights off, full attention, and immobility – were rejected in favor of a distracted experience. Like radio, TV would be just one aspect of home life alongside demanding children, husbands, and tasks. Its visuals would reinforce a message that could be understood in another room or while doing chores – the volume would go up when the commercials came on (Morley 2007: 277).

These discourses about the emerging device and its broadcasts have formed a lasting trend, which I call the "televisual sublime." In his 1954 testimony before an anti-leftist hearing held by the US Atomic Energy Commission, the noted physicist J. Robert Oppenheimer, who led the group that had developed the atomic bomb, and which ironically included many progressives like himself who were soon removed from office, talked about the instrumental rationality that animated the people who created this awesome technology. Once these scientists saw that it was feasible, the bomb's impact diminished in intellectual and emotional significance. They had been overtaken by the "technically sweet" quality of the technology (United States Atomic Energy Commission 1954: 81).

This "technically sweet" element is part of the love of new technology, the drive for innovation, early adoption, and the mix of the sublime – the awesome, the ineffable, the uncontrollable, the powerful – with the beautiful – the approachable, the attractive, the pliant, the soothing. In philosophical aesthetics, the sublime and the beautiful are generally regarded as opposites. The unique quality of consumer technology, especially television, has been to combine them. This is true at an industrial as well as an experiential level; many of the companies involved in developing then broadcasting TV, such as Westinghouse, General Electric, and Du Pont, also participated in the development of nuclear energy and weaponry – and advertised *on* TV from the earliest days. The US Advertising Council even sponsored television's coverage of bomb tests in 1952, under the auspices of the Atomic Energy Commission (Nelson 1992: 12, 37, 42, 44).

As it spread around the globe after World War II, TV became the most important cultural and political device in people's homes. Ever since, there has been widespread cultural anxiety at the supposed lack of "active choice" entailed in watching it (Carson 1983). The famous twentieth-century architect Frank Lloyd Wright called television "Chewing gum for the eyes" (quoted in Kellner 1990: 1). Novelist and attorney Andrew Vachss' hard-bitten, damaged criminal Burke, denizen of Manhattan's underworld, says: "If America is a nation of sheep, TV is the shepherd" (2006: 132). White Dot: The International Campaign Against Television (whitedot.org) peddles keychains designed to turn off any set, and signs for restaurants boasting that they do not have TVs. It invites people who grew up before television to publish their memories online of that "better" time. And Wilco's noted album *Kicking Television* (2005) sets up live music as a means of losing one's addiction to the apparatus. In Philip Roth's *The Dying Animal* (the inspiration for Isabel Coixet's 2008 feature film, *Elegy*), David Kepesh, a professor and cultural critic, defines himself and his tastes in opposition to popular culture. Kepesh bitterly, glibly inveighs against "TV doing what it does best: the triumph of trivialization over tragedy" (2002: 145). But his philandering with graduate students, he realizes, relies not on his sagacity but its platform – television itself, where he presents a regular slot avowing how dreadful TV is (2002: 1)! In *From Russia, With Love*, James Bond's faithful housekeeper, May Maxwell, calls it "the sinful thing" (Fleming 1984: 92). But away from her monitorial gaze in *You Only Live Twice*, Bond finds a consoling feeling of modernity in his Kyoto hotel room thanks to a crime series (Fleming 1964: 117). The same logocentric interdependence on what is both loathed and loved, the sublime and the beautiful, can be seen in the snobbery that creates hierarchies within the industry – HBO promotes itself with the slogan: "It's not television. It's HBO."

Educators are often greatly afeared of television. A slew of studies seeking to account for the alienation between college students and their professors places the blame for student disinterest in pedagogy on the popular, and especially TV, which is held responsible for "prolonged immaturity" (Bauerlein 2006: B8; Lasch 1979: 226–8). Britain's Association of Teachers and Lecturers surveyed 800 members in 2009 on this subject, and gleaned the following:

> 66 per cent said that *Big Brother* [2000–] was the programme that caused most poor behaviour among pupils, closely followed by *Little Britain* [2003–] at 61 per cent and *EastEnders* [1985–] at 43 per cent. Staff say these programmes led to general rudeness, such as answering back, mimicking, using retorts and TV catch-phrases (mentioned by 88 per cent), and swearing or using inappropriate language (mentioned by 82 per cent). Aggressive behaviour was highlighted by 74 per cent of those surveyed, and sexually inappropriate behaviour by 43 per cent.
>
> (atl.org.uk/media-office/media-archive/Inappropriate-behaviour.asp)

Neil Postman's *Amusing Ourselves to Death* (1987) tropes Aldous Huxley to condemn popular culture, especially television. Postman favored writing and reading over filming and watching. He contrasted a lost past of creative civilization with a pesky present of dishpan dross dominated by mindless consumerist entertainment. *Amusing Ourselves to Death* sold over 200,000 copies and was translated into several languages. It inspired a Roger Waters album (*Amused to Death* (1992)) and public-broadcasting debates in Canada and the US, became a memorable phrase in the English language, and made its author a noted figure within the media, where, Kepesh-like, he would appear on television denouncing the very forum that opened up to him.

Postman's argument against technology was made at a personal level, with his own subjectivity a guarantor of its validity – he famously wrote in longhand and declined to type. (Of course, that meant others performed such labor on his behalf.) He wouldn't use social-science or semiotic methods to analyze television. In fact he declined to deploy most academic knowledge about TV, apart from work done by his own inspirations, mentors, or students, paying virtually no heed to media, cultural, or communication studies. For instance, John Fiske and John Hartley's *Reading Television* (1980), which preceded his own success by several years and sold over 100,000 copies across seven languages, may as well never have happened. But the work Postman did fits into a very powerful critique of television. Alive only to shifts in the forces of production, he occupied a determinedly anti–Marxist frame that disavowed labor and conflict. His contempt for ordinary people as audiences, and his valorization of a better day long gone, effortlessly buys into nostalgia. Postman's allegedly halcyon era – the mid-nineteenth century – saw women disenfranchised, African-Americans enslaved, and the culture he favored being delivered by, to, and for white, property-owning men. In short, his better day was the supposedly quiet, deliberative domain before the crowd expressed itself. Yet this wistful, willful nostalgia continues to draw people into its mythic historical vision.

Policy-makers, too, are troubled by the people's device. The US-based Trilateral Commission, a foundation of corporate leaders and coin-operated intellectuals dedicated to strengthening capitalist societies, was founded in 1973 to solve, *inter alia*, the problem of awkwardly ungovernable populations in the era of TV. The Commission argued that television promoted an adversarial approach to political culture, emphasizing difference and debate rather than legitimacy and leadership. It distinguished a need for order from a need for democracy. TV was found wanting because it had made excessive contributions on behalf of the latter. Neoconservative and neoliberal critics continue to warn that it has become anti-free-enterprise, anti-family, anti-development, and anti-authority. The leading bourgeois economist Jagdish Bhagwati is convinced that television is partly to "blame" for global grass-roots activism against globalization, since it makes people identify with those suffering from capitalism. Bhagwati deems this TV empathy to be counterproductive, because it has not led to rational action (i.e. support for the neoclassical economic policies he supports, which many would say caused the problem). But he also maintains that television can be a savior! There is no need to litigate against companies that pollute the environment, or impose sanctions on states that enslave children, because "in today's world of CNN ... multinationals and their host governments cannot afford to alienate their constituencies" (Bhagwati 2002: 4, 6).

On the left, TV is frequently identified as a crucial component of advanced capitalism, a site for delimiting, molding, and controlling people's needs, and ensuring routinely high levels of consumption. Television is the key point of articulation between the requirements of a massively complicated economic system and the daily lives of people whose individual patterns of purchasing and laboring both service and are serviced *by* it. It is an effective device of ideological mystification, where economic travail in search of meeting basic needs is never adequately addressed, and viewers are subject to a false consciousness of happiness through the presentation of misleading versions of what their lives should be like. For feminists and anti-racists, TV is often derided for the demeaning, inaccurate, and stereotypical ways that it represents women and minorities (Kellner 1990; Miller 2002).

Of course, many people say TV is finished today, that it no longer matters. The rhetoric of newer audiovisual media is inflected with the phenomenological awe of a precocious child set to heal the wounds of modern life, magically reconciling public and private, labor and leisure, commerce and culture, citizenship and consumption. The alleged upshot? It's *La fin de la télévision* [*The End of Television*] (Missika 2006) or *La televisión ha muerto* [*Television is dead*] (De Silva 2000) and the Internet is the future. The grand organizer of daily life over half a century has lost its pride of place in the physical layout of the home and the daily order of drama and data. We must all say "Bienvenidos al mundo de la postelevisión" ["Welcome to the post-television world"], where dual monopolies have been broken: the physical object no longer dominates, and nor does its model of unidirectional production. TV has lost its identity (Verón 2008).

Yet the evidence for such claims is sparse and thin. Historically, it is true that most new media have supplanted earlier ones as central organs of authority or pleasure, as per books versus speeches, films versus plays, and records versus performances. But TV blended all of them, becoming a warehouse of contemporary culture that converged what had gone before (Newcomb 2005,

110; Standage 2006). It is true that the corporate music industry is shrinking due to the Internet, with double-digit decreases in compact-disc sales over the last decade, and that the Internet is displacing newspapers in the Global North as a key source of political and commercial information. But corporate and public TV continue to grow by every indicator imaginable (Friedman 2008d; Pew Research Center 2008; Spangler 2009). Television still occupies vast amounts of people's time and money, because it delivers information and entertainment with astonishing speed and ease. The early signs are that the Internet and TV will transform one another. After all, what are computer and telephone screens based on as entertainment forms anyway? In the words of Steve Ballmer, Microsoft's chief executive, "we will see TVs become more sophisticated and more connected. The boundary between the PC and the TV will dissolve" (quoted in Moses 2009; for more on the company's views, see Microsoft 2009). Similarly, *La Tempestad*'s 2008 dossier on the subject asked: "¿Está en la televisión el futuro del cine?" ["Does the future of cinema lie in TV?"].

Consider the United States, often a harbinger of media futures (for better or worse); as the editors of *A European Television History* put it, "American television becomes a horizon towards which all television seems to progress" (Bignell and Fickers 2008a: 4). In 2006, more than 98 percent of US homes had at least one set, while 64 percent had cable, up twenty points in twenty years. Consumers spent US$20 billion buying new TVs that year. By 2007, 51 percent of people owned three or more (the proportion was 44 percent in Britain) (Motion Picture Association of America 2007: 35, 37; Borland and Hansen 2007; Ellis 2007: 40). In 2008, the number of US households owning televisions increased by 1.5 percent, with particularly significant growth among migrants and their recent descendants. Of the top 100 brands recognized by residents in 2009, sixteen were TV or film-related, with CNN and MTV in the top ten (Reynolds 2009).

The US population watched more television in 2005 than a decade earlier – *an hour more* than in that basically pre-web era. In 2007, AOL Television and the Associated Press polled US residents on their viewing habits. Over one-quarter of the population said they watched more than three hours a day, while 13 percent watched more than thirty hours a week, up five points on 2005.

TV is more popular than ever. Ratings disclose that the average household watched eight and a quarter hours of television daily, and individuals four and a half hours in 2006 – record numbers. And in 2008, the statistically most significant change in leisure activities was the increase in time watching TV. Even the venerable (if un-venerated) Academy Awards saw a ratings increase of 13 percent in 2009 ("Precious Little Time" 2008; "What Impact" 2008; Grindstaff and Turow 2006: 119; "Nielsen Media" 2006; Cabletelevision Advertising Bureau 2007; Rash 2009).

In the US, children between the ages of six and fourteen are tuned to television at rates unprecedented for twenty years; 69 percent of them have sets in their bedrooms, versus 18 percent with Internet access and 49 percent owning or subscribing to video-games (Pew Research Center 2005). Those aged between two and eleven watched 17.34 hours of TV a week in 2006, an increase on the previous year; in Britain, they watch more than fifteen hours. The keenest viewers are young girls. They quite like new technology, and adopt it at a frenetic pace – but "TV is king," in the words of The Tubes' album *Remote Control* (1979) (Downey 2007a; Ofcom 2009: 109; Friedman 2009h).

The average US resident watched 127 and a quarter hours of television a month in 2006, as opposed to spending twenty-six-and-a-half hours online and two-and-a-quarter hours with their cells; in 2009, 93 percent of adults watched at least an hour of TV a day, but just 4 percent watched an hour of video online each day. Video texts are mostly consumed on television and in real time: time-shifting occupies 5 percent of spectators, and the same proportion of cell-phone owners watch video on them. People under the age of twenty-four spend fewer hours on the Internet than older users, but watch more video. Three-quarters of people have viewed TV at some point or another online – but they spend seventy times more hours a month doing so via a conventional set. Those born between 1984 and 1990, a desirable demographic both commercially and politically because their fundamental desires are not yet formed in terms of preferred brands, choose television over the Internet and the cell-phone, for both entertainment and information. Half the Internet sites that children aged between six and eleven visit attract their attention through advertising on TV or in print. Right across the age spectrum, television is the most influential advertising medium, and its influence is greater than during the pre-Web period. Hundreds of case studies undertaken over the past two decades confirm that TV is the principal source of raising brand awareness. But as there ceases to be a one-stop location for viewers, the larger stations face huge difficulties in maintaining their level of advertising ("Nielsen Reports Growth" 2008; "Majority of Americans" 2007; Shields 2009; "Nielsen Reports" 2008; "Kids Motivated" 2009; Gonsalves 2008; Neff 2009; Thomasch 2009). In Britain, people turned more and more to television as the twenty-first-century recession deepened, with distinct increases in ratings across 2008, while 94 percent of the population say TV news is their principal resource for understanding both global events and local politics (Fitzsimmons 2009; Graf 2008; Ellis 2007: 23; Gray 2009).

During the 2004 US Presidential election, 78 percent of the population followed the campaign on television, up from 70 percent in 2000 (Project for Excellence in Journalism 2005; Pew Research Center for the People & the Press 2005). Political operatives pay heed to this. Between the 2002 and 2006 mid-term elections, and across that 2004 campaign, TV expenditure on political advertising grew from US$995.5 million to US$1.7 billion – at a time of minimal inflation. That amounted to 80 percent of the growth in broadcasters' revenue in 2003–4 (vanden Heuvel 2008: 34). The 2002 election saw US$947 million spent on TV election advertising; 2004 US$1.55 billion; and 2006 US$1.72 billion. The correlative numbers for the Internet were US$5 million in 2002; US$29 million in 2004; and US$40 million in 2006 (Gueorguieva 2007). The vast majority of electronic electoral advertising takes place on local TV – 95 percent in 2007 (TNS Media Intelligence 2007; Bachman 2007).

Consider the famous Barack Obama campaign of 2008 and its much-vaunted use of the Internet. The campaign spent the vast majority of its energy and money on television. The Internet was there to raise funds and communicate with supporters. The US Presidency cycles with the summer Olympics, broadcast by General Electric (GE) subsidiary NBC, but few candidates commit funds to commercials in primetime during this epic of capitalist excess, because more powerful homologues of competition vie for screen time – athletes and corporations. Obama, however, took a multimillion dollar package across the stations owned by GE: NBC (Anglo broadcast), CNBC (business-leech cable), MSNBC (news cable), USA (entertainment cable), Oxygen (women's cable), and Telemundo (Spanish broadcast). TV was on the march, not in retreat: during the 2008 campaign, US\$2.2 billion was spent on TV and less than half a billion on radio, newspapers, magazines, and the Internet combined. On election night, CNN gained 109 percent more viewers than the equivalent evening four years earlier. And the Internet-enabled "citizen's democracy" heralded after Obama's victory? The first three months after his inauguration saw more money spent on political advertising by lobby groups (US\$270 million) than was normally the case in non-election years until September. Why? His reform agenda attracted huge expenditure by left and right on TV commercials addressing energy, labor, the environment, and health (Teinowitz 2008; Atkinson 2008; Gough 2008; Vogel 2009).

What about the old barriers to amateur producers sending and receiving sounds and images across distance? Haven't they been eroded, with YouTube open to all (5.8 billion video streams in January 2009 alone) and television soon to be forgotten? In fact, YouTube videos are the greatest boon imaginable to mainstream US TV. Rather than substituting for television programs, these excerpts and commentaries promote them, promising new business opportunities provided they can be legalized. Although amateur content forms the majority of what is on the service, it is barely watched by contrast with the vastly more popular texts of the culture industries: fifteen of its top twenty search terms are for US TV programs, and there has been a 600 percent increase since 2007 in people watching news videos from the Associated Press, Reuters, and similar corporate services. Along with the English Premier League, the Scottish Premier League, and Rodgers & Hammerstein, MTV's owner, Viacom, sued YouTube for copyright infringement because of the number of their texts that it re-screened. YouTube has been unpopular with advertisers because the amateurish texts are so variable in quality and theme and the professional ones are often illegally reproduced. So its owner, Google, reluctant to continue expending vast sums on server farms for a financially failed service at a loss of half-a-billion dollars a year, set up a new site of premium content, drawing on US TV and cinema. MTV arranged with MySpace to overlay advertising on clips that it owned, and more and more firms made deals with YouTube to license their texts (Kruitbosch and Nack 2008; Tancer 2009; Donohue 2009; "Hulu Who?" 2009; Vascellaro *et al.* 2009; DeBord 2009; Learmonth 2009a, b; Pace 2008; *Viacom et al.* v. *YouTube et al.* 07 Civ. 2103).

Television continues to proliferate. There are tens of thousands of broadcast, cable, and satellite TV stations: over 7,000 in Russia; 3,000 in China; 2,700 in the European Union; and 2,200 in the US. Almost 100 million people now subscribe to satellite television, with massive growth in the Global South (Central Intelligence Agency 2007; Euroconsult 2008). And the Global Internet TV portal global-itv.com lists over 9,000 stations available on the Web. The Organisation for Economic Co-operation and Development (OECD), the peak body of advanced capitalist democracies from the European Union to Australasia, says that its members have witnessed an explosion of television across the first years of the twenty-first century, mostly via satellite and cable. The number of networks increased from 816 in 2004 to 1,165 in 2006 – 43 percent growth. The amount of time watching TV has also increased. In 2004, people in OECD countries spent one-third of their time using the media watching television and one-fifth online. Although other OECD members exhibit only half the loyalty to TV of US viewers, it remains the most popular medium (2007: 175, 177). European data illustrate the ongoing power of television to attract advertisers. The Internet is growing slowly, and drawing money and people away from print rather than TV (see Table I.2).

In the decade since deregulation opened Europe up to more and more commercial stations and niche channels, viewing has consistently increased across dozens of nations by twenty minutes per day (Open Society 2005). And in the Global South, a "television set (or a better television set) is the main consumer priority for most people" (Straubhaar 2007: 1). In 2007, 2.5 billion people averaged over three hours a day watching TV worldwide (Thussu 2007: 593). In many parts of the world, such as southern Europe, uptake of the Internet remains slow by contrast with the Nordic countries or northern Asia (Microsoft 2009). And consider Argentina, a country on the cusp between the Third and First Worlds in living standards. For young

Table 1.1 Average household TV viewing time per day (hours)

	1997	1998	1999	2000	2001	2002	2003	2004	2005
Australia	–	–	–	–	3.3	3.3	3.2	–	–
Austria	2.37	–	2.45	2.47	2.53	2.7	2.68	2.73	2.77
Belgium (Wallonia)	3.33	–	3.47	3.5	3.6	3.6	3.6	3.67	3.83
Canada	3.25	–	3.09	3.07	3.19	3.09	–	–	–
Denmark	–	–	–	–	–	–	2.6	3	3
Finland	2.48	–	2.68	2.8	2.78	2.85	2.88	2.93	2.82
Ireland	–	–	–	–	–	2.6	2.55	–	–
Italy	–	–	–	–	–	–	3.83	4	4.1
Japan	3.56	3.7	3.58	3.75	3.85	3.61	3.7	3.91	3.71
Korea	–	–	–	3.3	3.1	3.2	3.2	3.17	–
New Zealand	2.77	2.83	2.77	2.8	2.8	2.85	2.88	2.88	2.68
Portugal	2.75	2.62	3.37	3.38	3.22	3.08	3.45	3.57	3.53
Spain	–	–	3.73	3.7	3.77	3.92	4.1	3.63	3.62
Sweden	–	2.4	2.38	2.5	2.47	2.45	–	2.52	2.43
Switzerland	2.2	2.3	2.4	2.4	2.43	2.47	2.47	2.47	2.45
Turkey	–	–	–	–	–	–	4	4	5
United Kingdom	–	–	–	–	–	–	3	–	–
United States	7.2	7.25	7.38	7.52	7.65	7.7	7.92	8.02	8.18

Source: Organisation for Economic Co-operation and Development (OECD Communications Outlook 2007: 191, OECD 2007, www.oecd.org/ sti/telecom/outlook).

Table I.2 Developments in advertising market shares for different media types in Europe (%)

	2000	2001	2002	2003	2004	2005	2006	2007
Television	31.6	31.9	32.7	33.2	33.7	33.8	34.1	34.6
Newspapers	35.0	34.0	33.1	32.3	31.9	31.7	31.3	30.8
Magazines	20.1	20.4	20.0	19.5	18.9	18.6	18.4	18.1
Billboards	6.1	6.5	6.6	6.7	6.6	6.6	6.6	6.6
Radio	5.0	5.0	5.0	6.0	6.0	6.0	6.0	6.0
Internet	1.1	1.2	1.3	1.7	2.2	2.7	2.9	3.1
Cinema	0.8	0.9	0.9	0.9	0.9	0.9	0.9	0.9

Source: Organisation for Economic Co-operation and Development (OECD Communications Outlook 2007: 192, OECD 2007, www.oecd.org/sti/telecom/outlook).

people, television is by far the medium with the greatest credibility and use – just one in twenty adolescents privilege the Internet for social and political knowledge (Morduchowicz 2008: 114, 116). The fear is that rather than being "hiper-conectados" ["hyper-connected"] people are really "hiper-segmentados e hiper-individualizados" ["hyper-segmented and hyper-individuated"] (Carboni and López 2008). In the case of Brazil, one of the world's largest economies and populations, 68 percent of people have never used the Web, while South Africa has seen the spread of television-set ownership amongst black citizens with the spread of electricity (Nigro 2008; Becker and González de Bustamante 2009: 57; van Vuuren 2004: 11).

TV is expanding the kinds of spaces where it is seen, as well. Wal-Mart, the largest retail chain in the world, has its own network, broadcast over 3,000 stores in the US; 140 corporations advertise on its six channels. The model has been emulated in China, Brazil, and Britain ("How Not" 2008). India is seeing an explosion of channels and networks, just as it is with newspapers (one more instance where cybertarians are as inaccurate as they are solipsistic in saying papers are dying out). And the core customers in the explosion of South Asian television advertising? Car manufacturers – they increased expenditure by 29 percent in 2008 and dominate the national scene (one more instance where cybertarians are as inaccurate as they are solipsistic in saying car advertising is dying out). The vaunted Indian film industry has entered the television warehouse, with big and little stars alike charging toward TV, and television actors brokering their way into cinema through mass exposure. The glamour of the industry is increasing at the same rate as its size and reach (Kamat 2009; "Overview" 2009). China has gone from fifty sets in 1958 to over 500 million today (Feng *et al.* 2008). In Brazil, about 200 sets in 1950 grew to the point where 98 percent of the nation has access. The huge TV network Globo continues to dominate public-interest knowledge – 42 percent of households with sets are tuned to its nightly news (Becker and González de Bustamante 2009: 45; Porto 2007: 368).

So it is silly to see the Internet in opposition to television; each is one more way of sending and receiving the other. The fact is that television is becoming *more* popular, not less. It is here to stay, whether we like it or not. I suspect that we are witnessing a *transformation* of TV, rather than its demise. What started in most countries as a *broadcast, national* medium, dominated by the state, is being transformed into a *cable, satellite, Internet,* and *international* medium, dominated by commerce – but still called "television." And it can shift beyond this narrative, as per the reintroduction of state ownership in twenty-first-century Russia, or the BBC winning audiences away from commercial systems and revolutionizing online viewing. A TV-like screen, located in domestic and public *spaces,* and transmitting signs from other *places,* will probably be the future.

This little book aims to help you understand television by providing a brief tour of the field of knowledge dedicated to TV. *Television Studies: The Basics* explains television theory, in Chapter 1; institutions, in Chapter 2; content, in Chapter 3; audiences, in Chapter 4; renovating TV studies, in Chapter 5; and the future, in the Conclusion. Some books about the study of television focus almost exclusively on what other academics have to say. I think that's worth knowing, but ideas about TV – and research into it – are produced by regulators, pediatricians, journalists, judges, viewers, activists, advertisers, producers, churches, women's groups, and governments as well as scholars. So you won't find endless references in this book to academic theorists, as if they alone constituted the field of knowledge about television. I'm concerned to show you how to study TV, not just cite professors.

Chapter 1 notes that television studies draws on a variety of theories and methods: ethnography to investigate production and reception; experimentation and clinical observation to connect watching television and subsequent conduct; textual and audience interpretation to speculate on psychological processes; content analysis to evaluate programming in terms of generic patterns; textual analysis to identify ideological tenor; and political economy to examine ownership, control, regulation, and international exchange.

Chapter 2 outlines the history of TV technology, the emergence of television around the world, and the role of the state, business, and labor in its development. We'll investigate public- and private-sector models, Third-World television, and the arrival of new technology, addressing regulation, deregulation, and globalization.

Chapter 3 highlights TV genres from the medium's origins to today; from the comprehensive service that provided sport, news, weather, music, comedy, and drama to contemporary stations dedicated to single kinds of programming.

Chapter 4 looks at television audiences as objects of anxiety, desire, and control via research instruments derived from communication studies, sociology, demography, the psy-function (psychoanalysis, psychology, and psychiatry), and marketing. These methods have been used by various constituencies: regulators, the psy-function itself, religionists, propagandists, and, above all, capital.

Chapter 5 offers examples of how to do TV studies by analyzing policies, programs, and topics. It draws on what has been outlined in previous chapters to offer some practical applications that should prove valuable across these three key domains.

The Conclusion thinks about the future of television. New digital environments, specifically telephones, PCs, and the Web, are transforming TV. Just as they are modeled on it, so television tries to look like them. Television tries to play well with others, as it learnt to do with earlier rivals such as radio and film.

QUESTIONS FOR DISCUSSION

(1) Is television very new or very old?
(2) Have early predictions about TV come true?

(3) How does television's history resemble the promises and panics associated with the Internet?

(4) What is the televisual sublime?

(5) Is TV over?

FURTHER READING

Arnheim, Rudolf. (1969). *Film as Art*. London: Faber & Faber.

DeLillo, Don. (1986). *White Noise*. London: Picador.

Fiske, John and John Hartley. (1980). *Reading Television*. London: Methuen.

Postman, Neil. (1987). *Amusing Ourselves to Death: Public Discourse in the Age of Show Business*. London: Methuen.

TELEVISION THEORY
TV STUDIES 1.0 AND 2.0

The finale of *The West Wing* included a quick shot of a copy of Michel Foucault's *"Society Must Be Defended": Lectures at the College de France, 1975–1976* being taken off a shelf as the office of former president Jed Bartlet (Martin Sheen) was packed up to make way for the new president, Matt Santos (Jimmy Smits).

(Dana Polan 2006)

I guess too much TV *can* rot your brain.

(Andrew Vachss 2008)

In its relentless drive to keep current … media studies has found its objects of study seemingly dictated by *Entertainment Weekly*.

(Bart Beaty 2009)

Technology is the opiate of the educated public … an end to poverty … equality of opportunity … a radical increase in individual freedom … the replacement of work by leisure … permanent but harmless social revolution … the final comeuppance of Mao Tse-tung and all his ilk … the triumph of wisdom over power … the end of ideology.

(John McDermott 1969)

I was losing my students in a ferment of curriculum changes that would eventually lead to the descheduling of Latin and Greek and their replacement by cultural and media studies. My refusal to sue the university, Elaine decided, was a sign of my innate weakness, a frailty that soon extended to the marriage bed.

(J.G. Ballard 2009)

"Television is vast" – both as an institution and an object of analysis (Hilmes 2005: 113). That vastness contributes to the televisual sublime already described. It's not surprising, then, that TV studies is characterized by major debates and differences, since its analysts "speak different languages, use different methods," and pursue "different questions" (Hartley 1999: 18). Perhaps "the most salient feature of the study of television may be its institutional dispersal" (Attallah 2007: 339).

TV has given rise to three major topics of scholarly inquiry:

- technology, ownership, and control – its political economy;
- textuality – its content; and
- audiences – its public.

Within these categories lie three further divisions:

- approaches to technology, ownership, and control vary between neoliberal endorsements of limited regulation by the state, in the interests of protecting property and guaranteeing market entry for new competitors, and Marxist critiques of the bourgeois media for controlling the socio-political agenda;
- approaches to textuality vary between hermeneutics, which unearths the meaning of individual programs and links them to broader social formations and problems, and content analysis, which establishes patterns across significant numbers of similar texts, rather than close readings of individual ones; and
- approaches to audiences vary between social–psychological attempts to validate correlations between TV and social conduct, political–economic critiques of imported texts threatening national culture, and celebrations of spectators making their own interpretations.

These tasks in turn articulate to particular academic disciplines, which are tied to particular interests of state and capital:

- engineering, computing, public policy, and "film" schools help create and run TV production and reception via business, the military, the community, and the public service;

- communication studies focuses on socio-economic projects such as propaganda, marketing, and citizenship;
- economics theorizes and polices doctrines of scarcity, and manages over-production through overseas expansion;
- Marxism points to the impact of ownership and control and cultural imperialism on TV and consciousness; and
- cultural criticism evaluates representation, justifies protectionism, and calls for content provision.

Lest this appear to be a tendentious insider's guide, you can visit the US National Center for Education Statistics' *Classification of Instructional Programs (CIP 2000)*, which categorizes mass communication/media studies as "the analysis and criticism of media institutions and media texts, how people experience and understand media content, and the roles of media in producing and transforming culture" via foci on law, policy, history, aesthetics, effects, economics, and literacy (09.0102), or the British Government's Quality Assurance Agency for Higher Education. It says that critical media literacy is essential equipment for citizenship and "mapping the contemporary" (2002) using tools from political economy, representation, aesthetics, discourse, consumption, identity, and ideology, frequently wrapped into production training (2007). The British model provides a less positivistic and reactionary set of skills, informed by social theory and progressive politics. This is in keeping with the fact that Western-European academia, for all its shortcomings, is less stitched-in than its US equivalent to either the welfare and warfare social-science bureaucracy or the high-aesthetic privilege of the philanthropic humanities and art worlds.

Many regulatory bodies with responsibility for the medium have more restrictive ideas about how to study television, especially in the US. Reed Hundt, Chair of the Federal Communications Commission (FCC) under Bill Clinton, argues that TV regulators must be "instructed at least rudimentarily in economics, antitrust, network operation, and administrative procedure" (Hundt and Rosston 2006: 33) − a drastically limited toolkit typical of the welfare−warfare bureaucracy/social-science nexus. What would be the impact if we supplemented or supplanted those skills by the labor theory of value, critiques of monopoly capital, content and textual analysis, ethnography, and effects research? This would loosen agencies like the FCC from a direct and necessary tie to the *données* of neoclassical economics, which define the public interest in narrow terms. It would jeopardize the hegemony of forms of knowledge that have no engagement with content, audiences, or producers, so certain is their lofty judgment that laissez-faire theory fits all. Right now, though, what matters is "up[-]to[-]date technical competence in law, engineering, economics, or other appropriate disciplines" (Hundt and Rosston 2006: 33). This has led to a dominant mixture of either extremely reactionary, pro-corporate cost–benefit analyses and technical specifications, or a faith in abstract empiricism, such that matters of minor import are elevated to great moment because they are amenable to statistical manipulation under controlled circumstances. The great labor historian E.P. Thompson made fun of this half a century ago with a famous essay summarizing faux research that he planned to publish in the mythic "*American Journal of Communicational Guphology*" (1959: 4n. 3).

Fractured by politics, nation, discipline, theory, and method, this dispersed field of knowledge can be bifurcated as TV Studies 1.0 and TV Studies 2.0 – both of which are subject to the televisual sublime. Television Studies 1.0 derived from the spread of new media technologies over the past two centuries into the lives of urbanizing populations, and the policing questions that posed to both state and capital. What would be the effects of these developments, and how would they vary between those with a stake in maintaining society versus transforming it? By the early twentieth century, academic experts had decreed media audiences to be passive consumers, thanks to the missions of literary criticism (distinguishing the aesthetically cultivated from others) and the psy-function (distinguishing the socially competent from others). Decades of social science have emphasized audience reactions to audiovisual entertainment: where they came from, how many there were, and what they did as a consequence of being present.

When new cultural technologies emerge, young people are identified as both pioneers and victims, simultaneously endowed by manufacturers and critics with power and vulnerability – the first to know and the last to understand cheap novels during the 1900s, silent then sound film during the teens and 1920s, radio in the 1930s, comic books of the 1940s and 1950s, pop music and television from the 1950s and 1960s, satanic rock as per the 1970s and

1980s, video-cassette recorders in the 1980s, and rap music, video games, and the Internet since the 1990s. Each of these innovations has brought an expanded horizon of texts to audiences, such that they come to be defined both in market terms and via the regulatory morality of administrators of conscience and taste. A "new practice of piety" accompanies each "new communications technology" (Hunter 1988: 220). Moral panics emerge, in scientistic frames that are created and populated by the denizens of communication studies, paediatrics, psychology, and education, who largely abjure cultural and political matters in favor of experiments on TV viewers. This is the psy-function (psychology, psychiatry, and psychoanalysis) at work. It is the heart of Television Studies 1.0.

Television Studies 1.0 also covers political economy, which focuses on ownership and control rather than audience response. Like the psy-function, this part of TV Studies 1.0 is frequently functionalist on its political–economy side, neglecting struggle, dissonance, and conflict in favor of a totalizing narrative in which television dominates everyday life and is all-powerful. TV is said to force people to turn away from precious artistic and social traces of authentic intersubjectivity by taking control of individual consciousness. The demand for television is dispersed, but its supply is centralized, so political economy regards it as one more industrial process subordinated to dominant economic forces within society that seek standardization of production. Far from reflecting preferences of consumers in reaction to tastes and desires, TV manipulates audiences from the economic apex of production. Coercion is mistaken for free will. The only element that might stand against this leveling sameness is said to be individual consciousness. But that consciousness has itself been customized to the requirements of the economy and making television programs.

There are significant ties in TV Studies 1.0 between the critical-theory tradition, which calls for a resistive consciousness through artistic rather than industrial texts, and political economy, which calls for diverse ownership and control of the industry. The first trend is philosophical and aesthetic in its desire to develop modernism and the avant garde, the second policy-oriented and political in its focus on institutional power. But they began as one with lamentations for the loss of a self-critical philosophical address and the triumph of industrialized cultural production. The two approaches continue to be linked via political economy's distaste for what is still often regarded as mass culture (Adorno and Horkeimer 1977; Garnham 1987). Conflicts to do with labor and interpretation are forgotten in favor of a pessimistic, top–down, leftist functionalism.

For Television Studies 2.0, by contrast, TV represents the apex of modernity, the first moment in history when central political and commercial organs and agendas became receptive to the popular classes. This perspective has offered a way in to research that reverses Television Studies 1.0's faith in the all-powerful agency of the apparatus. For, in TV Studies 2.0, the all-powerful agent is the television audience, not the industry. TV Studies 2.0 claims that the public is so clever and able that it makes its own meanings, outwitting institutions of the state, academia, and capitalism that seek to measure and control it. In the case of children and the media, anxieties from Television Studies 1.0 about turning Edenic innocents into rabid monsters or capitalist dupes are dismissed. TV supposedly obliterates geography, sovereignty, and hierarchy in an alchemy of truth and beauty, as per Houghland and Arnheim's 1935 hopes. The "interstellar death ray" and the nefarious, manipulative designs of governments and firms have failed. Today's deregulated, individuated world of television allegedly makes consumers into producers, frees the disabled from confinement, encourages new subjectivities, rewards intellect and competitiveness, links people across cultures, and allows billions of flowers to bloom in a post-political cornucopia. It's a kind of Marxist/Godardian wet dream, where people fish, film, fuck, frolic, and fund from morning to midnight. Sometimes, faith in the active audience reaches cosmic proportions. It has been a *donnée* of TV Studies 2.0 that television is not responsible for – well, anything. Consumption is the key – with production discounted, labor forgotten, consumers sovereign, and research undertaken by observing one's own practices of viewing and one's friends and children. This is narcissography at work, with the critic's persona a guarantor of assumed audience resistance and Dionysian revelry (Morris 1990).[1] New technology even sees some adherents of TV Studies 1.0 resigning from their former lives and signing up to join 2.0 due to their investment in a revised televisual sublime. Jean-Louis Missika argues that the classic era of television was a period of absolute domination by producers, editors, and schedulers over audiences, but it has been superseded by the freedoms of new technology (Cristiani and Missika 2007). His fellow-cybertarian Vincent Cerf, one of the seemingly limitless white men jostling to claim authorship of the Internet while boasting that no-one owns it, claims that TVs are becoming iPods – downloading devices subject to audience mastery (Martin 2007).

This strand of research, which lies at the core of Television Studies 2.0, is a very specific uptake of venerable and profound UK critiques of cultural pessimism, political economy, and current-affairs-oriented broadcasting. These critiques originated from a heavily regulated, duopolistic broadcasting system – 1950s–1970s Britain – in which the BBC represented a high-culture snobbery that many leftists associated with an oppressive class structure. Hence the desire for a playful, commercial, anti-citizen address as a counter. When this type of TV made its Atlantic crossing to the US, there was no public-broadcasting behemoth in need of critique – more a squibby amoeba "financially suspended in a vegetative state" (Chakravartty and Sarikakis 2006: 85). And there were lots of not-very-leftist professors and students seemingly aching to hear that US audiences learning about parts of the world that their country bombs, invades, owns, misrepresents, or otherwise exploits was less important, and less political, than those audiences' interpretations of actually existing soap operas, wrestling bouts, or science-fiction series. When a group of Yanqui Television Studies 2.0 scholars intervened in policy, it was to support video-game industrialists in a law case against a commercial ordinance that required manufacturers to advise parents that their products were risky for young people ("Brief" 2003; see Kline 2003).

Greg Dyke and David Putnam, famous British media executives, are highly unusual in boosting media studies as good for both citizenship and professional awareness (Burrell 2008; Beckett 2004), although Ofcom (2008b) has a *Media Literacy E-Bulletin*, amongst other initiatives. This is not surprising, because despite their complicity with many dominant ideas from neoclassical economics and the psy-function, TV Studies 1.0 and 2.0 are frequently associated with the more critical, textual, political–economic and ethnographic side of my summary. This alternative tradition attracts intense opprobrium. So Robert W. McChesney laments that the study of the media is "regarded by the pooh-bahs in history, political science, and sociology as having roughly the same intellectual merit as, say, driver's education" (2007: 16). Similar attitudes abound across the humanities (Hilmes 2005: 113): for the *Times Literary Supplement*, media and cultural studies form the "politico-intellectual junkyard of the Western world" (Minogue 1994: 27). Pet Tory philosopher Roger Scruton denounces media studies as "sub-Marxist gobbledook [*sic*]" (quoted in Beckett 2004). Probably the most-read academic work on television, *The Simpsons and Philosophy* (Irwin *et al.* 2001) sold a quarter of a million copies within six years and had no relationship to the work done over many decades in TV studies, so Olympian were its views of the world (as per *Amusing Ourselves to Death*) (Asma 2007). Britain's former Inspector of Schools denounces media studies as "a subject with little intellectual coherence and meager relevance to the world of work" (Woodhead 2009). Critics hold it "responsible for everything from undergraduates arriving at university unable to write proper sentences to the precipitous decline in the numbers taking Latin and Greek. No subject is the focus of so much sneering" and Cambridge, for example, derides it *tout court* (Morrison 2008). In Australia, where some media courses are very difficult to get into and require high entry scores, reactionaries decry the area as obscurantist, "degenerate" (a wonderful term) and misleading, because it supposedly attracts students through pseudo-vocationalism while in fact lacking articulations to industry (Windschuttle 2006).

Similar attitudes are expressed by the bourgeois British and Yanqui media, business leeches, and politicians. The *Observer* scornfully mocks us with a parental parody: "what better way to have our little work-shy scholars rushing off to read an improving book than to enthuse loudly in their presence about how the omnibus edition of *EastEnders* is the new double physics?" (Hogan 2004). The *Village Voice* dubs TV studies "the ultimate capitulation to the MTV mind ... couchpotatodom writ large ... just as Milton doesn't belong in the rave scene, sitcoms don't belong in the canon or the classroom" (Vincent 2000). The *Wall Street Journal* describes media studies as "deeply threatening to traditional leftist views of commerce," because its notions of active consumption are close to those of the right: "cultural-studies mavens are betraying the leftist cause, lending support to the corporate enemy and even training graduate students who wind up doing market research" (Postrel 1999). The *Daily Telegraph* thunders that media studies is "quasi-academic" (Lightfoot 2005; Paton 2007a), while *Guardian* newspaper columnist Simon Hoggart could be seen on British television in 2000 chiding local universities for wasting time on this nonsense when they should be in step with Harvard and MIT. Chris Patten, a former Conservative Party politician and the last Governor of Hong Kong, refers to the discipline as "Disneyland for the weaker minded" (quoted in Morley 2007: 17). The Conservative Party and Alan Sugar, UK inquisitor for *The Apprentice* (2005–), then a Labour Party politico, worry that TV Studies "may be putting future scientific and medical innovation under threat" and "undermining the economy" (Paton 2007b, 2008).

Media studies' popularity with students (in 1997, 31,000 English school pupils took it; in 2008, the number was 58,000) often irritates right-wing anti-intellectuals working in the media (Morrison 2008; Ellis 2005). Such people favor market-based education derived from preferences – other than when they lead people to learn about television! So we see the study of the media being simultaneously more vocational than many other subjects, due to its commitment to production skills and news-and-current affairs research; more populist, given its legitimization of the everyday and its success with students; and more politicized, because in the British tradition it has been influenced by leftists and feminists (Turner 2007). At the same time, much as it might decry the radicalism of some of these influences, the shameless UK government claims that Britain "leads the way worldwide in the study of media-related subjects, and is highly respected." Chinese students flock there to take these classes, which are lacking at home and are seen as more practical than traditional information-technology courses, because they emphasize textuality rather than wires, meaning rather than manufacture (British Council 2009; Hodges 2009).

It is worth recalling that new subject areas always cause controversy when they enter universities, as the British experience with the introduction of the natural sciences in the nineteenth century, and politics, philosophy, English, and sociology in the twentieth, indicates. These were practical responses to major socio-economic transformations – industrialization, state schooling, class mobility, and public welfare (Fox 2003; Whittam Smith 2008). Many of the claims made against our work are as silly as were critiques of those developments. For example, Hoggart's dismissiveness is ill-informed. Two minutes' research would have told him that Harvard long-hosted a journal of media studies (the ungainly-titled *Harvard International Journal of Press/Politics*, now thankfully free of its oxymoronic Yanqui moniker and its retro housing) and a New Approaches to International Law colloquium that engaged with cultural studies, while MIT held major conferences called "Media In Transition" to trope its acronym. Foucault proposes that we think of the media on a continuum with universities, journals of tendency, and books – all are media, and it is strange to treat one or the other as more or less significant or powerful as a venue or topic (2001: 928).

Where did TV studies come from? In the United States, it derives from university participation in the emergence of radio. The discipline of speech communication had been formed in the early-twentieth-century US to help white non-English-speaking migrants assimilate into the workforce. It became the first home of media education, because the engineering professors who founded radio stations in colleges during the 1920s needed program content, and drew volunteers from that area after being rebuffed by literature mavens. These stations doubled as laboratories, with research undertaken into technology, content, and reception. At the same time, schools of journalism were forming to produce newspaper workers (Kittross 1999). This was also a period of massively complex urbanization and the spread of adult literacy, democratic rights, labor organization, and socialist ideas. First radio then TV were prized and feared for their demagogic qualities. In the twentieth century, with the standardization of social-science method and its uptake and export by US military, commercial, and governmental interests, audiences came to be conceived as empirical entities that could be known via research instruments derived from communication, sociology, demography, the psy-function, and marketing. Such concerns were coupled with a secondary concentration on content. Texts, too, were conceived as empirical entities that could be known, via research instruments derived from sociology, communication, and literary criticism. Universities across the US began preparing students to work in the media. As they grew in size and opened up both to highly instrumental, conservatory-style training and to more critical tendencies within the human sciences, influenced by oppositional social movements, so TV studies was simultaneously deemed by many traditionalists to be overly applied and overly progressive. In Britain, a research position into TV was first endowed by Granada TV at Leeds University in 1959. Then the Society for Education in Film and Television and the British Film Institute began sometimes separate, sometimes overlapping, forms of stimulus in the 1960s and 1970s, from teaching posts to publishing, which ultimately fed into major formations of media studies influenced by continental Marxism and feminism and social movements. Classes grew as the subject developed from film appreciation to media critique and media training, in concert with shifting research agendas, a changing cultural economy, and the latter's applied, conservatory approach (Bignell *et al.* 2000a: 81; Bolas 2009; Fox 2003).

Today, major engagements with TV come from the psy-function, other social sciences (sociology, economics, communication studies, anthropology, and law), and the humanities (literature, cinema studies, media studies, and cultural studies). There are seven principal forms of inquiry, which:

- borrow ethnography from sociology and anthropology to investigate the experiences of audiences;
- use experimentation and testing methods from psychology to establish cause-and-effect relations between media consumption and subsequent conduct;
- adapt content analysis from sociology and communication studies to evaluate programming in terms of generic patterns;
- adopt textual analysis from literary theory and linguistics to identify the ideological tenor of content;
- apply textual and audience interpretation from psychoanalysis to speculate on psychological processes;
- deploy political economy to examine ownership, control, regulation, and international exchange; and
- utilize archival and historiographic methods to give TV a record of its past.

Relevant professional associations housing TV Studies 1.0 and 2.0 include those listed in Table 1.2.

Some of these bodies see themselves as feeder groups and even advocates for the industry; some identify as purely scholarly entities; and others call for progressive change. AEJMC describes itself as "a multicultural network of practitioners." Founded in 1912, it seeks to "advance education in journalism, cultivate better professional practice and promote the free flow of information, without boundaries." (Does the Association really mean this? Isn't copyright the longest-standing and most brutally enforced device for retarding such "free flow," by imposing boundaries and empowering police to enforce them?) BEA commenced in 1948 as an educational arm of the US radio then TV industry through the National Association of Broadcasters, which eventually provided it with

Table 1.1

Topics	*Objects*	*Methods*	*Disciplines*
Regulation, Industry Development, New Technology	State, Capital, Labor	Political Economy, Neoliberalism	Engineering, Computer Science, Economics, Political Science, Law, Communication Studies
Genre	Text	Content Analysis	Communication Studies, Sociology
Genre	Text	Textual Analysis	Literary/ Cultural/Media Studies
Uses	Audience	Uses and Gratifications	Communication Studies, Psychology, Marketing
Uses	Audience	Ethnography	Anthropology, Cultural/Media Studies, Communication Studies

resources to fund events and publications (Kittross 1999). It bears the lineaments of a heritage "preparing college students to enter the radio & TV business." MeCCSA, among the newer of these bodies, argues that media studies gets "negative publicity" because it "involves studying things which are generally seen as entertaining but trivial" or "for making things too complicated by using complicated theoretical language." MeCCSA presents itself as a service to students, rather alarmingly suggesting that "Many of the jobs you will go into once you have finished your degree have not yet been invented." It suggests that obtaining employment in the television sector may flow from "the ability to produce high[-]quality research, to analyze sociological trends, to work effectively

Table 1.2

International Association for Media & Communication Research	Union for Democratic Communications
Broadcast Education Association	Association for Education in Journalism and Mass Communication
National Communication Association	International Communication Association
Society for Cinema and Media Studies	American Association for Public Opinion Research
American Journalism Historians Association	Asociación Latinoamericana de Investigadores de la Comunicación
Association for Chinese Communication Studies	Association of Internet Researchers
Chinese Communication Association	European Consortium for Communications Research
European Society for Opinion and Marketing Research	Global Communication Research Association
Australian and New Zealand Communications Association	Southern African Communication Association
International Association for Media and History	Canadian Communication Association
Media, Communications & Cultural Studies Association	Association for Cultural Studies

with people, to organize events, to think creatively and to write well." SCMS says it is "devoted to the study of the moving image." Founded in 1959 "to be to film what the Modern Language Association was to literature" (Doherty 2008), the Society aims to "promote all areas of media studies" and "advance multi-cultural awareness and interaction." (Does the "moving image" include how the image is, quite literally, "moved," i.e. its political economy and ethnography of distribution?) Attempts to bring television studies into the former Society for Cinema Studies were roundly rejected in the 1990s by the operatic elite of cinephiles. It may be that the eventual expansion of their rubric to incorporate "media studies" derived not from an appreciation of the importance of TV, but because of "the propinquity of television studies to the higher-prestige if loosely defined field of new media studies" (Boddy 2005: 81). Universities "tend to value anything called new media" thanks to its applications to militarism and Mammon, and its ability to draw hefty research money through governmental and commercial fetishes for new technology. The upshot is that "studying anything that comes over the Internet ... has somehow become more legitimate than studying television itself" (Spigel 2005b: 84). By contrast with the jobs/jobs/jobs emphasis of several Associations, and the aesthetico-historical emphasis of SCMS, UDC sees itself as dedicated to the "critical study of the communications establishment" in the interests of "democratically controlled and produced media ... alternative, oppositional, independent and experimental production ... democratic communications systems locally, regionally and internationally." This is a transformative rather than a parthenogenetic project: UDC works toward a better world in preference to generating new cohorts of docile workers and aesthetes. IAMCR is the only truly international body in the figure above, because it has not been centered in the English-speaking behemoths of media studies, and has therefore featured a greater variety of epistemological, political, and geographical concerns.

Clearly, there is no single professional association to go to in order to see how academia makes sense of TV. The same applies to journals. It's a huge list! But consulting these and other titles will keep you abreast of debates in television studies – it may even put you ahead of your teachers:

International Journal of Cultural Policy, Entertainment Law Review, Transnational Television Studies, Global Media Journal, Television & New Media, Global Media and Communication, Poetics, Journal of Media Economics, Media International Australia, European Journal of Communication, Media Culture & Society, International Communication Gazette, Media Law and Practice, Feminist Media Studies, Comunicaço & Politica, International Journal of Communication, International Journal of Communications Law and Policy, Asian Journal of Communication, Games & Culture, Journal of Broadcasting & Electronic Media, Revista Electrónica Internacional de Economía Política de las Tecnologías de la Información y de la Comunicación, Entertainment and Sports Law Journal, Asian Media, Comunicaçao e Sociedade, Convergence, Loyola Entertainment Law Journal, Columbia VLA Journal of Law and the Arts, Loyola Entertainment Law Journal, Cultural Studies Review, Mediascape, Communication Review, Cultural Politics, Critical Studies in Media Communication, Quarterly Review of Film and Video, Cinema Journal, Journal of Media Sociology, Democratic Communiqué, Television Quarterly, Cultural Sociology, Journal of Arab and Muslim Media Research, Journal of Creative Communications, Comunicar, Catalan Journal of Communication & Cultural Studies, MedieKultur, Journal of Consumer Marketing, International Journal of Advertising, Journal of Marketing, European Journal of Marketing Media Development, Canadian Journal of Communication, Visual Anthropology, Visual Anthropology Review, NORDICOM Review of Nordic Research on Media and Communication, Journal of International Communication, Asian Journal of Communication, Journal of Radio Studies, New Media & Society, Journalism & Mass Communication Quarterly, Journal of Communication Inquiry, Historical Journal of Radio, Film & Television, Journal of Communication, European Journal of Cultural Studies, Journalism History, Journalism: Theory, Practice and Criticism, Media History, Women's Studies in Communication, Public Opinion Quarterly, Political Communication, Gamasutra, Federal Communications Law Journal, Fordham Intellectual Property, International Journal of Press/Politics, Popular Communication, Media & Entertainment Law Journal, Topia, Cultural Studies, Communications, International Journal of Cultural Studies, Journal of British Cinema & Television, Social Semiotics, Journal of E-Media Studies, Critical Studies in Television, Jump Cut, Screen Education, Screen, Velvet Light Trap, Flow, Journal of Film & Video, New Review of Film and Television Studies, Journal of Popular Film & Television, Middle East Journal of Culture and Communication, Journal of Sports Media, Central European Journal of Communication, Journal of Advertising, International Journal of Market Research, Journal of Advertising Research, Asia Pacific Journal of Marketing

Some journals are the organs of professional associations, which authors may have to join then obediently cite the work of powerful members in order to be published; some are journals of tendency, which seek new and transformative work rather than the reiteration of normal science; and some are dedicated to particular regions or languages.

TV studies also exists in the medium itself and in museums. Many channels are dedicated to repertory replays of old programming. Nostalgia is a staple, and television itself is a source of programs. For example, TV that is about television began in the US with *The Dick van Dyke Show* (1961–6) and moved on through such shows as *The Mary Tyler Moore Show* (1970–7), *Max Headroom* (1987–8), and *Murphy Brown* (1988–98) (Caldwell 2008b; Wallace 1997: 35). There is now a huge public archive of programs, even though many texts were lost because their makers saw them as ephemeral rather than of lasting aesthetic or historical value. Despite that assumption, what was once regarded as passing entertainment has become perennial art, perforce its collection and cataloguing within leading museums such as New York City's Museum of Modern Art (the creature of the Rockefeller family, but regarded as one of the major art centers in the world). In the 1950s, the Museum looked to US TV as an avantgarde device that would speak to the masses even as it generated museologically worthy creativity. Two decades later, New York's Museum of Broadcasting opened, with a clearer mission, one that analyzed broadcasting in the way that most US cultural policy works – as propaganda for capitalism and the industry, as a site of canon formation, and as a tourist attraction. And in the ten years prior to his death, Andy Warhol taped a large amount of television, which is now held at Pittsburgh's Andy Warhol Museum. The archive offers two kinds of cultural analysis. First, because Warhol represents the pop-art tradition, his tastes become hermeneutic clues to that world and his own oeuvre. Second, the Museum is a body of broadcast history (Spigel 2005a: 74–5, 82, 86, 67). And there are significant physical and electronic museums of television and the moving image in La Libertad, Ankara, New York, London, Paris, Chicago, Toronto, Los Angeles, Bradford, Canberra, Berlin, and Tokyo.

Core sources for studying television via the Internet are listed in Table 1.3.

Most of the significant psy-function and neoliberal contributions to Television Studies 1.0 have come through journals and policy

Table 1.3

UNESCO (unesco.org/culture)	Digital Divide Network (digitaldivide.net)
Culture Statistics Observatory (culturestatistics.net)	Urban Institute Arts and Culture Indicators Project (urban.org)
Centre for Cultural Policy Research (culturalpolicy.arts.gla.ac.uk)	Council of Europe Cultural Policy (coe.int)
Basel Action Network (ban.org)	Creative Commons (creativecommons.org)
Sarai (sarai.net)	Free Software Foundation (fsf.org)
Alternative Law Forum (altlawforum.org)	Cultural Democracy (culturaldemocarcy.net)
Cultural Policy & the Arts National Data Archive (cpanda.org)	Feminists for Free Expression (ffeusa.org)
European Commission Education Audiovisual & Culture Executive Agency (eacea.ec.europa.eu)	Observatory of Cultural Policies in Africa (ocpa.irmo.hr)
Pew Charitable Trusts (pewtrusts.com)	Fairness in Accuracy and Reporting (fair.org)
AfricaMediaOnline (africamediaonline.com)	Asian Media (asiamedia.ucla.edu)
Asia Media and Information Center (amic.org.sg)	Audiovisual Observatory (obs.coe.int)
Global Public Media (globalpublicmedia.com)	

reports, because they are the preferred publishing locations for those areas. If we look at key books from TV Studies 1.0 and 2.0 over the past four decades, which tend to come from more critical, progressive tendencies, certain common themes and developments become clear.[2] I have prepared two matrices of such foundational texts. After all, as Foucault said: "On ne me fera jamais croire qu'un livre est mauvais parce qu'on a vu son auteur a la télévision" ["You'll never persuade me a book is no good simply because its author has been on television"] (2001: 925).

The first matrix features notable contributions from the late 1960s through the 1980s (Table 1.4).

Table 1.4

Form of analysis	Example
Feminist Studies	Ien Ang, *Het Geval Dallas*, Muriel G. Cantor and Suzanne Pingree, *The Soap Opera*, Richard Dyer *et al.*, *Coronation Street*, Helen Baehr and Gillian Dyer, *Boxed-In*, Dorothy Hobson, *Crossroads*, Michèle Mattelart, *Women, Media and Crisis*, Tania Modleski, *Loving with a Vengeance*, Gaye Tuchman *et al.*, *Hearth and Home*
Genre Study	Samir Allam, *Fernsehserien, Wertvorstellungen und Zensur in Ägypten*, Raymond Williams, *Television*, Robert C. Allen, *Speaking of Soap Operas*, Jane Feuer *et al.*, *MTM*, Albert Moran, *Images & Industry*, Cristina Lasagni and Giuseppe Richeri, *L'altro mondo quotidiano*, Brian G. Rose, *TV Genres*, George W. Brandt, *British Television Drama*, Jim Cook, *Television Sitcom*, Stanley Cohen and Jock Young, *The Manufacture of News*
Political Economy and Cultural Imperialism Analysis	Herbert I. Schiller, *Mass Communications and American Empire*, Luis Ramiro Beltrán and Elizabeth Fox, *Comunicación dominada*, Ariel Dorfman and Armand Mattelart, *Para leer al pato Donald*, Armand Mattelart, *Multinationales et systèmes de communication*, Raymond Williams, *Communications*, Philip Schlesinger *et al.*, *Televising "Terrorism,"* Stuart Hood, *On Television*, Richard Collins *et al.*, *The Economics of Television*, Jack G. Shaheen, *The TV Arab*, Kaarle Nordenstreng and Tapio Varis, *Television Traffic*
Ideology Critique	Edward Buscombe, *Football on Television*, Colin McArthur, *Television and History*, Herbert I. Schiller, *The Mind Managers*

continued

Table 1.4 continued

Form of analysis	Example
National Television History	Erik Barnouw, *The Sponsor*, Asa Briggs, *The BBC*, Erik Barnouw, *Tube of Plenty*, KS Inglis, *This is the ABC*, Asa Briggs, *Sound & Vision*, Masami Ito, *Broadcasting in Japan*, Tom Burns, *The BBC*, John Tulloch and Graeme Turner, *Australian Television*
Production and Audience Ethnography	Manuel Alvarado and Edward Buscombe, *Hazell*, John Tulloch and Manuel Alvarado, *Doctor Who*, Gladys Daza Hernández, *TV.cultura*, David Morley, *The Nationwide Audience*, Bob Hodge and David Tripp, *Children and Television*, Todd Gitlin, *Inside Prime Time*, Philip Elliott, *The Making of a Television Series*, Albert Moran, *Making a TV Series*, Muriel G. Cantor, *The Hollywood TV Producer*, Horace Newcomb and Robert S. Alley, *The Producer's Medium*, Herbert Gans, *Deciding What's News*, Roger Silverstone, *Framing Science*, Manuel Alvarado and John Stewart, *Made for Television*, John Tulloch and Albert Moran, *A Country Practice*
Media Criticism	Horace Newcomb, *TV: The Most Popular Art*, Hal Himmelstein, *Television Myth and the American Mind*, John Fiske and John Hartley, *Reading Television*, Stuart Hall and Paddy Whannel, *The Popular Arts*
Anthology Readers	James Curran et al., *Mass Communication and Society*, Tony Bennett et al., *Popular Television and Film*, E. Ann Kaplan, *Regarding Television*, Len Masterman, *Television Mythologies*, Horace Newcomb, *Television: The Critical View*, Phillip Drummond and Richard Paterson, *Television in Transition*, Phillip Drummond and Richard Paterson, *Television and its Audience*, Michael Gurevitch et al., *Culture, Society and the Media*

This formation has grown and changed in the last two decades, as the second matrix below (Table 1.5) indicates. Generalized cultural imperialism critique and national television history have been transformed into more specific analyses, represented by national, regional, global, diasporic, First Peoples, and activist television. Ideology critique has been subsumed by racialization analysis and policy critique. Feminism has been supplemented by gender studies, including queer analyses. As the field has become academically institutionalized, media criticism has fallen away,[3] but anthology readers and textbooks have proliferated. Genre study and ethnography have remained significant, and new areas have emerged, such as cultural and institutional history. This is in keeping with intellectual growth and institutionalization as well as a reaction to broader trends, such as social–movement activism and the globalization and privatization of television in the wake of the Cold War and the rise of neoliberalism.[4] Foundational categories and texts since 1990 are listed in Table 1.5.

We are witnessing a shift here of some significance. John Hartley expertly describes the terrain:

> Sometime during the 1970s and 1980s, TV theory … [began] to grow out of an amalgam of critical humanities and behavioral social sciences. It was devoted to understanding, on one hand, *values* (human, aesthetic, cultural) – the domain of the critic – and, on the other hand, *behaviors* (psychological, social) – the terrain of the clinic. Mix in the influence of politicized "high theory" (structuralism, psychoanalysis, Marxism, postmodernism) and countercultural "new social movements" associated with identity (class, gender, race, ethnicity, sexual orientation, age, first peoples, subcultures based on consumption) and you had the makings of television theory.
>
> (2005: 103)

The only amendment I'd make to this useful capsule account is that critics were not content with describing values based purely on texts – they also went hunting for audiences to buttress their opinions; and clinicians were not content with describing impacts based on viewers – they also went hunting for texts to buttress their opinions.

Table 1.5

Form of analysis	Example
Gender Studies	Sujata Moorti, *The Color of Rape*, Mary Ellen Brown, *Television and Women's Culture*, Marlene Sanders and Marcia Rock, *Waiting for Prime Time*, Julie D'Acci, *Defining Women*, Lynn Spigel, *Make Room for TV*, Mary Beth Haralovich and Lauren Rabinovitz, *Television, History, and American Culture*, Helen Wood, *Talking with Television*, Charlotte Brunsdon, *Screen Tastes*, Ann Gray, *Video Playtime*, Lynn Spigel and Denise Mann, *Private Screenings*, Lisa Lewis, *Gender Politics and MTV*, Beretta E. Smith-Shomade, *Shaded Lives*, Andrea L. Press, *Women Watching Television*, Lorna Jowett, *Sex and the Slayer*, Helen Baehr and Ann Gray, *Turning it On*, Charlotte Brunsdon, et al., *Feminist Television Criticism*, Jane Shattuc, *The Talking Cure*, Jane Arthurs, *Television and Sexuality*, Sarah Projansky, *Watching Rape*, Frances Bonner, *Ordinary Television*, Bonnie J. Dow, *Prime-Time Feminism*, Marsha F. Cassidy, *What Women Watched*, Amanda D. Lotz, *Redesigning Women*, Elana Levine, *Wallowing in Sex*, Janet Thumin, *Inventing Television Culture*, Andrea L. Press and Elizabeth R. Cole, *Speaking of Abortion*, Glyn Davis and Gary Needham, *Queer TV*
Genre Study	Misha Kavka, *Reality Television, Affect and Intimacy*, Antonio Savorelli, *Oltre la Sitcom*, Brent MacGregor, *Live, Direct and Biased?*, Jason Jacobs, *Body Trauma TV*, Luciana Bistane and Luciane Bacellar, *Jornalismo de TV*, Jonathan Gray et al., *Satire TV*, Patricia Joyner Priest, *Public Intimacies*, Raymond Boyle and Richard Haynes, *Power Play*, Armand and Michèle Mattelart, *The Carnival of the Image*, Stig Hjarvard, *News in a Globalized Society*, Rod Brookes, *Representing Sport*, Vamsee Juluri, *Becoming a Global Audience*, Milly Buonanno, *Narrami o diva*, David Buckingham, *Small Screens*, John Tulloch, *Television Drama*, Steve M. Barkin, *American Television News*, Alfredo Vizeu et al., *Telejornalismo*, Charlton D. McIlwain, *When Death Goes Pop*, Katherine Fry, *Constructing the Heartland*, James Chapman, *Saints & Avengers*, Robert Chairs and Bradley Chilton, *Star Trek Visions*, Mark Andrejevic, *Reality TV*, Michael V. Tueth, *Laughter in the Living Room*, James Friedman, *Reality Squared*, Bernard M. Timberg and Robert J. Erler, *Television Talk*, Garry Whannel, *Fields in Vision*, Hugh O'Donnell, *Good Times, Bad Times*, Kristina Riegert , "*Nationalising" Foreign Conflict*, Gerd Hallenberger and Joachim Kaps, *Hatten Sie's Gewusst?*, Milly Buonanno, *The Age of Television*, Matthew J. Smith and Andrew F. Wood, *Survivor Lessons*, Mark Jancovich and James Lyons, *Quality Popular Television*, Janice Peck, *The Gods of Televangelism*, Jimmie L. Reeves and Richard Campbell, *Cracked Coverage*, Robert C. Allen, *to be continued . . .*, David Marc, *Comic Visions*, Jason Mitell, *Genre and Television*, Jeffrey P. Jones, *Entertaining Politics*, John Langer, *Tabloid Television*, Susan Murray and Laurie Ouellette, *Reality TV*, David Buxton, *From "The Avengers" to "Miami Vice*," Steve Neale and Frank Krutnik, *Popular Film and Television Comedy*, Michèle Barrett and Duncan Barrett, *Star Trek*, Richard Kilborn and John Corner, *An Introduction to Television Documentary*, Joseph Turow, *Playing Doctor*, Jostein

	Gripsrud, The "Dynasty" Years, Darrell Y. Hamamoto, Nervous Laughter, Andrew Goodwin, Dancing in the Distraction Factory, Thomas Tufte, Living with the Rubbish Queen, Nancy Bernhard, US Television News and Cold War Propaganda, 1947–60, Sara Gwenllian-Jones and Roberta Pearson, Cult Television, Lez Cooke, British Television Drama, Dana Heller, The Great American Makeover, Glenn Creeber, Fifty Key Television Programmes, Solange Davin and Rhona Jackson, Television and Criticism, Annette Hill, Reality TV, Cynthia Chris, Watching Wildlife, Dana Heller, Makeover Television, Lesley Henderson, Social Issues in Television Fiction, Elana Lavine and Lisa Parks, Undead TV, Michael Kackman, Citizen Spy, Laurie Ouellette and James Hay, Better Living Through Reality TV, Carol A. Stabile and Mark Harrison, Prime Time Animation, Glyn Davis and Kay Dickinson, Teen TV, Robert M. Jarvis and Paul R. Joseph, Prime Time Law, Greg M. Smith, Beautiful TV, Bill Osgerby and Anna Gough-Yates, Action TV, J.P. Telotte, The Essential Science Fiction Reader, Robert Gidding and Keith Selby, The Classic Serial on Television and Radio, Janet McCabe and Kim Akass, Quality TV, Graeme Turner. Ending the Affair, Gareth Palmer .Exposing Lifestyle Television, Jonathan Gray, Television Entertainment, Gary R. Edgerton and Brian G. Rose, Thinking Outside the Box, Kristina Riegert, Politicotainment, Dorothy Hobson, Soap Opera, Robin Nelson, TV Drama in Transition, Sarah Cardwell, Adaptation Revisited, Alfredo Vizeu, A Sociedade do Telejornalismo, Sue Thornham and Tony Purvis, Television Drama, Jane Stokes, On Screen Rivals, Alfredo Vizeu, O lado oculto do telejornalismo
Political Economy and Cultural Imperialism/ Globalization Analysis	Luis Reygadas, Ensamblando Culturas, Robin Andersen, Consumer Culture & TV Programming, Albert Moran, Copycat TV, César Bolaño, Indústria cultural informaçao e capitalismo, Yahya R. Kamalipour, Images of the US Around the World, Ralph Negrine and Stylianos Papathanassopoulos, The Internationalisation of Television, Lorenzo Vilches, Mercados globales, historias nacionales, Gerald Sussman and John A. Lent, Global Productions, Jeremy Tunstall, Television Producers, Peter Golding and Graham Murdock, The Political Economy of the Media, Jeanette Steemers, Selling Television, Michael G. Elasmar, The Impact of International Television, Eileen R. Meehan and Ellen Riordan, Sex & Money, Barbara J. Selznick, Global Television, Jean K. Chalaby, Transnational Television Worldwide, Lisa Parks and Shanti Kumar, Planet TV
Racialization Analysis	América Rodriguez, Making Latino News, Sarita Malik, Representing Black Britain, Kristal Brent Zook, Color by Fox, Chon A. Noriega, Shot in America, Darrell Y. Hamamoto, Monitored Peril, Donald Bogle, Primetime Blues, Sut Jhally and Justin Lewis, Enlightened Racism, Sasha Torres, Living Color, Herman Gray, Watching Race, Stephen Bourne, Black in the British Frame, Steven D. Classen, Watching Jim Crow, John Downing and Charles Husband, Representing "Race," Oscar H. Gandy, Communication and Race, Alan Nadel, Television in Black-and-White America, Darnell M. Hunt Screening the Los Angeles "Riots," Sasha Torres, Black White and in Color, Beretta E. Smith-Shomade, Pimpin' Ain't Easy, Yeidy M. Rivero, Tuning Out Blackness

continued

Table 1.5 continued

Form of analysis	Example
Regional and Global Television History	Thomas F. Skidmore, *Television, Politics and the Transition to Democracy in Latin America*, Amos Owen Thomas, *Transnational Media and Contoured Markets*, Jésus Martín-Barbero and Germán Rey, *Los ejercicios del ver*, Joseph Straubhaar, *World Television*, Jean K. Chalaby, *Transnational Television in Europe*, Miguel de Moragas Spa and Carmelo Garitaonandia, *Decentralisation in the Global Era*, Barbara J. Selznick, *Global Television*, Richard Collins, *From Satellite to Single Market*, Luis Albornoz, *Al fin solos …*, *La nueva televisión del MERCOSUR*, Brett Christophers, *Envisioning Media Power*, Michael Scriven and Monia Lecompte, *Television Broadcasting in Contemporary France and Britain*, Timothy Havens, *Global Television Marketplace*, Sydney W. Head, *Broadcasting in Africa*, Sofia Blind and Gerd Hallenberger, *European Co-Productions in Television and Film*, Elizabeth Fox, *Latin American Broadcasting*, Anthony Smith, *International History of Television*, Royce J. Ammon, *Global Television and the Shaping of World Politics*, Giovanni Bechelloni, *Televisione come cultura*, Anura Goonasekera and Paul S.N. Lee, *TV Without Borders*, John Sinclair, *Latin American Television*, Philip Kitley, *Television, Regulation and Civil Society in Asia*, David French and Michael Richards, *Television in Contemporary Asia*, Amos Owen Thomas, *Imagi-Nations and Borderless Television*, Fausto Colombo, *TV and Interactivity in Europe*, John Lent, *Mass Communications in the Caribbean*, Srinivas R. Melkote et al., *International Satellite Broadcasting in South Asia*, Alessandro Silj, *East of Dallas*, Yahya R. Kamalipour and Hamid Mowlana, *The Mass Media in the Middle East*, Alessandro Silj, *The New Television in Europe*, Zhenzhi Guo, *Zhongguo Dianshi Shi*, Stuart Cunningham et al., *New Patterns in Global Television*, Mohammed El-Nawawy and Adel Iskandar, *Al-Jazeera*, Phillip Drummond et al., *National Identity and Europe*, Ib Bondebjerg and F. Bono, *Television in Scandinavia*, Ensirah El Shal, *Satellite Television Channels in the Third World*, Jan Wieten et al., *Television Across Europe*, Shelton A. Gunaratne, *Handbook of Media in Asia*, Miguel de Moragas Spa et al., *TV on Your Doorstep*, Lynn Spigel and Jan Olsson, *Television After TV*, Stylianos Papathanassopoulos, *European Television in the Digital Age*, Naomi Sakr, *Satellite Realms*, Kay Richardson and Ulrike Meinhof, *Worlds in Common*, Denise D. Bielby and C. Lee Harrington, *Global TV*, Jonathan Bignell and Andreas Fickers, *A European Television History*, Albert Moran with Justin Malbon, *Understanding the Global TV Format*, Albert Moran and Michael Keane, *Television Across Asia*, Michael Keane et al., *New Television, Globalisation, and the East Asian Cultural Imagination*, Naomi Sakr, *Arab Television Today*, Nora Mazziotti, *La industria de la telenovela*, Graham Roberts and Philip Taylor, *The Historian, Television and Television History*, Michael Curtin, *Playing to the World's Biggest Audience*

Diasporic, First Peoples, and Activist Television	Marie Gillespie, *Television, Ethnicity and Cultural Change*, Stuart Cunningham and John Sinclair, *Floating Lives*, Donald B. Browne, *Electronic Media and Indigenous Peoples*, Tony Dowmunt, *Channels of Resistance*, Hamid Naficy, *The Making of Exile Cultures*, John Hartley and Alan McKee, *The Indigenous Public Sphere*, Faye D. Ginsburg et al., *Media Worlds*, Robert L. Hilliard and Michael C. Keith, *The Hidden Screen*, Lorna Roth, *Something New in the Air*
Production and Audience Ethnography and History	Karen E. Riggs *Mature Audiences*, Purnima Mankekar, *Screening Culture*, Viewing Politics, Barry Dornfeld, *Producing Public Television*, *Producing Public Culture*, Daniel C. Hallin, *We Keep America on Top of the World*, Richard Butsch, *The Making of American Audiences*, Henry Jenkins, *Textual Poachers*, Mirta Varela and Alejandro Grimson, *Audiencias, cultura y poder*, David Buckingham, *The Making of Citizens*, David Morley, *Television, Audiences and Cultural Studies*, Robin Means Coleman, *Say it Loud!*, Nilda Jacks and Ana Carolina Escosteguy, *Comunicação e Recepção*, Ellen Seiter et al., *Remote Control*, JoEllen Fisherkeller, *Growing up with Television*, Sonia Livingstone and Peter Lunt, *Talk on Television*, Pertti Alasuutari, *Rethinking the Media Audience*, James Hay et al., *The Audience and its Landscape*, Nancy K. Baym, *Tune In, Log On*, Justin Lewis, *The Ideological Octopus*, Vicki Mayer, *Producing Dreams, Consuming Youth*, Mirca Madianou, *Mediating the Nation*, Dafna Lemish, *Children and Television*, Lila Abu-Lughod, *Dramas of Nationhood*, John T. Caldwell, *Production Culture*, Máire Messenger Davies, *"Dear BBC,"* Ien Ang, *Desperately Seeking the Audience*
Policy Critique	Valerio Fuenzalida, *La television pública en América Latina*, Megan Mullen, *Television in the Multichannel Age*, Dominique Wolton, *Éloge du grand public*, Philip Green, *Primetime Politics*, Megan Mullen, *The Rise of Cable Programming in the United States*, Heather Hendershot, *Saturday Morning Censors*, Robert W. McChesney, *The Problem of the Media*, Bruce M. Owen, *The Internet Challenge to Television*, Thomas Streeter, *Selling the Air*, William Hoynes, *Public Television for Sale*, Douglas Kellner, *Television and the Crisis of Democracy*, Stuart Hood, *Behind the Screens*, Greg Philo, *Message Received*, Sakae Ishikawa, *Quality Assessment of Television*, Geoff Mulgan, *The Question of Quality*, Doris Graber, *Processing Politics*, Jay G. Blumler, *Television and the Public Interest*, Bob Franklin, *British Television Policy*, Octavio Getino, *Cine y televisión en América Latina*, Monroe E. Price, *Television, the Public Sphere, and National Identity*, Eduardo Giordano and Carlos Zeller, *Políticas de televisión*, Graeme Turner and Jinna Tay, *Television Studies After TV*, Laurie Ouellette, *Viewers Like You?*, Andrew Kenyon, *TV Futures*, A. Leurdijk, *Televisie Journalistiek over de multiculturele samenleving*, Michael Tracey, *The Decline and Fall of Public Service Broadcasting*, Stephane Olivesi, *Histoire politique de la télévision*, Javier Pérez de Silva, *La televisión ha muerto*, Jean-Louis Missika, *La fin de la télévision*, Hernan Galperin, *New Television*, Des Freedman, *The Politics of Media Policy*, Amanda D. Lotz, *The Television Will Be Revolutionized*, Sharon Marie Ross, *Beyond the Box*, Lisa Parks, *Cultures in Orbit*, Douglas Kellner, *From 9/11 to Terror War*, Douglas Kellner, *The Persian TV War*, Peter Dahlgren, *Television and the Public Sphere*, Eileen R. Meehan, *Why TV is Not Our Fault*

continued

Table 1.5 continued

Form of analysis	Example
Textbook Summation and Research	Victoria O'Donnell, *Television Criticism*, Ellen Seiter, *Television and New Media Audiences*, Bernadette Casey et al., *Television Studies*, Leah R. Vande Berg et al., *Critical Approaches to Television*, Jeremy G. Butler, *Television*, John Tulloch, *Watching Audiences*, Keith Selby and Ron Cowdery, *How to Study Television*, Denis McQuail, *Audience Analysis*, Graeme Burton, *Talking Television*, David McQueen, *Television*, Muriel G. Cantor and Joel M. Cantor, *Prime-Time Television*, Lawrence Grossberg et al., *Media Making*, Kristin Thompson, *Storytelling in Film and Television*, John Hartley, *Uses of Television*, Janet Staiger, *Media Reception Studies*, Karen Lury, *Interpreting Television*, John Hartley, *Television Truths*, Jonathan Bignell, *An Introduction to Television Studies*, Jonathan Bignell and Jeremy Orlebar, *The Television Handbook*, Nicholas Abercrombie, *Television as Text*, Glen Creeber, *Tele-Visions*, Ron Lembo, *Thinking Through Television*, John Ellis, *TV FAQ*, Arlindo Machado, *A Televisão levada a sério*, Christina Slade, *The Real Thing*
Anthology Readers	Robert C. Allen, *Channels of Discourse*, Marie Gillespie, *Media Audiences*, Andrew Goodwin and Garry Whannel, *Understanding Television*, Patricia Mellencamp, *Logics of Television*, John Corner and Sylvia Harvey, *Television Times*, Gary Burns and Robert J. Thompson, *Television Studies*, Gail Dines and Jean M. Humez, *Gender, Race and Class in the Media*, Horace Newcomb, *Encyclopedia of Television*, Christine Geraghty and David Lusted, *The Television Studies Book*, Jostein Gripsrud, *Television and Common Knowledge*, Mike Wayne, *Dissident Voices*, Robert C. Allen and Annette Hill, *The Television Studies Reader*, Janet Wasko, *Companion to Television*, Michele Hilmes and Jason Jacobs, *The Television History Book*, John Sinclair and Graeme Turner, *Contemporary World Television*, Douglas Gomery and Luke Hockley, *Television Institutions*, Helen Wheatley, *Re-Viewing Television History*

A synoptic survey in the *Annual Review of Sociology* proposes that "changes in the medium threaten to make past research on TV appear quaint and anachronistic" (Grindstaff and Turow 2006: 103). But as media forms proliferate and change, their intermingling with social change ensures an ongoing link between cultural analysis and television. And there are some excellent examples of productive work that engages, but is not beholden to, 1.0/2.0 binaries about audiences (vulnerability/power) and aesthetics (quality/banality). Vincent Mosco starts from cultural myths and "builds a bridge to political economy" in his excoriation of neoliberal phantasies about empowerment, insisting on "the mutually constitutive relationship between political economy and cultural studies" (2004: 6–7). Richard Maxwell (2002) links

> a critique of neo-liberalism and a cultural studies approach to consumption ... not by issuing nostrums against the pleasures of shopping[,] but by paying attention to the politics of resource allocation that brings a consumption infrastructure into the built environment.

Such attempts to criticize and draw upon both TV Studies 1.0 and 2.0 are standard practice in much analysis beyond Britain, the US, and their white-settler academic satellites (Israel, Australia, Canada, and Aotearoa/New Zealand). Arvind Rajagopal (2002) notes that because the television, the telephone, the Internet, and the neoliberal are all new to most Indians, "markets and media generate new kinds of rights and new kinds of imagination ... novel ways of exercising citizenship rights and conceiving politics." In the spirit of that radical contextualism – where television's significance is not fixed historically or geographically – the chapters to come seek both to shake up your understanding of what TV is, and to reinforce that understanding.

Television is many things, depending on where, when, how, why, and by whom it is being studied. The question is whether TV Studies 1.0 or 2.0 are adequate to the task of understanding television in all its manifestations.

Take the case of Mary-Kate and Ashley Olsen, who debuted on US network TV as babies in the situation comedy *Full House* (1987–95). During that period, a company was set up to feature them in music, videos, and books. By their fifteenth birthday, they had launched a clothing line, and *Hollywood Reporter* dubbed them "the most powerful young women in Hollywood." When the twins turned eighteen, each was worth over US$130 million, thanks to gross sales of their products of US$1.4 billion. The clothing line, heralded as a chic "homeless look," drew massive opprobrium from student activists because the New International Division Cultural Labor saw the line neatly – and gruesomely – index the difference in choices between the twins and their employees: the people who made the clothes owned and endorsed by the cute-as-a-button Olsens were Bangladeshi women, paid between US$189.28 and US$436.80 a year and denied the paid maternity leave legally mandated for them (Shade and Porter 2008). Meanwhile, the sexism that restricts strong roles in Hollywood movies for women aged over forty had seen middle-aged women migrating to leading roles on television, including cable, in ways that would have been unthinkable a decade ago, adding luster to US TV (McNamara 2007) and offering a wider variety of femininity than the Olsens and their ilk.

This account draws on Television Studies 1.0 in its address of the material conditions underpinning the Olsen media corporation, alerting us to a dialectical struggle between the cute and sometimes traumatic life of the twins, lived under public scrutiny, and the infinitely harsher (and largely un-scrutinized) labor exploitation that they depend on. Such an analysis forces us to transcend a TV- and celebrity-focused form of analysis that works with materials handed out by the publicity department and the fan's gaze. So does a psy-function account of how pro-anorexia websites value the twins (Lipczynska 2007). A second account draws on Television Studies 2.0 to focus on the ideological and material transformations that create the discourse of the Olsens and their semiotic value.

This other way in to the Olsens locates them in shifting discourses of femininity, where women have moved from representing domestic values to being high-profile, individual actors in public life. As part of that shift, which has certain continuities to do with consumption, women such as the Olsens become, from very early ages, both embroiled in, and representative of, complex commodity and labor relations for which they are, quite remarkably, held responsible. At the same time, the twins' struggles with education, weight, and love make them subjects of identification for many others dealing with the effect of feminism – without its ideological and interpersonal buttressing (Probyn 2008).

Can these two versions be brought together (as I suspect each of these brilliant analysts would wish to see)? That would take us to the next level of TV theory, which we'll consider in Chapter Five.

QUESTIONS FOR DISCUSSION

(1) What are the key disciplines feeding into TV Studies?
(2) What are the seven forms of inquiry of TV Studies?
(3) What is TV Studies 1.0?
(4) What is TV Studies 2.0?
(5) What are the major research topics about television according to publishing trends in the field?

NOTES

(1) I engage in some narcissography in this book, drawing on personal experience to suggest larger claims.
(2) I have tried to be very inclusive in this list but my apologies to authors whose important work has been excluded. For what it's worth, I left my own books out.
(3) For accounts of television criticism, see Benn 1990; Caughie 1984; Newcomb 1986; Poole 1984.
(4) Series of short monographs about programs have also emerged, from the BFI/Palgrave, Blackwell, and Wayne State University Press.

FURTHER READING

Gray, Herman. (1995). *Watching Race: Television and the Struggle for "Blackness."* Minneapolis: University of Minnesota Press.

Grossberg, Lawrence, Ellen Wartella, D. Charles Whitney, and J. McGregor Wise. (2005). *Media Making: Mass Media in a Popular Culture*, 2nd edn. Thousand Oaks: Sage Publications.

Hartley, John. (1999). *Uses of Television*. London: Routledge.

Seiter, Ellen. (1999). *Television and New Media Audiences*. Oxford: Clarendon Press.

Wasko, Janet, ed. (2005). *A Companion to Television*. Malden: Blackwell.

TELEVISION INSTITUTIONS

MARILYN: What does he do, your father?
RANSOM: He underestimates the intelligence of the American public and they pay him handsomely for it.
MARILYN: What does that mean?
RANSOM: He works in television.

(Jay McInerney 1987: 135)

Us, the creative industry, the wishy-washy liberal Marxist-poncy pony-tailed Hari Krishna dancing quality-worshipping impoverished public-service TV pussy-drips.

(Armando Iannucci 2008)

TV is the object of policies, programs, and users – an institution that is itself governed by institutions. This chapter explores television's institutional history, examining its emergence, who has controlled it, and where it has traveled. The first epigraph above captures the ambiguous, conflicted way in which people who work in it regard TV. It comes from Jay McInerney's novel, *Ransom*, the *Bildungsroman*-like tale of a Yanqui child of the culture industries who goes to Japan to reinvent himself. The second is a rather risqué, self-mocking remark from a television producer who is dedicated to things that others deride.

In Britain, 40 percent of television revenue comes from satellite subscriptions, 36 percent from advertising, and 24 percent from public money. The proportions are similar in Holland, Ireland, and Sweden, whereas advertising is the predominant source of revenue in Japan, Italy, and the US. The BBC is primarily funded by a fee on TV sets, which was set at £2 when introduced in 1946; it will be £151.50 from 2012 (Low 2009; Ofcom 2007: 20–1). Public broadcasters do not eschew competition – in fact, they operate internal markets for resources in addition to commissioning a large amount of programming from private producers, and compete for audience attention. Some, such as Canada's CBC and Australia's SBS, run commercials. In this chapter, we'll uncover the history to this story by looking at the rise of television, the shifting roles of the public and private sectors, the labor that makes TV happen, and its global impact.

HISTORY

In April 1927, US politician (and future President) Herbert Hoover's luckless features, soon to preside over the Republican Party's inept erosion of the global capitalist economy via the Great Depression, emerged on television thanks to a narrow beam transmitted by telephone and wireless from Washington to Whippany to New York. It could be seen through holes in a spinning disc (Borland and Hansen 2007). That same year, the BBC was granted a Royal Charter. The state was present, then, from the first broadcasts: endorsing, controlling, and performing.

TV was introduced onto the market, tentatively and briefly, in the 1930s. Ethel Lina White's 1936 novel, *The Wheel Spins* (the source for Alfred Hitchcock's classic film *The Lady Vanishes* two years later) recalls these early days in this description of its heroine: "Iris watched the smoke curling up from her cigarette. Occasionally she saw a vague little puckered face swaying amid the haze, like an unsuccessful attempt at television" (1955: 58). Decades of research and experimentation dedicated to transcending such dismal images were not matched by successful commodification. Britain had perhaps 3,000 sets prior to World War II, the US 6,000–10,000, and the Soviet Union about 400 (though all these numbers are in dispute). The Propaganda Ministry of the Nazi Party favored TV as a collective experience, so public settings were crucial to German television rather than domestic ones (Kersta 1942: 116; Gomery 2008: 231; Rantanen 2002: 93; Uricchio 2008: 298; Hickethier 2008: 73). TV was "a fully explored but wholly unexploited field" (Fly 1942).

The war halted experimental broadcasting and commercial supply, but even in 1942, regulators were sure that television would turn out to be a key industry, "a cushion against unemployment and depression" (Fly 1942). In the US, its development continued in the early days of the conflict. In the proud words of CBS President William S. Paley, TV shifted "from painting peacetime pictures in quiet living rooms to the lethal job of war." Paley went to work in psychological warfare to master propaganda. He believed that "improvement in television which emerges from this wartime work" would bring "pleasure" and "national pride" (Paley 1942). And within moments of the attack on Pearl Harbor, when information was fragmentary, TV went on the air to report, simulating the assault via pre-prepared visuals of what a battle in that region of the Pacific would resemble. (Despite what we are told today, journalists knew for months that an event such as this was likely.) Lessons in civil defense became common on New York television, while weather forecasts were banned in case they were picked up by enemy submarines. War bonds were sold through a drive whereby viewers telephoned in with pledges, and 50,000 air-raid wardens plus thousands of civil-defense groups were trained via television sets located in police stations. In the run-up to European hostilities, the BBC had run many programs on anti-aircraft defense, until its service was halted in order to focus industrial energies on the war effort more directly. In Germany, TV was removed from commercial circulation when the war began. It was reserved for entertaining injured and deployed troops (Hubbell 1942: 192–8; Kersta 1942: 26; Hickethier 2008: 72).

Once the war ended, television's uptake was spectacular. In the US, suburbanization and televisualization coincided, as returning servicemen set up families away from city centers due to incentives from government to buy homes. The penetration of TV went from 0.2 percent of houses in 1946 to 9 percent in 1950 and 65 percent in 1955. In the UK, signals extended beyond London from 1949. Over the next ten years, television spread across the US and Europe, then into the Third World, as newly free peoples emerged from colonialism, and claimed TV as a rite of passage and a right of communication. Television became *the* postcolonial object of desire, the most coveted object in homes around the world (Hickethier 2008: 74). This was not, however, a free-for-all. It was a very managed domain. In 1944, the nascent US Television Broadcasters Association stressed its wish to avoid "any repetition of the errors that marked radio's beginnings" (quoted in Boddy 1994: 114). What were these errors? Radio was initially a two-way device that required technical mastery. In place of these qualities, the Association sought a one-way, easy-to-use technology that would encourage audiences to watch and buy, not participate and create. And they wanted no tinkering, inventing, or frustration with the appliance.

Television was a fundamentally national phenomenon from the 1950s to the 1980s, in that its technology, content, and spectrum were regulated by governments. At the same time, it had international and commercial influences. Fashions were adopted by newcomers from pathbreaking nations and places with which they had affinities and histories based on colonialism, regionalism, or language. Both technology and content were sold as commodities. Countries with sizeable commercial radio networks developed similar TV systems (Australia and the US stood out) and countries with large public-service radio structures brokered them into television (India and Britain, for example). The US was unusual in eschewing national public television until its system had matured, while Australia was unusual in its spread of private and public from the very beginning. National networks in the US and Australia mixed stations that they owned and operated with numerous affiliates. There were also many independent stations, especially in the US. Through the 1960s and 1970s, local TV properties had massive profit margins, with networks competing to buy them or sign them up to take shows. The US pioneered the widespread use of cable and was the first place where systems other than broadcast television became dominant, because so many places had difficulty picking up broadcasts as a consequence of their topography. Then cable was stimulated by deregulation in 1977. By 1980, one-fifth of households had cable television, a proportion that increased to well over half of all homes ten years later and is now nearly 90 percent if one includes satellite. That led to a shift, with networks finally selling programming to cable stations from 1993 – a long, slow process of the end of local stations that began long before the Internet proliferated (Schechner and Dana 2009; Richardson and Figueroa 2005). The US also pioneered color television. All three principal networks were offering comprehensive color schedules by 1966, and by 1972 over half the population owned the new sets (Attallah 2007: 328). In the Second World, by contrast, TV was state- and Party-dominated, and its uptake was slow. Just 5 percent of the Soviet population had sets as late as 1960, though virtually everyone did by the mid–1980s (Mickiewicz 1999: 24, 26).

Public broadcasters have played a special role in this history. John Reith, the first head of the BBC, and his successors promoted the Corporation as a bulwark against rampant commercialism (i.e. the United States and its successful cinema exports) and political extremism (i.e. the Soviet Union and Italy and their successful ideological exports) (McGuigan 1996: 56). The task of public broadcasting was to inform, educate, and entertain, and it has largely remained that, albeit updated to reflect the wordy jargon of creative-industry discourses that has come to dominate European policy discussions of TV. Public broadcasters continue to transcend the idiotic limits of markets, because they seek to be universally available across geographical space to all citizens, to sustain national culture, to be independent of political and commercial pressures, to show impartiality, and to encourage textual diversity (Ofcom 2007; Slabbert *et al.* 2007: 333). Public broadcasting's remit involves such tasks as bringing the arts to the working class, teaching the population in school, informing and diverting unpaid female labor in the home, covering nation-building events such as sport and news, and addressing religious differences. The Australian Government refers to the ABC as "an important community space," a "virtual village square" that is "an essential component of our democracy" thanks to its core principles of universal availability, local engagement, national textuality, and comprehensiveness and diversity of content (Conroy 2008: 1; Department of Broadband, Communications and the Digital Economy 2008: 5).

In Britain, the BBC was the only TV network from 1936 to 1955, when ITV became a commercial alternative. BBC 2 appeared in 1964. In 1982, Channel 4 began. Then satellite networks arrived, based both locally and abroad. Post-War German TV was modeled after the UK, but with the institutionalization of governance through interest groups, such as the church and labor, in order to avoid the concentration of power that had characterized Nazi rule. Turkey had a state monopoly on TV from 1964 to

1993. In France, TV had no advertising until 1968, and private stations were allowed from 1982; today, there is a huge array of choice by contrast with the first three decades of television. Bizarrely, a key contemporary issue for the French left is maintaining advertising on public TV, which was removed by government decree in 2009 in order to aid the plutocracy by reserving commercial revenue for private stations, with the alibi that this change would create a Francophone BBC. Progressive activists worried that the real impact would be to diminish resources for the public service (Open Society Institute 2005; Chrisafis 2009).

Sometimes public TV has been straightforwardly propagandistic, with the state directly ruling the airwaves, for instance during Soviet-backed dictatorships in eastern and central Europe and US-backed dictatorships in Spain and Greece. Such strong-arm propaganda was in contradistinction to the indirect, autonomous concept of the BBC. Then the West's deregulatory policy fashions of the 1980s coincided with the decline of state socialism. Words such as "free" became clichés of for-profit networks as opposed to public services. In the emerging democracies of eastern and central Europe, news and current affairs offered few protections for journalists to ply their trade, either through legislation or codes that guaranteed editorial independence from the interlocking business and political interests of station proprietors (Open Society Institute 2005). In East Asia, fundamentally state-centric TV was gradually supplanted both by the desire of capital to shift toward culture and services and the emergence of satellites that outran regulation (Curtin 2007). At the same time, cultural agencies such as public TV were increasingly expected to reflect diversity as much as unity, paying heed to differences within populations as well as between them (Chakravartty and Sarikakis 2006: 88–9, 95).

Depending on their scale and polity, many countries followed more devolved strategies than the centralized public model – China was too poor to create a national TV service, so after television began in 1958 to just fifty sets, all of them in Beijing, the state established both centralized and provincial broadcasters. By 1966 and the Cultural Revolution, there were 12,000 receivers, which were generally collectively owned. Local and provincial municipalities made their own programs as well as being network members from the 1980s, and the thawing of state socialism saw the first commercial air in 1979. Small-scale stations began transmogrifying into commercial outlets as cable and satellite technology proliferated through the 1990s. By 1998, there were more than 4,000 networks. Today, the nation has more cable subscribers than anywhere else. Education stations affiliated with various levels of government have become for-profit, nationally available enterprises, frequently refusing to carry programs from central public TV on commercial grounds. These tendencies reflected both wider national-policy issues and the banal models of the capitalist West. The inevitable taste for mergers and consolidations in the 1990s infected local practice, further complicating the distinction between private and public TV, and weakening localism – a story we are familiar with from elsewhere. A condition of joining the World Trade Organization was met in 2004 when China permitted minority foreign investment in local media corporations, but news has remained Soviet-like both in its content and the requirement that it be screened on all stations at the same time (bar the elite preserve of satellite): when it wasn't being a source of entertainment, TV was still there to serve the Party (Zhao 2008: 95–6, 99; Hung 2008: 65–6; Fung 2008: 66; Feng *et al.* 2008; Chen 2007).

In Zambia, when freedom from colonial enslavement came in 1964, TV was nationalized. Shifting away from its stress on British expatriate audiences, television was transformed into a central part of self-reliance and nation-building until the 1990s brought privatization, internationalization, and commodification in obedience to Western and local elites (Kapatamoyo 2008) – a common African narrative. Throughout Latin America, big corporate interests have always been privileged, and public broadcasting has been dependent on governments for both funding and programming direction, apart from Bolivia and Chile, where services began only in the 1960s and under the purview of universities. Mexico was the first Latin American country to introduce TV, in 1950. The state granted licenses to a number of businesses for what were constitutionally defined as public airwaves. In one way or another, those favored firms have continued to dominate the landscape. The state did, however, reserve part of the spectrum for minority interests, catered to by Canal 11 from 1958. In 1983, Imevisión became a multifaceted state broadcaster, but the deregulatory wave of that decade and the next saw its privatization (Toussaint 2007). TV

Globo began in Brazil in 1965 as the offspring of a daily newspaper backed by Time Life. This was the year after a *coup/golpe* that ushered in military dictatorship for two decades, during which time the network was intimately involved with governmental priorities and personnel, a coziness that developed with the return to democracy in 1985. The twenty-first-century switch to digital TV saw the rest of the continent depending on decisions made in Brazil and Mexico on the choice of technology, so great was their sway throughout the region and beyond (Porto 2007: 368; Carboni and López 2008; Protzel 2005; Venegas 2008: 458–9).

REGULATION

Televisual regulation has routinely addressed several distinct but related elements:

- allocating and administering licenses and space on the electronic spectrum;
- censoring advertising, politics, sex, and violence;
- restricting cross-media and foreign ownership; and
- mandating local, regional, national, ethnic, sporting, and children's programs.

These regulations display fears and hopes for TV and its perceived power as a source of education, information, and distraction. Television has turned into a site of struggle between the idea of a technology that binds peoples together in national or regional formations versus pure entertainment. As was indicated above, the first discourse draws from a notion of public service and the second from private gain. They lead to distinct modes of production and distribution.

As may already be clear, if I had been writing this book in the first four decades of TV, this section would have been characterized by a Cold-War division. The principal systems were the Western-European, which mixed a dominant public-service model with a subordinate commercial one both at home and in former colonies, and the Soviet, which made for direct control across the state-socialist world and eschewed private-sector enterprise both at home and in its sphere of influence. But today, the US model is triumphant, with untrammeled commercialism rapidly becoming a norm since the 1980s. For that reason, I shall dedicate some space here to debates within the US as exemplary of the trouble and strife that follow upon this hyper-commercialism.

The enabling legislation that birthed and still governs the FCC supposedly guarantees citizens that broadcasters serve "the public interest, convenience and necessity," a tradition that began when CBS set up a radio network in the 1920s founded on news rather than its rival NBC's predilection for entertainment (Scardino 2005). What has been the Commission's record with TV?

When veteran US newsman Edward R. Murrow addressed the country's Radio–Television News Directors Association in 1958, he used the description/metaphor that TV needed to "illuminate" and "inspire," or it would be "merely wires and light in a box." In a famous speech to the National Association of Broadcasters three years later, John F. Kennedy's chair of the FCC, Newton Minow, called US television a "vast wasteland" (1971). He urged broad-casters to embark on enlightened Cold-War leadership, to prove that the US was not the mindless consumer world that the Soviet Union claimed. The networks must live up to their legislative responsibilities and act in the public interest by informing and entertaining, transcending what he later recognized as "white sub-urbia's Dick-and-Jane world" (Minow 2001). They responded by doubling the time devoted to news each evening, and quickly became the dominant means of Yanquis learning about current affairs (Schudson and Tifft 2005: 32). Twenty years later, however, Ronald Reagan's FCC head, Mark Fowler, celebrated the reduc-tion of the "box" to "transistors and tubes." He argued in an inter-view with *Reason* magazine that "television is just another appliance – it's a toaster with pictures" and hence in no need of regulation, beyond ensuring its physical safety as a commodity (1981). (Not surprisingly, Alfred Hitchcock had said it earlier and better: "Tele-vision is like the American toaster, you push the button and the same thing pops up every time" (quoted in Wasko 2005a: 10)).

Minow's and Fowler's expressions gave their vocalists instant and undimmed celebrity (Murrow already had it as the most her-alded audiovisual journalist in US history). Minow was named "top newsmaker" of 1961 in an Associated Press survey, and appeared on television and radio more than any other Kennedy official. The phrase "vast wasteland" has even, irony of ironies, provided raw material for the wasteland's parthenogenesis: it has been the answer to questions posed on numerous game shows, from *Jeopardy!* (1964–75, 1978–9, 1984–) to *Who Wants to Be a Millionaire?* (1998–) (Minow and Cate 2003: 408). But network profits rose even as Minow's criticisms resonated during his time as FCC Chair. Minow postured that stations' licenses might not be renewed, but his DC masters needed TV for electoral purposes, so these threats were hollow. By 1965, he was comfortably back practicing law – with CBS as a client (Gomery 2008: 220).

The "toaster with pictures" slogan is less celebrated, but has been more efficacious as a slogan for deregulation across successive Administrations. It remains in *Reason*'s pantheon of famous libertarian quotations, alongside Reagan and others of his ilk. Where Minow stands for public culture's restraining (and ultimately conserving) function for capitalism, Fowler represents capitalism's brooding arrogance, its neoliberal lust to reject use value in favor of exchange value. Minow decries Fowler's vision, arguing that broadcasting "is not an ordinary business" because of its "public responsibilities" (Minow and Cate 2003: 415). But Fowler's phrase has won the day, at least to this point. Minow's lives on as a recalcitrant moral irritant, rather than a central policy technology.

Ideas of deregulation appealed to the left as well as the right. The free-cable, free-video social movements of the 1960s and 1970s and the neoclassical, deregulatory intellectual movements of the 1970s and 1980s each imagined a people's technology emerging from the wasteland of broadcast television, as porta-pak equipment, localism, and unrestrained markets provided alternatives to the numbing nationwide commercialism of the networks. The social-movement vision saw this occurring overnight. The technocratic vision imagined it in the "long run." One began with folksy culturalism, the other with technophilic futurism. Each claimed it in the name of diversity, and they even merged in the depoliticized "Californian ideology" of community media, much of which quickly embraced market forms. Neither formation engaged economic reality. But together, they established the preconditions for unsettling a cozy, patriarchal, and quite competent television system that had combined, as TV should, what was good for you and what made you feel good, all on the one set of stations; i.e. a comprehensive service

(Mullen 2003; Barbrook and Cameron 1996). These discourses remain at work in Television Studies 2.0 and cybertarianism.

In place of the universalism of the old networks, where sport, weather, news, lifestyle, and drama programming had a comfortable and appropriate *frottage*, highly centralized but profoundly targeted consumer networks emerged in the 1990s that fetishized lifestyle and consumerism *tout court* over a blend of purchase and politics, of fun and foreign policy, of consumption and citizenship. The fashion for this deregulation swept the TV world, hand in hand with an end to the idea that media organizations should be run by media people, who had commitments to the public interest as well as the bottom line. As media companies were acquired by large conglomerates, the cash flow guaranteed by television was expected to support other firms, leading in many cases to a drain on TV resources. A classic instance is the US ratings leader, Spanish-language station Univision. An enormously popular network, it was hit hard by the 2008–9 downturn in automobile advertising, losing 25 percent of revenue. But its real difficulties lay in the fact that it had been purchased by a private-equity firm which went into huge debt to buy it, and whose mad loans it must service (Szalai 2008).

The febrile fetish of deregulation spread around the world from the FCC across the 1980s. The decline of state socialism in Europe and dictatorship in Latin America coincided with a deregulatory fervor that gripped policy-making in capitalist democracies and international organizations, exerting a major impact on communication infrastructures and wreaking havoc on media workers' chances of fulfilling, secure employment. States that had once regarded broadcasting as too influential to be left to commerce were persuaded by this new cult to sever their allegiance to public ownership and control, in the name of efficiency, effectiveness, and freedom. Countries that already had extensive commercial networks diminished regulatory controls on private-sector television, while those with public-sector systems opened up the airwaves to profit. At the same time, new technologies made TV less easily controlled by national governments, because audiences could draw signals from beyond political boundaries via satellite and the Internet. Today, a worldwide television system mixes public and private on an unequal basis. The former is increasingly scrambling for funding and legitimacy, while the latter is rampant. A gigantic corporate-welfare scam enables private-sector TV. Not having to bid for licenses in an open way that is free to all renders ridiculous the assertion that television is laissez-faire, but this reality is camouflaged by corporations claiming to benefit local communities through a "special obligation to serve the common good." They even argue that "Fowler was famously wrong" in his reduction of the industry to toast-burning (Eggerton 2008).

Another former head of the FCC avows that "[t]he key goal of communications policy is to promote the welfare of our citizens, primarily through productivity gains" which will "increase business productivity and increase the benefits to consumers." The overriding concern is "to maximize the operation of markets" (Hundt and Rosston 2006: 2). This bald statement puts democracy out of the picture other than as a servant of capital. It subordinates – in fact denies – the fact that many consumers are also employees and citizens. Their welfare may be jeopardized or minimized by "productivity gains" without democratic worker control, fair redistribution of returns on investment, and competent circulation of knowledge about domestic and foreign politics, economics, and culture. (It is in keeping, however, with the broad swathe even of TV research, which, whether or not it is blindly wedded to the preferred discourses of business, pays hardly any heed whatsoever to the fact that people work to make television, or that citizens work and learn when they watch it (Grindstaff and Turow 2006: 118).) This leads to grotesque racial and gender imbalances in job opportunities, as well as exploitative labor practices and low levels of public awareness of crucial political–economic matters. In the US, we see multicultural talent on-screen, for example among newsreaders and journalists, but off-screen, whiteness prevails, because there are no audience targets decreeing otherwise. The BBC's workforce, too, is "hideously white" (Burrell 2008).

The transformation of communications systems by neoliberal processes (privatization, deregulation, and the elimination of services provided by the welfare state for both political and economic reasons) has resulted in the recomposition and resignification of territories and publics. The transnationalization and (neo)liberalization of the culture industries imposes entry into the global economy, and domestic restructuring, according to a "dialectic of uniformization and differentiation." On the one hand, juridical protocols, technologies, and administrative procedures become singular; on the other, accommodating to transnational markets requires the generation of local differences to facilitate content that will sell across borders:

> Each geographic space needs to differentiate itself and construct its media image in order to valorize itself in relation to the exterior and in that way insert itself into international networks; culture is amply utilized in the construction of that media image.
>
> (Herscovici 1999: 58–9)

These things materialize in the light of different policy purposes and histories. So if we look at how Britain and the US pursued digital TV, we can discern some significant variation. In the UK, there were paradoxical desires, to promote more and more competition within and between public and private broadcasters, even as public broadcasting was protected and urged to innovate. In the US, the overweening intent was to shore up existing private oligopolies and minimize disruption to corporate dominance, despite technological changes (Galperin 2004: 23).

Deregulation and the proliferation of commercial and technological alternatives to public-service broadcasting has sent the sector into one of its periodic crises of confidence. The damp squib that is PBS in the US, with 3 percent of the audience, might seem a desperate harbinger for the more-successful examples that inspired it, such as the BBC. Many critics of today's BBC want it to air unpopular content that does not threaten commercial fare. But the Corporation has resisted the idea of serving only a minority. Like ARD and ZDF in Germany and SVT in Sweden, it continues to deliver high-quality as well as popular programs. ZDF spends a great deal on local production, which stimulates private stations to rely less on imported materials. SVT faced commercial competition for the first time in 1991, but maintained viewership while encouraging private alternatives to invest in programming that would match its traditions, though as its commercial rival TV4 became more and more profit-oriented, SVT both lost audiences and became more populist. Denmark and Norway also have systems where advertiser-supported stations discharge certain public-service obligations. In Canada, when the CBC began investing more in French-language services, its for-profit competitors followed suit. Again and again, real risk-taking and innovation come from strong public broadcasters (Riegert 2008; Blake *et al.* 1999; Lund and Berg 2009). Despite the assault by deregulatory politicians, capitalists, and bureaucrats over the past quarter of a century, right across Europe, public television remains the principal source of news across the continent (Open Society Institute 2005). The BBC's role has expanded from its original purposes of informing, educating, and entertaining the citizenry to helping "build digital Britain" and developing the Corporation's centrality to national culture by making it a portal and a model of technological innovation (Thompson 2006). The iPlayer, which attracted 237 million viewings in 2008, its first year, embodies these abilities, as public culture outstripped for-profit inventiveness. Australia's ABC has been similarly innovative by contrast with commercial rivals (Department of Broadband, Communications and the Digital Economy 2008: 8).

In the case of the new democracies in Eastern and Central Europe, the old days of command television, dominated by strong state-socialist governments, have been succeeded by an incomplete, underfunded, and under-regulated transition to public-service television. Commercial stations have bloomed, both in legal and pirate forms, and are moving toward consolidated oligopolies that typify advanced economies, with massive Western investment taking advantage of the end of foreign-ownership restrictions. So Estonian TV is run from Norway, for example. The process can be as political as it was under state socialism – in Poland, public TV changes controllers when governments change. Older capitalist democracies that deregulated created similarly dependent relationships: Austria, which only opened television to commercial services in 2001, is dominated by German private concerns. Italian deregulation of cross-media ownership rules has seen massive concentration of media power in the hands of one man – Silvio Berlusconi, a politician whose routine electoral success was ensured despite numerous indictments because of his tight-fisted control of news as owner of three channels and controller of state ones, *inter alia* (Open Society Institute 2005; Hasebrink and Herzog 2007; "Tragedy or Farce?" 2009; Hibberd 2007; Eco and Solomon 2007).

Like the Nordic countries, Britain's notion of public-service broadcasting is not restricted to the traditional flagship of the BBC. S4C in Wales is required to provide an alternative to the hegemony of English; Channel Five is expected to be commercial but to stress British material; Channel 4 must innovate and educate; and ITV's remit is to ensure the provision of regional programming, including current affairs and news (Ofcom 2007). For over two decades, those arrangements functioned effectively. But with more channels and more media seeking advertising revenue, only the BBC, with income guaranteed through the license fee, feels able to discharge its public-service obligations. Current projections suggest that UK TV advertising revenue will decline by 20 percent from 2006 to 2012. Channel 4 faced a shortfall in its funding of £150 million late in 2008 due to failed investments in a digital radio network plus diminished money from commercials, even though its audience had grown by 12 percent and its advertising revenue by one-quarter over the previous five years (Sweney 2008; Duncan 2009). Part of the back story is that advertising on TV is massively more costly in Britain than the US, since there are so many fewer outlets, which has sent capital scurrying toward cheaper Internet alternatives. And two decades of viewer choice had also decimated ITV's audience. Its income was so imperiled that Ofcom estimated in 2009 that ITV would invest £235 million less in programs each year through 2012 (Richards 2009). And, on another front, the evidence shows that children's television suffers hugely when concentration of ownership is achieved due to deregulation (Children Now 2007). So ITV wants to cut its public-service obligations, without losing its prime place on remote controls, a privilege given in return for this remit (Robinson 2009; Ofcom 2009: 36; Gibson 2008; Swearingen and Chapman 2008).

LABOR

Clearly, television companies are now producing, distributing, and exhibiting texts through a wide array of platforms, mechanisms, and funding systems, beyond their origins in broadcast TV. This proliferation, alongside technological, regulatory, and wider macro-economic changes, has dramatically altered the landscape and experience of media work. When I migrated to New York City in

1993, interviewers for broadcast stations' news shows would come to my apartment as a team: a full complement of sound recordist, camera operator, lighting technician, and journalist. Now they are rolled into one person. More content must be produced from fewer resources, and more and more multi-skilling and multi-tasking are required. In my example, the journalist has taken over the other tasks. The job of the editor is also being scooped up into the new concept of the "preditor," who must perform the functions of producer and editor. And if journalists work for companies like NBC, they often write copy for several websites *and* provide different edited versions of the original story for MSNBC, CNBC, CNBC Africa, CNBC Europe, and CNBC Asia, in addition to the parent network and individual channels in various countries.

In the British case, whereas the BBC used to do the vast majority of its production in house, via full-time employees, 39 percent of its texts now come from independent small businesses (Thompson 2009). TV executive Dawn Airey (2007) warns against this "casualisation of the industry" because it leads to less thorough and committed institutions and workers, and undermines collegial memory and practice. Veteran producer Irene Shubik remembers a time when "a nucleus of directors, story editors, designers and writers" worked together, sharing skills and ideas over numerous projects and many years. Such teamwork and innovation may not be so easily generated with more fetishized work practices (2000: 43).

For decades, employment in television has expanded above US national averages, with cable a particular source of job growth (Toto 2000). Today, the Bureau of Labor Statistics warns that "a large number of jobseekers" remain "attracted by the glamour of this industry" (2008), even though projections for employment are dismal. Before the recession was officially decreed, in 2007, writers' employment was the lowest for eleven years (Writers Guild 2008). The figures below paint a declining number of jobs in US broadcast TV, although cable continues to grow. This disparity is partially due to the change in viewing numbers toward cable and satellite, and partially to the fact that it is a largely un-unionized sector by comparison with broadcast, so wages, security, and health insurance decline while profit margins increase.

The US media as a whole lost 200,000 jobs in the decade after the 2000 dot-com bubble, more than half in newspapers ("Media

Jobs?" 2008). The key difference emerging in 2009 was the collapse of non-media firms that paid huge sums of money for national television coverage, such as car companies and big-box or high-street retail stores. The previous year, the weakness of the advertising economy had been hidden by two gigantic stimuli in an Olympic Games and a Presidential election. But even as the recession hit and the broadcast networks' ratings dropped, advertisers remained firm believers in the efficacy of TV over other media – budgets were being cut everywhere, but less for television ("Most Media" 2008; Consoli 2008).

Cable profits surged even as broadcast ones tumbled in 2008, and the indications were for renewed growth in cable advertising despite the recession (Atkinson 2009; Steinberg 2009b). Cable and satellite were the site of conflicts between those who just owned texts versus those who owned platforms as well. Viacom threatened to remove stations from Time Warner in 2008, at a time when it provided 20 percent of the audience, because it was only receiving 2 percent of monthly receipts from subscribers (Friedman 2009a). At the same time as "good," ongoing jobs in TV were diminishing in number, cable networks continued to emerge – 13 percent more in 2004 by contrast with the year before – and gain profitability, with each year of the past decade bringing advertising growth due to the discounts available by comparison with the old networks. But this is no index of an open market. Rather, it signals additional ownership concentration, with 90 percent of the major cable networks owned by five conglomerates, which also own many of the companies that make the shows they buy. Before deregulation in 1995, networks had to abide by an anti-trust logic. Instead of screening shows they had produced, they bought the right to put on programs made by others; as a consequence, independent houses proliferated – there were forty major independents until these rules were rescinded. All the small businesses fell apart as big TV corporations moved production in-house so that they could sell texts on through infinite other territories and media. The people who made the creative decisions about everything from storylines to wallpaper were over-ridden again and again by men in suits who lacked relevant expertise. And these desk-bound businesspeople want to prevent the Web from being subject to the same wage conditions as television ("Most Media" 2008; Richardson and Figueroa 2005; Herskovitz

2007; Dobuzinskis 2009). All this has an impact on the programs you enjoy or the sector of the economy you want to work in.

> In India, the number of TV commercials per channel per day increased by 41 percent between 2004 and 2008. Cable systems, which had been localized and were celebrated as oppositional because so many engaged in illegal downloading, became national and legal in 2008 through the emergence of multi-system firms via investments of around seven billion rupees, consolidation of the industry from chaos into oligopoly, and the spread of digital cable. As this growth took place, workers went on strike for improved pay from producers, and 2008 was the first time in history that Indian television featured reruns. More and more stars from cinema were brought in to headline shows, and high-end audiences were targeted by specialized new stations. Costs spiraled (AdEx India Analysis 2008; Jayaraman 2009; "2008" 2009).

GLOBALIZATION

Former US Secretary of State and master of the dark art of international relations Henry Kissinger (1999) says "globalisation is really another name for the dominant role of the United States." His consulting firm advises that the US must "win the battle of the world's information flows, dominating the airwaves as Great Britain once ruled the seas," not least because

> Americans should not deny the fact that of all the nations in the history of the world, theirs is the most just, the most tolerant, the most willing to constantly reassess and improve itself, and the best model for the future.

Less magically and self-interestedly, Jacques Attali (2008) explains that a new "mercantile order forms wherever a creative class masters a key innovation from navigation to accounting or, in our own time, where services are most efficiently mass produced, thus generating enormous wealth." New eras in communication also index homologies and exchanges between militarism, colonialism, and class control. The networked-computing era has solidified the US as the world's dominant economic actor. Alongside Japan and Western Europe, it forms the power triad of the cultural world. None of that has changed or been even mildly imperiled by the newer media or anything else. China and India provide many leading software engineers, but they lack domestic venture capitalists, military underpinnings to computing innovation, and histories of global textual power at the mainstream level as per Sony, the BBC, Hollywood, or the Pacific North-West; so the triad still accounts for 80 percent of the globe's programming market, for example ("World Television Market" 2009).

Over the past forty years, the New International Division of Cultural Labor has seen production of both TV sets and shows go offshore. Britain, for instance, had over thirty different manufacturers of televisions after World War II. In 2009, the last one shuttered its doors, because low-wage rivals in Turkey, Eastern and Central Europe, and Asia were able to produce flat-screen TVs more cheaply – often thanks to state subvention or suppression of workers' wages and organizations (Low 2009; Shim and Jin 2007: 163). From the very first, the US sought to bind the export of sets and texts and the export of ideology. So Sarnoff wrote an editorial for *Look* magazine in 1950 avowing that "[t]o be believed, the American way of life must be seen as well as heard." TV was the ideal means (2004: 309). And in the 1960s, a Vice-President of NBC International discussed difficulties in exporting programs to Saudi Arabia to do with lip-sync dubbing: "This problem has been encountered before with such languages as Japanese, and will be overcome as American television know-how continues to expand throughout the world" (Anderson 1965: 21). The export of televisual technologies, texts, and tastes made the US a dominant presence on screens wherever markets were open to it from the 1960s (Miller *et al.* 2005).

The subsequent development of a cultural-imperialism thesis, in Latin America in particular, argued that the US, as the world's leading producer and exporter of television, was transferring its dominant value system to others. There was said to be a corresponding diminution in the vitality and standing of local languages and traditions, and hence a threat to national identity. As Herbert I. Schiller expressed it: "the media-cultural component in a developed, corporate economy supports the economic objectives of the decisive industrial-financial sectors (i.e., the creation and extension of the consumer society)" (1991: 14). This position attributed US political, military, and economic hegemony to dominance over news agencies, advertising, market research, public opinion, screen trade, technology, propaganda, and telecommunications. The long history of US participation in Latin-American politics, followed by involvement in South-East Asian wars during the 1960s, led to critiques of its military interventions against struggles of national liberation, which in turn targeted links between the military–industrial complex and the media. Critics pointed out that communications and culture bolstered US foreign policy and military strategy and enabled the more general expansion of multinational corporations, which were substantial power brokers in their own right.

From the early 1970s, most notably via the United Nations Educational, Scientific and Cultural Organisation (UNESCO) and the Non-Aligned Movement, Third World countries lobbied for what was variously termed a New International Information Order or New World Information and Cultural Order (NWICO), mirroring calls for a New International Economic Order and a revised North–South dialog. The 1973 meeting of Heads of State of Non-Aligned Countries spoke of a "need to reaffirm national cultural identity" (quoted in Sinclair 1982: 8). UNESCO set up the Mac-Bride Commission to investigate cultural and communication issues in North–South cultural flows and power. It reported in 1980 on the need for equal distribution of the electronic spectrum, reduced postal rates for international texts, protection against satellites crossing borders, and an emphasis on the media as tools of development and democracy rather than commerce. There continue to be annual roundtables on the Commission's legacy, but the insistence by the US on the free flow of communications, including TV, proved to be a successful riposte to NWICO, in keeping with the deregulatory ideas discussed earlier.

These concerns are not solely the province of the Global South. The Canadians have a unique purchase on anxieties about US screen domination. Even before the inception of television there in 1952, affection for Yanqui culture was officially derided as unpatriotic, because there were 150,000 TV sets in Canada tuned to US signals prior to the advent of local broadcasting. There has been over half a century of battling what is perceived as "an ideological misrecognition whereby Canadians mistake American television for what they really like while simultaneously neglecting the Canadian television that they ought to like." By contrast with these overwhelming Anglo anxieties, French-Canadian television is avowedly populist and commercially successful (Attallah 2007: 331, 334, 338, 344).

For its part, the EU has attempted to balance continental culture and commercial success through TV, while acknowledging the medium's national specificity and the difficulties of dealing with so many linguistic groups. The default international language of much television is English, which has enabled and, in turn, *been* enabled by the popularity of US material, a further cause of concern to many nations in the Union. EU agencies have been torn between the notion of an unfettered regional market for the exchange of programs that will appeal across 465 million people, by far the wealthiest TV market in the world; the desire to generate a continental sense of belonging; and the complexities of so many member-states, with so few having strong, embedded television systems. The Union's neoliberal elements are opposed to public-service broadcasting, as are parts of the World Trade Organization. But there can be a *rapprochement* between these drives, via the notion of viewers as consumers with rights to quality, just as they exercise with regard to appliances, food, politics, or universities (Open Society Initiative 2005; Celot and Gualtieri 2007).

There is a significant contrary view to the theories and policies that engage media imperialism. A 1994 television survey by the *Economist* remarked that cultural politics is always so localized in its first and last instances that the "electronic bonds" of exported drama are "threadbare" (Heilemann 1994: Survey 4). Clearly, part of the talent of TV texts is that they can be altered to suit new circumstances. Sony, Time Warner, and Disney all produce thousands of hours of television texts in foreign markets each year, designed for local audiences. Similar stories apply to material produced by the Spanish-owned Endemol in the Netherlands, and Action Time, Granada, and All American Fremantle. In Italy, *The Nanny* (1993–9) was dubbed to make Fran Drescher's character Sicilian rather than Jewish, thereby connoting someone adjacent yet still marginal to the dominant culture. In the 1960s, Disney television in Australia consisted of US programs rebroadcast on local stations;

by the 1990s, these shows were superficially localized, via young, cute, and guileless Australian presenters. And General Motors translated its "hot dogs, baseball, apple pie, and Chevrolet" jingle into "meat pies, football, kangaroos, and Holden cars" for the Australian market. Granada customized the British soap opera *Coronation Street* (1960–) for China (*Joy Luck Street* (2000)) (Miller *et al.* 2005). *La malinche*, the complex female icon of Latin American sexual conquest and collaboration implicated with the Spanish invasion, appears in struggles over *ikhtilat*, the concept of illicit sex in Arab reality television (Kraidy 2009). In South Africa, former African National Congress Communist Party leader Tokyo Sexwale, now a billionaire, played the business leech in the localized version of *The Apprentice* (Glenn 2008).

"The West" finally won over a key segment of the Indian market with a localized *Who Wants to be a Millionaire?* (memorable for its "role" in *Slum Dog Millionaire* (Danny Boyle 2008)). While the original program was British, it met many Yanqui criteria stylistically and ideologically with its game-show consumerism and sexual objectification. It was also said to have "softened up the general public for the 'knowledge economy'" (Hartley 2008: 244; for the fullest version of such claims, see Ott 2007). The program was sold to 107 countries by 2009. In the Middle East, it was remade as a pan-Arab Islamic game show (Gray 2009; Bielby and Harrington 2008: 113). The managing director of Celador, which sold the format, says: "It's a bit like the old days of the British empire. We've got a map of the world in the office colored in pink where we've placed the show" (quoted in Freedman 2008: 213).

Modeled on the 1950s US game show, textual formats are traded in both regulated and pirated ways, with multinational firms moving easily between high moralism and sharp practice. The Format Recognition and Protection Association represents over 100 TV companies worldwide that charge for re-use of their intellectual property. Agile format firms are aware that local-content regulations are designed to stymie TV imports, so they point out to companies based in small nations which protect local industries and culture through state quotas that buying a format and customizing it may satisfy such policies (Moran with Malbon 2006: 9). Not all format exchanges go easily. A famous case concerns the 1999 Mexican program *TeleChobis*, an unauthorized TV Azteca version of the BBC children's program, *Teletubbies* (1997–2001). *Teletubbies* was screening on Azteca's rival, Televisa. Azteca responded by introducing many national signifiers and live children to its unauthorized copycat *TeleChobis* – but was ultimately stymied through intellectual-property regimes (Kraidy 2005: 104–14).

Then there is the question of entire channels broadcasting overseas. Since the 1980s, CNN and MTV have come to symbolize that truth and fun can be sold not just as shows, but networks. The US continues to be the major source of TV news and current affairs around the world, while Britain has about one-fifth of global exports. This power is exerted via CNN and the BBC on the one hand, and news agencies – Associated Press Television News and Reuters Television – on the other. CNN broadcasts to over 130 nations across the principal world languages, with globally generated as well as regionally specific content a key to its prominence. Germany has two news networks in Asia, received by over 1,000 satellite systems, with three-quarters of programming in German and one-quarter in English ("Deutsche Welle" 2009). Such inequality in the source and ideology of stories about the Global South has led to renewed NWICO-like calls for a *contra*-flow of news (Thussu 2004). US governmental and civil-society action produces specifically propagandistic television – the US bombards Iran with satellite TV in Farsi (twenty-five networks in 2005, many of which focused on politics), generated by "Persian" expatriates in southern California who define themselves against the Islamic Republic (Semati 2007: 151–2), Cuba receives State Department "information" day after day, and the Pentagon has a channel.

While criticisms were long made of MTV when it started to globalize, because of a preponderance of US material, the network quickly became regional rather than local or Yanqui in its programming. By 2008, MTV was in 162 countries across thirty-three languages, with revenue not only from the sale of shows but massive merchandising tie-ins as well – toys, clothes, and, of course, *Rock Band* (2007–), the video game which has sold millions of copies. Nevertheless, customization to local markets never prevented Sumner Redstone, its owner, from boasting about MTV's universal influence (Miller *et al.* 2005; Bignell and Fickers 2008a: 41; "Listen to the Music" 2008; "Job 1 at Viacom" 2009). For its part, 80 percent of programming for children outside the white-settler colonies and China comes from the US. The only large cross-national study of children's TV shows the absolute dominance of US programs. The US children's channel Nickelodeon is available in well over 150 countries. So young people across Ghana, Kenya, Nigeria, and South Africa are familiar with *SpongeBob SquarePants* (1999–) (Götz *et al.* 2008; Osei-Hwere and Pecora 2008: 16, 19).

ESPN, a series of Yanqui sports cable channels owned by Disney, has thirty-one networks outside the US, in addition to related interests in promotions and other media. Its texts are on sale in 194 countries and territories across fifteen language groups. ESPN customizes programs established in the US, notably the highlights show *SportsCenter* (1979–), and emphasizes local interests in materials devised for particular audiences, especially football. A Latin American network started in 1989 and operates alongside three sub-regional networks. ESPN owns five networks in Canada, is screened throughout the Middle East on satellite, has several EU channels, and runs thirteen customized stations across Asia (ESPN International 2009). At issue here are the expropriation of profit and the consolidation of already-dominant sports.

When it comes to films shown on television, US exports remain extremely powerful. In 1995, 89 percent of films screened on Brazil's cable channels were US imports, which occupied 61 percent of time dedicated to cinema on Mexican TV. Cable and satellite opened up the Middle East across the 1990s, producing a scramble to "secure access to Western content" and partially "Arabize" it. US film channels and a special Arab-dedicated Disney service were strikingly successful – by 1999, Disney was making US$100 million a month in the Middle East. Three years later, Showtime debuted ten new channels through Nilesat. Since its earliest days in the 1960s, Malaysian television has relied on US cinema for content, which dominates prime time. The same is true in Sri Lanka and the Philippines, where local movies are rarely seen on television. Eurodata TV's analysis in 1999 of films on television found that fourteen Hollywood pictures drew the highest audiences in twenty-seven nations across all continents (Miller *et al.* 2005).

Television drama more generally shows the same trend. In 1983, the US was estimated to have 60 percent of global TV sales. By 1999, that US figure had grown to 68 percent, thanks to 85 percent of exported children's programming and 81 percent of TV movies. The only sizeable trade the other way was Britain's paltry export (worth US$85 million); the following year, the UK's share of world television exchange stood at 9 percent, France's and Australia's at 3 percent. Britain went from a small TV trade surplus in 1989 to deficits of £272 million in 1997 and £403 million in 2000 – the difference arising from fashions in public policy, because the proliferation of channels following deregulation created new opportunities for English-language texts from Hollywood's archive. UK exports dropped by 10 percent in 1999 and 11 percent in 2000, victims of the tendency to buy British formats rather than programs, which minimized price and maximized local re-signification. A key function of BBC America, a cable network that has been on the air in the US since 1998, is to showcase reality programs that might then be sold as formats. The BBC boasts that Britain exports more than half the world's formats (Steemers 2004: 142–3; Gray 2009). As noted above, Britain's Channel Five is meant to turn a profit but stress national programming. Yet, in 2006, its six most popular programs included two Hollywood movies and *CSI: Crime Scene Investigation* (2000–), *CSI: Miami* (2002–), and *CSI: New York* (2004–) (Ofcom 2007: 107). Cool Britannia, anyone? Best television in the world?

How is US dominance achieved? In part because Hollywood can set export prices below the cost to importing nations of making their own programs – its initial expenditures have already been largely recouped via the sizeable domestic market. To give a sense of how differential pricing can aid in entering other countries, consider the key world television market, MIPCOM. Sales are made on a sliding scale. The fees paid reflect wealth, gullibility, and domestic competition rather than audience desire (see Tables 2.1 and 2.2).

Ideological change can matter as much as pricing. In 1974, the Soviet Union imported 5 percent of programming and in 1984, 8 percent; but after the collapse of state socialism, Russia imported 60 percent of its TV in 1997, much of it from the US. This was associated with a comprehensive re-articulation of the way the US was described on Russian television, a transformation from demonization to sanctification. Yanqui programs, propaganda, and products proliferated (Mickiewicz 1999: 21). Almost all commercials in the

Table 2.1 Sites, genres and US$ prices for US texts in television market, 2002 (drama per hour, others per half-hour)

Site	Feature	TV movie	Drama	Comedy	Documentary	Child
Australia	1 million	30,000	10,000	5,000	4,000	3,000
Brazil	60,000	16,000	9,000	2,500	3,000	2,250
Canada	125,000	100,000	50,000	35,000	5,000	25,000
Czech Republic	30,000	3,500	3,000	800	800	500
France	2 million	90,000	55,000	25,000	12,000	10,000
Germany	5 million	200,000	75,000	20,000	18,000	14,000
Italy	1 million	100,000	30,000	10,000	7,000	7,000
Japan	1.4 million	30,000	23,000	7,000	16,000	5,000
Mexico	40,000	15,000	8,000	6,000	2,000	2,000
Nordic	200,000	18,000	7,000	4,500	3,500	2,500
Spain	1 million	50,000	20,000	6,000	5,000	3,000
Britain	2 million	35,000	50,000	25,000	20,000	22,500

Source: Miller et al. 2005.

Table 2.2 Sites, genres and US$ prices for US texts in television market, 2008

Site	Documentary	Drama	Format	Animation
US	100,000–1m	300,000–1m	20,000–50,000	5,000–100,000
UK	10,000–200,000	20,000–120,000	15,000–40,000	12,000–34,000
Australia	3,000–10,000	16,000–50,000	7,500–35,000	1,000–4,500
Mexico	1,000–3,000	2,500–10,000	2,000–10,000	1,500–4,000
Japan	6,000–50,000	16,000–35,000	10,000–30,000	8,300–20,000
China	1,000–2,000	1,000–2,500	1,000–3,500	1,200

Source: Based on figures from *Television Business International*, 2008.

1990s, for instance, were imported US materials dubbed into Russian (Morris 2007: 1390–1). Though many commercials are now localized, the promise of transcendence through consumption remains marked with US diacritics. The Soviet Union had been a major exporter of television to East Germany and Bulgaria. When state socialism was displaced by authoritarian capitalism, the picture changed dramatically. By 1997, the US had displaced Soviet sales to eastern and central Europe. The de-Sovietization process of privatizing TV stations also decimated the screening of local films – previously the most significant genre in terms of time on the schedule – in favor of imported drama (Rantanen 2002: 86, 97).

Even when the volume of US television exports decreases, revenue may increase due to foreign-exchange fluctuations and other factors. In 2000, receipts from US programming in Europe grew by 15.9 percent although sales diminished from 223,000 hours to 214,000. The audiovisual imbalance of trade stood at US$8.2 billion, up 14 percent on 1999. In 2001, volume diminished again, by 1 percent. Sometimes co-productions account for the change in imported hours, as many are made in concert with the US but count as European for the purposes of public subsidies. The few competitors to the US in the European market have fallen away recently, notably New Zealand/Aoteraoan and Australian soap operas, which were briefly successful. By the late 1990s, Indonesia's five commercial stations were importing 7,000 shows annually, mostly from the US (Boellstorff 2003: 37). Kenyan television remains over 70 percent dominated by material from the First World, from international news to drama and reality (Evusa 2008: 209–10).

Dedicated genre stations (known as thematic channels in Spain) rely massively on US imports. They are mostly excluded from official statistics, which tend to focus on broadcast television. An exception is Australia, where numbers show a massive jump in imported TV with the advent of genre stations. The only year of net exports was due to the Sydney Olympics.

Although prime time on broadcast TV worldwide is usually occupied by local shows, in the wealthiest market, Europe, the dominant drama series in 2007 were *CSI: Miami*, *Desperate Housewives* (2004–), *Lost* (2004–), *Without a Trace* (2006–), and *The Simpsons* (1989–) (Bignell and Fickers 2008a: 8). In Asia, twenty-five-million fans watch the three *CSI* shows on Sony's AXN satellite network, while Britain's Channel Five meets its quality mandate through that franchise shows at the same time as it brands itself as US TV for the UK (Cohan 2008: 4; Goode 2007). US influence continues to apply under new technology: when TV commercials are displaced by the Internet – in Britain, revenue for the two media are close to equal at £3 billion annually – the majority goes to US companies (Duncan 2009).

The main element of difference within these globalizing yet centralizing tendencies is the Latin American *telenovela*. *Telenovelas* began when US companies looked to sell the same cleaning

Table 2.3 Geographical origins of television fiction programmed by major networks (sample week March 12–18 2000)

		Domestic (%)	US (%)	European (%)	Other (%)
United	Whole day	47	43	0	10
Kingdom	Prime time only	51	49	0	0
Germany	Whole day	36	57	5	2
	Prime time only	56	44	0	0
France	Whole day	25	56	15	5
	Prime time only	75	25	0	0
Italy	Whole day	19	64	4	13
	Prime time only	43	51	6	0
Spain	Whole day	20	56	7	17
	Prime time only	51	37	12	0

ιcts to women overseas they had sold domestically through
became known as the soap opera. The genre quickly underwent local customization (Straubhaar 2007: 9). Starting in the
1950s, by 2002 the foreign trade in these *novelas* amounted to
US$300 million. Televisa, the Mexican network, has been able to
export both across Latin America and to Spanish-language stations
in the US. Encouraged by the wealth of the Latin@ audience
north of the border, Mexico launched a satellite in 1984 and was
selling *telenovelas* to nearly 100 countries within fifteen years. TV
Globo was exporting shows from Brazil to Europe by the 1970s,
and reached 130 nations in 2001. In 2009, it featured a 200-episode
novela filmed and set in India (Protzel 2005; Havens 2005: 271,
275; Cajueiro 2009). In the US, the most popular programs on
Spanish-language Univision are Latin-American imports, such as
Las Tontas no Van al Cielo (2008–) [*Stupid Girls Don't Go to Heaven*]
and *Sin Tetas no Hay Paraíso* (2006) [*There's No Paradise Without
Breasts*]. They are also the most-pirated downloads on YouTube of
any TV programs, and led to a gigantic legal battle with the network's Mexican supplier (Goodwin 2009; Wentz 2009; James
2009a). *Yo Soy Betty, la fea* (1999–2001) was remade as *Ugly Betty*
(2006–) for the US from its Colombian origins following focus-
group research on behalf of the US producer and network. The
firm undertaking the work (one psychologist = "the firm") was
anglo parlante, and the program drew entirely negative reactions
from trial viewers. But the network proceeded anyway, probably
due to Salma Hayek's influence and the mythology then surrounding NBC's Ben Silverman. No wonder many Latin critics bemoan
the pressure to standardize that has come with international sales,
resulting in a loss of specificity, localism, and cutting-edge critique
of social relations (Mazziotti 1996: 113)!

Despite this notable exception of the *telenovela*,[1] the overall weight
of the evidence on globalization is clear. The volume of US exports
may be unstable, but their relative significance increases, and their
symbolism continues to resonate as both an index and a cause of the
power of that country to bewilder, horrify, and enchant people
everywhere. And TV's capacity to travel and sell is undimmed. In
2008 the trade in television programs across the Americas, the Asia-
Pacific region, and Europe was worth €271.6 billion, up 5 percent
on the previous year ("World Television Market" 2009). India has

been very open to overseas ownership, so Viacom entered the fray with its network Colors in 2008, quickly achieving second place in national ratings among Hindi channels ("2008" 2009; Fung 2008: 85). The fantasy of a post-US era of world TV remains just that.

QUESTIONS FOR DISCUSSION

(1) What was the story of television prior to World War II?
(2) How would you distinguish public from commercial TV?
(3) How has deregulation changed television?
(4) What is the debate about media imperialism and globalization – does the United States dominate world television?
(5) What do you think about the different prices charged to TV stations for the same shows around the world?
(6) How do you explain the success of *telenovelas*?

NOTE

(1) For a fascinating account of attempts to create a *novela* away from the dominant countries, see Gregory (2007: 116–29).

FURTHER READING

Bignell, Jonathan and Andreas Fickers, eds. (2008). *A European Television History*. Malden: Wiley-Blackwell.

Gomery, Douglas. (2008). *A History of Broadcasting in the United States*. Malden: Blackwell.

Kraidy, Marwan M. (2005). *Hybridity, or the Cultural Logic of Globalization*. Philadelphia: Temple University Press.

Schiller, Herbert I. (1969). *Mass Communications and American Empire*. Boston: Beacon Press.

Straubhaar, Joseph. (2007). *World Television: From Global to Local*. Thousand Oaks: Sage.

CONTENT

One night in Miami, still dazed from a week on an Atlantic liner, I began watching a film and at first had some difficulty in adjusting to a much greater frequency of commercial "breaks." Yet this was a minor problem compared to what eventually happened. Two other films, which were due to be shown on the same channel on other nights, began to be inserted as trailers. A crime in San Francisco (the subject of the original film) began to operate in an extraordinary counterpoint not only with the deodorant and cereal commercials but with a romance in Paris and the eruption of a prehistoric monster who laid waste New York. ... [T]he transitions from film to commercial and from film A to films B and C were in effect unmarked.... I believe I registered some incidents as happening in the wrong film, and some characters in the commercials as involved in the film episodes, in what came to seem – for all the occasional bizarre disparities – a single irresponsible flow of images and feelings.

(Raymond Williams 1978: 91–2)

Cloistered away in a Tokyo hotel, hemmed in on all sides by oppressive black frames, we watch through [Chris] Marker's lens a numbing day of television programming: first, there are the sacred deer of Nara; then a cultural program on NHK about the nineteenth-century French writer and dandy Gérard de Nerval; the Nerval program carries us to the grave of Jean-Jacques Rousseau, followed by an evening program on the Khmer Rouge in Cambodia; later still, after the killing fields, there is adult programming: "I did it all. All the way to the evening shows for adults – so called." Images from the day spent before Japanese television recur throughout the film; the persistence of the images suggests that the temporal vertigo of film – the "insane memory," as one Krasna letter describes the temporality of modern, cinematic and televisual imagery – is borrowed from the small screen. The narrator senses as much. In trying to juxtapose the Nerval/Rousseau show against images of Pol Pot, the voiceover wonders aloud: "From Jean-Jacques Rousseau to the Khmer Rouge: Coincidence? Or, the sense of history?"

(Adrian Switzer (2009: 93) describing *Sans Soleil* (Chris Marker 1982))

I really cannot read another cultural studies analysis of ... *The Sopranos* [1999–2007].

(Stuart Hall, in MacCabe 2008)

Williams' fuddy-duddy epigram draws on a moment of discombobulation, time as a magazine critic, and years as a left Leavisite, to propose a "central television experience: the fact of flow." Each program is related to what precedes and follows it through memory, mood, and expectation, denying the possibility of critical viewing (1978: 95).[1] A more aesthetic, pleasurably delirious sensibility informs the account of *Sans Soleil*. And three decades later, Williams' fellow cultural-studies maven Hall complains about their discipline's approach to television. I suspect he was expressing *ennui* in the face of TV Studies 2.0: resistive readings of texts that endow them with magical properties of feminism, socialism, anti-racism, art, redemption, and so on, derived from the critic's persona. No wonder Olympian social science negatively juxtaposes TV Studies that has "merely performed readings of individual television programs" with "real research" (Grindstaff and Turow 2006: 115).

Whatever the merits of such readings – and critiques of them – analysts continue to write about *The Sopranos*, for example, because it engages so many key themes of US culture: the quotidian mundanity of family life; irresolvable discrepancies between ideology and reality; hyper-masculine white violence; ethnic stereotypes; state and corporate corruption; and mendacity as a way of life, all amplified beyond what a feature film can do in terms of time, and a commercial TV series can do in terms of risk (Speranza 2008; for an engagement with some of these issues, see Polan 2009). HBO subscribers in 2007 could watch the last season of *The Sopranos* eight times a week, while those who had digital on-demand could do so at any moment, as could people taping it. Official ratings gave the program 7.4 million viewers for Sunday-night premieres, but 11.1 million watched if one includes other accounting methods

(Thornton 2009; Bauder 2007; Lemmonier 2008). That seems like a program worthy of analysis, given its themes and their uptake.

Half-a-century ago, Smythe called for an analysis of television texts as "a group of symbols" that "serve as a medium of exchange between the mass media and the audience" (1954: 143). This can be undertaken in ways that do not create qualities in either programs or viewers that are products of critics' desires. Genre-based study is crucial to understanding content, given the serial, repetitious nature of much television, especially with channels dedicated to one topic, from shopping to Manchester United. Genre is central to TV, as evidenced by, for example, the routine practices of classification undertaken by program guides. Paul Attallah suggests that "the entire television industry is organized around the production of specific genres.... Television could be said not to exist outside of its genres" (1984: 227). The concept derives from the Latin *genus*, which in turn comes from the word for giving birth. Genre originally referred to kinds of people, often by class or race – "an act of classification and classification" and hence "a strategy of control" (Hodge 1990: 21). Certain genres are deemed intrinsically worthier than others because of their moral stance or the special qualities required of their creators. This aspect of theorizing genre dates back hundreds of years (Hunter 1988: 213–14). Its traces are apparent in TV Studies 1.0 and the way regulators and critics create hierarchies of pleasure and worth. For example, Ofcom, the UK's guardian of the electronic media, shies away from deriding reality television, but can't bring itself to catalog reality in the same way as current affairs or science, so it has constructed a distinction between "factual entertainment" (reality) and "Serious Factual" (documentary) (which rates capital letters) (2007: 5). Generic tendencies have been emphasized and perhaps even endorsed by Television Studies 2.0, which prefers the popular over the avant garde, the audience over the author. Television Studies 1.0 favors the opposite (Edgar 2000: 75; Bignell *et al.* 2000b: 81).

Genres are about the interplay of repetition and difference, and their organization and interpretation by producers, audiences, and critics. This can happen during production, scheduling, reviewing, and watching. We may even plan our viewing by genre (Saturday is sport, or Wednesday is British comedy). There is enough in common between these descriptions to justify grouping them together, and enough that is different to mean we watch more than just one part of a program or schedule. This represents continuity in the history of literary and televisual genres: they are always related to the cultural attributes of a population at a certain moment, sometimes as reactions to those attributes, and sometimes as sources of them (Hunter 1988: 215). Just as the expansion of printing and literacy held implications for the emergence of the novel, so the spread of TiVo and technological familiarity influence the mixed genres of latter-day TV.

Knowing how to construct programs and schedules along generic lines is both a matter of dramatic rules and economic ones: having one's product quickly and easily recognized as a reality show, a crime series, or a science–fiction serial. Genre in television works in varied ways: stations may themselves be genres (such as film or sport channels); viewers may reorganize TV to suit their own schedules, via delayed replay; and domestic satellite dishes may pick up signals that are dispatched promiscuously and with no interest in organizing the audience's time, given that the projected audience is globally spread out. Genres are industrial categories that make series recognizable. Industrial innovation involves both repetition and difference, which in turn can discourage taking risks, curbing costly newness with cheap formulae.

Genre is also about relations between topics, camera angles, colors, sounds, and actors (Curti 1988: 156). John Caughie foregrounds visual style (how the camera moves and shots are put together), *mise-en-scène* (what appears in front of the camera), and narrative structures (1991: 137). As Fiske and Hartley show, the shot in television depends for its meaning on the genre in which it is located as well as how it is combined with other shots. They instance footage of children leaving school, which may signify the routine of life for a family member, if it occurs in a documentary; characterization and tension, in a television play; or risk, in a public-service announcement (1980: 53).

Genres are fluid guides to TV, rather than laws with rigid distinctions. For example, principally factual programs must have entertaining elements or risk losing their audiences, while primarily fictional ones must touch on fact and impart knowledge (Smythe 1954: 147). So a genre such as the wildlife documentary undergoes fascinating mutations. In the US, it was a fringe interest until themed channels such as Discovery Animal Planet emerged in response to deregulation based on pieties about consumer power. It needed to be sealed off from environmental and animal-rights discourse in order to draw corporate backing (Chris 2006). Contemporary instances of comedy as social comment and news, such as *The Daily Show* (1996–) on Comedy Central, transgress boundaries and become popular and influential. Rather than being welcomed as an indictment of bourgeois TV norms whose valuable *bricolage* – as per the best traditions of committed journalism – blends, like life itself, parody and reporting, this alarms traditionalists who want news to be news (Grindstaff and Turow 2006: 111).

DRAMA

Thirty years ago, Horace Newcomb positioned television drama alongside novels rather than radio or film, because its "sense of density" explores complex themes in lengthy treatments with slow build-ups and multi-sequenced sites of character development and interaction (1974: 256). Newcomb was making his claim in the context of an appeal to the central question for the humanities-based study of television of his day, i.e. whether it was worthy of formalist (or any) textual analysis, as opposed to behavioral research or generic condemnation. For Douglas Kellner (1982), television provides "stories which dramatize society's values, ideals and ways of life; they are enacted in story-telling media." TV is "the electronic ideology machine" whose formulaic drama series offer "hegemonic ideology for advanced capitalism." These are generally realist texts, meaning that they have neat aetiological chains, an everyday *mise-en-scène*, and continuity editing. They are unchallenging, familiar, and within everyday cultural competence. But while some critics always subordinate television drama to the stage and the cinema, the noted playwright and scriptwriter David Hare argues that "the vitality of British film came from television," specifically its support for one-shot drama and series with a small number of episodes (Billington and Hare 2009).

TV drama has interesting semiological and sociological intertexts; for instance, police-procedural series draw on signage associated with both earlier shows and public concerns about crime, blended with ideological and interpersonal tropes. The genre constructs a viewing position that accepts the state monopoly on the exercise of "legitimate" violence in the protection of private property, private morality, and human safety. Police drama increasingly moves between public and private spheres, through officers' emotions. Whereas 1960s shows concentrated on the social landscape and professional policing – its public face – programs since then have tended to construct interiority for their characters. Emotional tendencies merge with action sequences and office life to produce soap-operatic forms (Tulloch 1990: 69–70, 72). A powerful instance is *Dexter* (2006–), where personal and professional lives intertwine inexorably, creepily, and multi-generationally.

For the founding parents of TV production, drama was a familiar genre that could meet the needs of either prestigious or commercial dictates. Despite Gerald Cock, the BBC's inaugural Director of Television, announcing in 1936 that drama would not be important for the new medium, because people "were already sated with entertainment," it was one of the first sources of programming for TV. Early dramatic forms included live filming of theatrical plays that were not repeated (and sometimes not taped) – the BBC's first was Luigi Pirandello's *The Man With a Flower in His Mouth* in 1930; radio serials and novels that were adapted; aged movies no longer earning money in cinemas; live broadcasts from theaters; and collaborations (in the US instance) with major film studios, once they decided to cooperate rather than compete with the industry (Cock, quoted in Giddings and Selby 2001: 14).

This type of convergence, TV's thoroughgoing reach across media, is part of its capacious warehousing project. So in the US, programs such as *The Man from U.N.C.L.E.* (1964–8) were made by studios for television, then edited together to form feature films (in this case, for overseas release). The ultimate example was *Star Trek* (1966–9), which became a feature-film franchise in the 1980s and 1990s and generated several TV series (1973–4, 1987–94, 1993–9, 1995–2001, and 2001–5). For decades, the networks borrowed from Hollywood by offering made-for-TV movies, until CBS abandoned the genre in 2006 in favor of low-cost alternatives. But they were soon resurrected on cable via the Sci Fi Channel, Lifetime, and Hallmark (Attallah 2007: 327–8; Bourdon *et al.* 2008: 107; Lowry 2009).

The most durable dramatic form borrowed from radio has been the soap opera and *telenovela*. John Tulloch says the special intimacy that audience members experience in successful soap opera exemplifies a myth being taken up by a commercial cultural apparatus "to provide social order at times of cultural crisis" (1990: 58). In many parts of the world, soaps/*novelas* have normalized extramarital sexual pleasure, same-sex relationships, health issues, and gender politics. They have been likened in their barometric sensitivity to "the nineteenth-century weekly sermon to a packed congregation" (Graham 2000: 7). Their visual styles coalesce with their narrative concerns. Interior sets and close-ups of people in pairs with pastel colors surrounding them synchronize with plot lines about emotional interiority and the circularity of love. Neither is ever really individual and neither can ever conclude, in that both the genre and actual emotional life lack obvious closure (Curti 1988: 153–4, 157–9). Viewers are more likely to chat about soaps and draw on them to think about everyday life than other genres, whether the subject matter be marital frustration versus televisual romance, TV glamour versus suburban dross, or a raft of social issues ("Women's Favorites on TV" 2009; Brown 1990; Ang 1982).

What about so-called quality drama, prime-time "event" television that addresses major historical themes and is rarely spun into lengthy series over many years? The efflorescence of the detail-rich, sociology-poor, anally-retentive, period-piece British TV drama of the late 1960s and since – what Rupert Murdoch (1989) haughtily calls "drama run by the costume department" – was tied to a realization on the screen of past days of class equanimity, thereby redirecting attention from the political economy of the present (for a rather kinder appreciation, see Giddings and Selby 2001). But when it took hold, historical drama was extraordinary in its purchase. In the UK, major mini-series that embodied these issues included *The Forsyte Saga* (1967), *The First Churchills* (1969), and *The Pallisers* (1974). Adaptations of British novels and histories proved so popular in the US that heroic reconstructions of a lost Englishness became a means of garnering export sales even if they drew opprobrium for faux-historical, elite foci.

A strong contrast comes with Britain's *Days of Hope*, a 1975 mini-series about working-class politics from World War I through to the General Strike. It was made by committed Marxists Ken Loach, Tony Garnett, and Jim Allen, who hoped contemporary viewers would interpret the series in the light of class struggle in 1970s Britain. This led to an unparalleled debate about the value of socialist realism as a means of laying bare complex social issues, versus commitments to the avant garde that thought conventional narratives could never radicalize their audiences, due to the reactionary nature of dramatic conventions that position spectators as perfectly knowledgeable. The debate thrived for five years in the columns of *Screen* and *Edinburgh '77 Magazine* (see Bennett *et al.* 1981: 305–52).

In the US, *Roots* (1977) and *Holocaust* (1978) were massively successful, profoundly political US mini-series about slavery and the Holocaust, the greatest contradictions of the Enlightenment apart from misogyny and private property (Turnock *et al.* 2008: 192–3). Stuart Cunningham's work on historical mini-series of 1980s Australian TV argues for a high level of aesthetic and political sophistication in such long-form drama. Engaging *The Dismissal* (1983) and *Vietnam: The Mini-Series* (1987), he argues that these sprawling yet condensed narratives displaced a fixation with events through attention to causes and outcomes. At their best, they made for "an unparalleled upgrading of the terms within which historical information and argument is mediated through mainstream television," dealing (in these instances) with the political backdrop to a CIA-backed coup and conflict within a high-profile family during an unpopular war.

A multi-perspectival element was provided by the *Bildungsroman*-like "multiplication of authorising perspectives." *Vietnam: The Mini-Series* explained a nation torn apart inside the microcosm of a family by simultaneously engaging maturational questions and historical debates. It imbricated the self and the social at sites of interpersonal and political disagreement and negotiation that interpellated the engaged citizen rather than the "distracted consumer" (2008). Albert Moran argued: "[t]he central strategy of the Australian historical mini-series is to portray the development of national consciousness inside emergence of an individual consciousness" (1989: 252).

This references Aristotle's distinction between history and drama, favoring the latter because of its capacity for the general and the complex, the explanatorily powerful and conflictual (1961: 68, 111). That was also said to have been the great power of one-shot television drama, especially in the days when (for budgetary reasons) it was live and dominated by close-ups and dialog. So the TV version of "kitchen-sink" drama and cinema in 1960s Britain encouraged consideration of a class-based society, while 1950s US TV mounted a critique of suburbanization, pointing out the paranoia and violence underpinning the whitest of families sheltering behind their whitest of picket fences.

US network drama supposedly underwent a rebirth when ABC screened *Twin Peaks* (1990–1). It captured the hypocrisy of everyday middle-class life, turning network television to schizoid critiques with an intense, directly sexual gaze. The first episode drew a third of the US audience. It was instantly hailed as setting new trends and standards, due to the cinematic score, lush visuality, slow pacing, references to classical Hollywood films, and arty authorship via the participation of David Lynch – even as it drew on soap-operatic ensemble casting and indeterminacy alongside these high-prestige elements. Although some critics were puzzled by the show, baby-boomer viewers (many of whom were in the desired demographic group of their thirties) enjoyed its cinematic conceits. *Twin Peaks* became the most publicly-discussed program on the air, according to network research (Nelson 1992; Lavery 2004; Yehya 2008; Gomery 2008: 331).

Both the socialist realism of a *Days of Hope* and the avant gardisme of a *Twin Peaks* are derided by latter-day pro-business bureaucrats, intellectuals, and critics as too dark, slow, unattractive, gritty, and socio-political. Such condemnations appear in *Building a Global Audience*, a report commissioned by the Blair Labour Government on how to stimulate export sales of TV shows (Graham and Associates 1999). Long-form historical drama was compromised in Western Europe by the dire effects of deregulation and privatization across the 1980s and 1990s, although some notable series continued, such as the monumental *Heimat* on German TV (1984–2004). Internationally, the mini-series seemed to die off during the 1990s due to its costs, but in the US it became a successful source of high-quality drama on both the networks and cable (CBS, NBC, TNT, and HBO) in 2008–9, bolstered by revenue prospects through international and DVD sales, and there was a modest revival in France due to public investment (Bourdon *et al.* 2008: 118–19; de Leeuw *et al.* 2008: 134; Lowry 2009). The noted Scandinavian film movement Dogma 95, led by Lars von Trier, probably gained its greatest exposure through Denmark's *Riget*, a wry mid-1990s mini-series about medicine that undercut viewers' bourgeois safety in ultimate omniscience, the certitude that they would "understand" in the end, with all loose ends securely tied and genres clearly distinct (it veered ecstatically from humor to horror). *Riget* was released in movie form in the UK and the US (Cervantes 2008).

And some lengthy dramatic forms continue. In a country like Finland, with its history of imperial conquest and economic dependency on Russia and Sweden, issues of national identity and economic migration have long formed a core of TV drama, for example *Elämänmeno* [*The Way Life Goes*] (1978). The nation's status as an interstitial borderland caught in the dialectic of pastoralism and urbanism has been a central concern (de Leeuw *et al.* 2008: 135–7; Moring 2009). Or consider US medical dramas. For decades, the staple heroes of these stories were gallant, pioneering, risk-taking surgeons boldly experimenting to keep people alive. From the 1940s to the 1960s, this focus on acute care also characterized public policy and the profession, which worked closely with producers to ensure that series accurately reflected their view of medicine going boldly where none had ventured before. As that boosterish emphasis was superseded in policy circles because of inflationary costs and a new emphasis on economies rather than breakthroughs, heroic TV drama fell out of step until the moral ambiguity of such programs as *ER* (1994–2008), *Chicago Hope* (1994–2000), and *Grey's Anatomy* (2005–). Nevertheless, the system's grotesque capitalist inefficiencies remain unaddressed – healthcare is largely a wonderful, not a wasteful, thing in TV drama (Turow 1989; Turow and Gans-Boriskin 2007; Holtz 2008).

Drama in general continues to be important to public broadcasters. In Britain, it accounted for half of ITV's 2006 evening programs (Ofcom 2007: 31). *Pace* the fears of the Labour Party's business friends, challenging drama need not be done within an entirely naturalist frame – consider the mixed-genre, deconstructive *mélange* of Dennis Potter's *The Singing Detective* (1986) emerging from the drabness of Thatcherite Britain, Rainer Werner Fassbinder's epic *Berlin*

Alexanderplatz (1980), Ingmar Bergman's *Bildmakana* (2000), or Fernando Meirelles' *Cidade dos Homens* (2002–5) – testimonies to the creative *largesse* offered by high-budget, high-prestige, auteur TV drama, whether from the UK, Germany, Sweden, or Brazil. Cable networks in the US have always had much lower budgets than their network competitors. The top cable stations are now enjoying huge ratings increases through investing much more in drama than before, beyond the percentage changes for the networks – since 2005, up 8.5 percent for cable and 1.5 percent for network (Stutzman 2008). In the UK, reduced advertising revenue and the desire to extricate themselves from public-service obligations saw ITV and Channel 4 racing away from drama and toward reality in 2009; or specifically, giving up on drama series and investing in one-off or mini-series events (McLean 2009).

A decade after *Twin Peaks*, the *CSI* franchise arrived. It is noted for various technical investments – shot on 16 and 35 mm film then transferred to digital video, with helicopter shots abounding, animators creating scenes inside dead bodies through computing, and editors cutting as never before (there are a thousand shots per episode). This provides a rich look that cheaper series cannot match, because they are bounded by studio sets and video-taping. The original *CSI* was sold to 177 countries, and *CSI: Miami* was the most popular drama worldwide in 2006. In the US, the last *CSI* of 2004–5, directed by Quentin Tarantino, drew an audience of over forty million, and it has been a popular legally downloaded or -streamed text since 2006. A British spin-off began in 2009 (Gomery 2008: 342–4; Lury 2005: 45–6; Cohan 2008: 3; Hale 2008; Lotz 2008: 84).

Piety and technology merge in the *CSI* franchise. During the Presidency of George W. Bush, a regime characterized, *inter alia*, by a loathing of secular positivism and inquiry, these immensely popular programs indexed just such forms of knowledge, as inductive and deductive processes and criminological norms were applied to new and old technologies to solve problems on a rational basis. Inspired by expert exculpatory testimony in O.J. Simpson's 1995 murder trial, the franchise placed great faith in the possibility of objective truth delivering reliable outcomes through police procedures. Attorney-novelist Andrew Vachss bemoans that "Jurors think *CSI* is a documentary." Criminologists are perturbed by the series' cavalier attitude to the norms of video surveillance, eyewitness testimony, and forensic reliability and their impact on the viewing public. Nevertheless, they and science educators love the fact that student applications to forensic-science programs have skyrocketed due to *CSI*'s influence, which is extended thanks to official websites that inform visitors about forensics. Manufacturers of equipment for crime laboratories shower the shows with product placements to keep their *mises-en-scènes* up-to-date because they are effective as secret commercials, and the National Science Foundation sponsored a *CSI* "forensic web adventure" to accompany a traveling museum exhibit (Mooney 2005; Ott 2007: 166; Turow and Gans-Boriskin 2007: 278; Turow 2004; Goode 2007: 124; Jones and Bangert 2006; Caswell 2008; Vachss 2006: 132; O'Donnell 2007: 215–16, 218; Desmarais *et al.* 2008; Miller *et al.* 2008).

24, one of the longest-running spy Yanqui shows, is also screened around the world. In 2009, 100 million people watch it across 236 channels. *24* began in the fateful fall of 2001, right after airplane missiles had struck the north-east of the US. The program binds together two senses of realism in a classical dual verisimilitude that draws both on faithfulness to a genre (espionage) and on narrative cues, images, sounds, and editing associated with documentaries or news programs. This is in keeping with its central conceit of a season's action taking place over the twenty-four hours it takes to watch each set of episodes. *24* has been welcomed as a return of high-quality drama that runs counter to the hegemony of reality television, and even celebrated as a grand piece of existential philosophy – the solitary figure against an array of untrustworthy institutions. Yet it clearly borrows devices and story-lines from more critically derided genres, such as soap opera, reality, and vigilante action adventure, thanks to its cliffhanger episodic stories and macho violence – in addition to drawing on the avant garde, courtesy of fractured story-lines and points of view. Of course, this is all underwritten by corporate messages; the first episode in 2003 began and ended with a six-minute film promoting a Ford car. And *24*'s uniqueness became a formula in 2009, when CBS announced *Harper's Island*, an overtly self-destructing series in which it is guaranteed that a central character will die in each of thirteen weeks (Aitkenhead 2009; McPherson 2008; McMahon 2008; Attallah 2006; Miklos 2008; Lotz 2008: 173; Steinberg

2009a). Then there is the question of 24's politics. Produced by Republicans, it has featured cameos by their ideological *confrères* in politics (John McCain) and the news media (Laura Ingraham and Larry Elder) and was endorsed by the intellectual lackeys of the Bush regime such as the *ur*-disgraced-academic John Woo, who wrote legal justifications for inhumane brutality (Lithwick 2008). The show's creator, Joel Surnow, boasts of being a "rightwing nut job" (quoted in Aitkenhead 2009). The Heritage Foundation, a reactionary, coin-operated think-tank, held a press conference in 2006 in celebration of the series that featured Michael Chertoff, then the Secretary of Homeland Security, and extremist talk-radio host Rush Limbaugh, who announced that Vice-President Dick Cheney and Defense Secretary Donald Rumsfeld were fans of the program. 24 clearly endorses torture as a means of extracting information from terrorists, which has been a major ideological and policy distinction between US political parties since 2001. For some critics, it represents "la suma de los miedos americanos" ["the sum of American fears"] (Miklos 2008: 79). John Downing has termed the program "*the most extended televisual reflection to date on the implications of 9/11*" and an egregious argument in favor of the "need" for immediate and illegal action in the "public interest" (2007: 62). It's fine for the hero, Jack Bauer, "a man never at a loss for something to do with an electrode," to deny medical assistance to a terrorist whom he has wounded, shoot another's wife in the leg, then threaten a second shot to the knee unless her husband confides in him; and fine for the US President to subject a Cabinet member to electric shocks to interrogate him (Downing 2007: 72, 77; Lithwick 2008) as Bauer endlessly intones, "Whatever it takes." Similar questions of illegitimate process and authoritarian ideology have been posed of the *CSI* franchise (West 2008). A delegation from the major US officer-training site, West Point, visited 24's producers in 2007 to express anxiety that so many military recruits adopt illegal and immoral attitudes to torture based on their inter-pellation by the series, while interrogators reported a direct mimesis between the show and actual practices in Iraqi prisons by US forces inspired by the show. Human Rights Watch also weighed in. Yet 24 became the first carbon-neutral US TV drama in 2009, with offsets calculated against the impact of car chases, air travel, and use of coal-generated electricity, in addition to favoring wind and solar power. And its executive producer Kiefer Sutherland, the highest-paid TV actor in the world, is liberal in his politics, and disavows the notion that the program works ideologically at all – "it's good drama. And I love this drama!" (Glaister 2009; Kaufman 2009; M. Miller 2007; Sutherland, quoted in Aitkenhead 2009). Thank heavens for Stella Artois' Godardian spoof (www.guardian.co.uk/media/2009/mar/23/stella-artois-nouvelle-vague).

Either way, for viewers in search of entertainment delivered not just via broad-brush ideology but also through form and style, high-end US TV had become the repository of many values traditionally associated with art cinema – bravura montage editing, high-contrast yet subtle *mise-en-scène*, ellipsis and synthesis, direct address of a knowing audience, and stars chosen for the capacity to deliver lines over headlines. As the glossy, high-art inflected Latin American film magazine *La Tempestad* puts it, "el opio nuestro de cada día" ["our daily opium"] is offering "niveles altísimos de exigencia artística" ["the highest levels of artistic achievement"] ("La televisión y el futuro del cine" 2008). In the US, *24*'s staple audience was the most-educated and affluent demographic group (Sconce 2004: 99) – people not usually associated with the violence and anti-intellectualism of the program's far-right producers and public supporters.

In terms of this kind of aesthetic valuation, one might argue that the move by several shows toward webisodes, which last about half the duration of the program that they accompany and are only available online, signals a trend toward gossipy ephemera, since they add value only to diehard fans because they focus on comparatively insubstantial topics and characters. Or we could say that the trend makes artistic variations available to different kinds of viewers. In Australia, risky programming is tested through five-minute online versions that can be watched while audiences are allegedly busy at work; they may turn into fully-fledged TV shows if they draw followers (Marcus 2008).

SPORT

By contrast with most drama (with *24* a seeming exception – but not "really," since it is scripted, shot, and edited in advance of being screened), coverage of sporting fixtures must follow the passage of play in a contest involving many people over a brief period. It can be chaotic, but it's rule-governed. The narrative is open, like a soap: even the conclusion of a season is never the conclusion of the seemingly endless competition that marks out this genre. Sport is an intensely emotional program-type, but without recourse to close-ups or personal verbalization in quite the same way as drama. Instead, there is a direct address of such issues to the audience by commentators, as well as a textual mirror of the audience via the crowd.

Like theatre, live sport has been central to television from the first. In 1931, the *Encyclopedia Britannica* illustrated the possibilities of the new medium by referring to the prospect of live athletics coverage (Settel and Laas 1969: 35). And from very early on, sport and TV "got together like bacon and eggs.... Like algae and fungi in moss" (Claeys and van Pelt 1986: 98). They shared a sense of immediacy, of happening at the instant that they were seen. Sport offered television well-defined spatial and temporal co-ordinates alongside spontaneity and surprise, and costs met by event organizers. It epitomized the culture industries' blend of repetition and difference brokered through pleasure. Smythe saw televised sport as "a representation of the human condition," an

> image of skillful use of trained bodies ... or gross sex aggression ... competing for survival without the benefit of accepted law ... a form of folk-drama ... a sardonic morality story, or perhaps a means of reassuring cynical viewers that life is fixed from the start.
>
> (1954: 144–5)

The Nazis regarded sport as a key part of TV propaganda in the 1930s. Perhaps 150,000 Berliners saw the 1936 Olympics in public viewing rooms. London viewers watched cricket in 1938, and New York TV presented live wrestling, football, and baseball a year later. The first pictures of a disaster (a New York fire) came through because cameras were at a nearby swimming pool. In the US, prewar attempts to popularize TV-watching promoted collective viewing in bars of wrestling and boxing. In the 1950s, the networks discovered that Westerns and situation comedies were attracting large audiences, but comprised of people without large disposable incomes. The target viewer selected in their stead was the young adult urban male, for whom sport was a priority (Lever and Wheeler 1993: 127; Uricchio 2008: 298; Hickethier 2008: 71; Whannel 1985: 62; Geurens 1989: 57; Settel and Laas 1969: 43; Harmond 1979: 82–3; Kersta 1942: 117–18; Parente 1977: 130).

Technological developments made televised sport increasingly manageable and increasingly spectacular. An initial model that replicated the view from a grandstand seat has changed in the light of the capacity to flit between many seats in many places. This and other refinements took place over half a century via such innovations as parabolic reflector microphones, mobile cameras, color, video recording and editing, caption generation, computer-aided design and drafting, video amplifiers to adjust the framing of an existing shot, international switching grids, chalkboards, and cameras in stumps, nets, helmets, and dirigibles (for the early history, see Whannel 1992: 64–6).

The first network broadcast in the US was a 1945 football game with President Harry S. Truman in the stadium, binding together sport, politics, and corporate power in a symbolic whirl that presaged the central role of sport in the emergent TV system (Gomery 2008: 233, 235–6). In Canada, the stimulus to establishing television came from the fact that people were already viewing sport from across the border (Cavanagh 1992: 305). In the UK, the first slow-motion replay came in 1962, during coverage of the Grand National horse race. The 1970 World Cup from Mexico was the first major event carried via satellite in color. Color television enabled snooker to become a TV sport – in black and white, it had been too difficult to distinguish the balls being potted. And a boxing bout between Frank Bruno and Mike Tyson inaugurated pay-per-view in 1996 (Low 2009; Bignell and Orlebar 2005: 150).

This history informed Murdoch's infamously indelicate, albeit honest, remark in 1996 that his companies "use sports as a 'battering ram'" to draw in subscribers – in the UK, that's the only genre Murdoch and his fellow capitalists invest in significantly. By 2006, 60 percent of Sky subscribers who followed football bought its service just because of English Premier League coverage (Murdoch, quoted in Papathanassopoulos 2002: 197; Ofcom 2009: 4; Ofcom and Human Capital 2006: iii). Subscription television in Australia really grew because crucial sporting events were captured from broadcast networks in 2008 – qualifying games in the men's World Cup of football and Twenty20 cricket ("Subscription Television" 2008). In the US, the extraordinary intertextuality and variety of sport mean that cable stations that lack the financial backbone of broadcast networks to buy top events still see sport as a ratings winner. The strategy is proving crucial in the Kenyan struggle to dominate satellite, with British money that owns the rights to English football suddenly dominant (Wandera 2008). And despite the desire to bind the Canadian nation together through TV hockey, when networks wanted to target specific territories and could do so thanks to localizing technologies, they tailored coverage to particular markets. Neither tendency reflected or encouraged multiculturalism, as we can see from the racism and sexism of core commentators (Beaty and Sullivan 2006: 96–7, 141).

These technological and legal changes are siphoning sports away from broadcast TV and onto cable, satellite, and pay-per-view. As such, they are an instance of commercial television belatedly learning from public television. Many sports were built up by public broadcasters, only for cautious but wealthy capitalist companies to buy the innovations. This happened with basketball in the US, which was pioneered on television by San Francisco's public station; cricket and rugby union around the world (developed as spectator sports by public networks in Britain, Australia, and New Zealand); and football across Europe. In 1995, there were just three sports channels in Europe; by 2000, there were sixty (Papathanassopoulos 2002: 189). ITV tried to resurrect its business by purchasing rights to the 2008–9 FA Cup, a failing competition that had been restored to fame through heavy BBC marketing – which promptly lost the rights to its unimaginative commercial rivals at a price that helped to send ITV to the brink financially (Gibson 2009a; Dyke 2009).

Britain's regulator, Ofcom, promulgates a list of sports "of national interest" that should be available on broadcast rather than satellite TV (2008a). Why? Seven of the nine most popular programs on BBC 1 in 2006 and three of the top five on ITV1 were World Cup matches (Ofcom 2007: 106). Events such as the summer Olympics are held to be symbolic agents that display and generate consensual values in the community while it is undergoing structural adjustment to social change. The integrative and harmonious aspects of social life are celebrated and emphasized in such accounts. They represent a functionalist strand in public policy and social research that emphasizes the allegedly consensual aspects to very conservative views of family, economic, and audience life (for examples of such reasoning applied to US TV, see Rothenbuhler 1988, 1989).

Sports also come and go with TV history. Consider wrestling. After great successes with women viewers in the 1940s and 1950s on US television, its popularity with the networks fell away, a victim of their desire for the male spectator's disposable income. TV re-introduced the sport in the 1980s, using hand-held cameras in extreme close-ups of the action to emphasize spectacle. Wrestling's return involved a new address to women, and revised rules. Quick falls, tightly circumscribed moves, and rigorous refereeing were forsaken. In their stead came spectacular circus-like activity, dominated by absurd persons in silly costumes, adopting exotic personae and seeking the acrobatic and the showy as means of success, and TV Studies 2.0 narcissographers in search of carnival to celebrate (Geurens 1989: 57–8; 61, Sammond 2005).

This renewed interest in female spectators has had profound impacts on television sport. In the early 1990s Canada, a beer company that owned the sports cable network TSN, sought an isomorphism of sporting content, audience, and beer intake by living up to its advertising motto: "We deliver the male." As late as 1998, an advertisement for ESPN in *Broadcasting & Cable* magazine promised "More tackles, less tutus." But commercial and cultural changes are exerting tremendous pressure on the normativity of sport, endangering the seemingly rock-solid maleness at its core. Far from seeing sport as unacceptable and unwanted, female US spectators tune to the Olympics in large numbers. The 1992 Winter Games gained 57 percent of its US TV audience from women. Women's figure skating out-rated that year's World Series of men's baseball and the collegiate basketball championship game. And the women's technical skating program at the 1994 Winter Games drew the fourth-highest ratings of any program in US history, right alongside the final episode of *M*A*S*H* (1972–83). In 1995, more women than men in Britain watched Wimbledon tennis on television, and the numbers were nearly equal for boxing. In the 1998 professional basketball play-offs, more women were drawn to Game Seven of the Bulls–Pacers series than to *Veronica's Closet* (1997–2000) or *ER*. That year, the women's final at the US Open tennis out-rated the men's by 15 percent. Every major professional men's league in the US now has a women's media marketing plan. Male spectatorship of TV sport in the US is in serious decline, as more and more viewers turn to the History and Discovery Channels. The perennial savior of network sportscasters, the National Football League (NFL), saw 1998–9 and 1999–2000 ratings for *Monday Night Football* (1970–) at a record low, while a third of its audience was female. In 1999, more men aged 18–34 viewed professional women's softball on ESPN2 than watched Arena football, the National Hockey League, or Major League Soccer. So something is happening (Miller 2001a). A clue comes from ABC's coverage of Super Bowl 2000, which included Giants cornerback Jason Seahorn in uniform pants during a pregame show, to which journalist Meredith Vieira offered that football is "all about the butt" (quoted in Miller 2001a). Why does this matter? Because women in the US buy well over half the cars, TVs, and PCs that are sold, and 90 percent of the produce ("Hello, Girls" 2009).

US TV executives operate from the assumption that women are attracted to biographical and conceptual narratives about stars and their sports, rather than statistics or quests for success. So NBC initiated "a female-inclusive sports subgenre" at the 1992 Summer Games, offering "private-life" histories of selected contestants. NBC targeted women and families in 1996 to such effect that 50 percent of its Olympic audience was adult women and 35 percent men, with women's gymnastics one of the most popular events. Male boxing and wrestling were edged out of prime time (although there remained a disproportionate address in general of men's versus women's sport on screen). The network reported an increase of 26 percent in the number of women viewers aged 25–54 by comparison with the 1992 Barcelona Games. Similar tendencies have continued through successive Olympiads. In the 2004 Summer Olympics, NBC covered male athletes in individual events more than female, but airtime dedicated to women's teams was significantly higher than for men's (Miller 2001a; Tuggle *et al.* 2007).

In his widely-used manual for making TV (thirteen editions from 1961 to 2001), Gerald Millerson values "interpretative techniques" as crucial components of televising sport. He warns that "although your camera can show what is happening, it will often fail to convey the atmosphere or spirit of the occasion," so "selective techniques" may be better than "direct reportage." In the case of covering a mountain climb, this requires low angles to stress danger; a concentration on physical extremities, such as fingers; and audio of heavy breathing and slowly ascending music, so that "the illusion grows." The ultimate is achieved if the audience responds somatically, developing "dizziness, nausea," and other "sympathetic bodily reactions" (1990: 371).

Training in how to present TV sport lists these scopophilic and obedient prerequisites for getting a job: "Personality, audience appeal, diligence, loyalty, integrity, willingness to work, and the ability to learn." Such positions are divided between play-by-play/ball-by-ball commentary, expert or color remarks, highlights, male gossip shows such as HBO then Showtime's *Inside the NFL* (1978–), the BBC's *Football Focus* (2001–), and news bulletins. The two- or three-person commentary team derives from the stop–start nature of many sports covered, notably cricket, baseball, and US "football." But it can also be used as a relief for sports with little respite, such as Australian-Rules Football, and it allows for specialist statistical information and interpretation. A scorer here fulfils two purposes, providing the commentator with information and flashing it on-screen for the viewer. Spotters on the sidelines at football games give an additional perspective. Whereas the commentator from on-high has a seat in the grandstand, the spotter is amongst the struggle and controversy, the gossip and the medical center, providing a space for directors to cut to from action (Hitchcock 1991: vii, 1, 3–4).

The tight interplay of technology and emotion is clear in the instructions that Australia's Channel 9 used for many years to train its cricket commentators, which included, *inter alia*:

> Think constantly of voice-over cassettes, animations, computers and anything which will help the viewer enjoy the telecast.... As a commentator you will keep foremost in your mind that cricket contains venom and courage, drama and humour, and you will not be backward in bringing out in your commentary those aspects of the noble and ancient pastime.
>
> (Quoted in Benaud 1984: 117)

Commentators are urged to emphasize gladiatorial elements of difference, character, history, and conflict to add excitement (Morris and Nydahl 1985: 105; Bryant *et al.* 1977). They must

> [c]reate a feeling that the competitors don't like each other.... Studies have shown that fans react better, and are more emotionally involved, if aggressive hostility is present.... Work the audience at the emotional level and get them involved in the game.
>
> (Hitchcock 1991: 75)

As a baseball TV director explains, "I'm trying to establish that tense relationship between the pitcher and the batter ... that impression of a face-off." In Britain, television producers have made it clear to athletics officials that coverage requires "head-to-head confrontations" (Heuring 1988: 90; British Film Institute 1986). When the 1983 Indianapolis 500 was run without untoward incidents and injuries, ABC's replay of the race included a segment on safety issues, the alibi for featuring extended highlights of death and destruction from earlier, purportedly more riveting contests (Edgerton and Ostroff 1985: 276). And the BBC's instructions to its camera operators for the 1976 Montreal Olympic Games emphasized the need to capture male swimmers' "straight lines" in order to suggest "strength, security, vitality and manliness" rather than the "grace and sweetness" of female competitors' "curved lines" (quoted in Peters 1976).

National, technical, and commercial differences are important. Until the early-twenty-first century, viewers of Italian football received a broadly sweeping picture of play, a strategic view that rarely went beyond a medium long shot. But for the English game, there was an abundance of medium shots of the crowd and two-shots and close-ups of the players, thanks to the minimal number of largely low-angle cameras, which TV had persuaded football grounds to dig pits for, thus enhancing their effect (Whannel 1992: 51). That distinction ended with the triumph of the more distanced, sober continental aesthetic, which coincided with every major match becoming available live (as opposed to none during the 1970s and 1980s, with few on delay either). The English Premier League today requires TV to provide multi-camera coverage, which makes for more closely-edited replays and highlights from varied angles (Armstrong 2007).

Boxing is theoretically ideal for television, because it is so easy to track visually, but has been the subject of bitter controversy since its low-rent proletarian violence became less fashionable than the ruling-class violence of, for example, Formula One. Conversely, cricket presents immense technical difficulties: the ball is tiny and can travel vast distances at great speed without adequate warning, while commercial TV must always allow for camera operators to include advertising perimeters wherever possible (British Film Institute 1986). The potential is there to look foolish as shots of nothing accompany spoken events of substance. So cricket has a complex series of safety maneuvers involving multiple camera set-ups, edits, and pans. Australia's Channel 9 coverage dealt with this problem in a way that translated an obstacle into a virtue of entertainment; an average over of six deliveries would be comprised of fifty shots, compared to around thirty when the BBC was the source (Whannel 1992: 99).

By the early 1980s, it was commonplace for TV Studies 1.0 to bewail the transformative impact of television on sport. These critiques assumed sport to be a once (and potentially future) expression of human muscular grace that was being perverted by the grubbiness of commerce and the specifically non-redemptive nature of television because sport for sport's sake had been displaced by "competitive individualism, consumer capitalism and nationalist chauvinism." There have been intense debates from this perspective on sponsorship of sport by beer and tobacco companies, and TV has been criticized for its partiality toward male-dominated sports such as football, golf, motor cars, and cricket. The neglect of other sports has adversely affected their capacity to attract sponsors; coverage is vital to major investors and growth of the sport. In many nations, women's sport has received minimal airtime (Rowe 1991).

This position frequently borrows from aesthetics to valorize sport in high-culture terms, even as it presumes upon sport's popularity to cross-validate itself as "the people's" property. In place of this combination of artistry and mass appeal, sport has allegedly been commodified by marketers, sponsors, advertisers, unions, television, administrators, and governments. For the cultural critic with an abiding faith in sport as it was prior to television, and wary of fans' propensity to consume, this meant establishing rules for limiting personal excess: TV tennis only via Grand Slam events; cricket via Tests alone; football during the season proper (Attwood 1990). Such a process avoids what Colin Tatz refers to as "sponsorship and television's emasculation of the rules" by returning sports to their original continuity and metonymy, to the beauty and culture that once made cricket, for instance, "a sort of morality" (1986: 57–8). For Christopher Lasch, TV has had an entirely negative impact on US sports – tennis is now played on all-weather courts, which reduce the importance of speed and tactical acumen; entire sports are disarticulated from their seasonal rhythms; spectators become less knowledgeable; and players grow more violent. All these changes are allegedly due to television (1979: 192–3). As if to make the point, the legendary US coach Bear Bryant once said: "I'll play at midnight if that's what TV wants" (quoted in McKay 1991: 91).

Televised sport shifts attention away from the processes of sport and onto its outcomes. Participation becomes defined and evaluated in terms of relationship to ultimate success, according to such critiques (Goldstein and Bredemeier 1977: 155). It is tempting to conclude that television uses sport to "articulate capitalist rationality, masculine hegemony, Eurocentric racism, militaristic nationalism and liberal values" (McKay 1991: 93–4; also see Clarke and Clarke 1982: McKay and Kirk 1992). As Schiller puts it, "the audience is targeted in its most vulnerable condition, relaxed yet fully receptive to the physical action and the inserted sales pitch. It is the ideal ambiance for the penetration of consciousness by a wide variety of ideological messages" (1989: 130). It's no surprise that Peugeot Talbot decided to sponsor UK athletics in the 1980s because the company sought to connect its cars with health, success, and beauty: "a very necessary and important association," in the words of one executive (British Film Institute 1986). This industrialization eventually made the most famous sports announcer in US history, Howard Cosell, leave the scene in the mid-1980s, saying, "I have observed the disgusting extent to which television will go in order to get a rating ... sports today is endlessly complex, an ever-spinning spiral of deceit, immorality, absence of ethics, and defiance of the public interest" (1986: 3–4).

Critics locate sport and TV as sub-sections of the advertising industry (Parente 1977: 130). They say it has lost its nobility and become a creature of spectacle rather than action. Sporting organizations were initially wary of television but soon learnt of its potential as a source of revenue and hence growth. For, just as television was appearing, sports themselves were managerializing. They were no longer the province of amateur administrators. The desire for growth meant following the precepts laid down by broadcasters: simple rules, good facilities, reasonable duration, obvious skill, visual appeal, and large crowds. When broadcasters paid facilities fees to sporting organizations, to cover space taken up at grounds, electricity, and other overheads, this was reasonable. But once that transaction became a fee for the right to broadcast the event, a new order of corporatization was at hand (Whannel 1992: 22–3, 78). The same period saw an increasing governmental obsession with rearing hearty youths, and new corporate interest in recruiting and maintaining healthy employees. There came to be a significant national component to sporting policy and a trend toward nationalism in the coverage of global events, as research into successive men's World Cup football competitions indicates (Tudor 1992).

In terms of spectatorship, there is some evidence that sports that professionalized alongside and as part of the development of US TV coverage in the 1960s and 1970s saw attendance grow for major games, especially across genders. This quickly inflated the salaries of players, whilst diminishing their connections to teams and spatial communities via promiscuous transfer systems (Harmond 1979: 86–7, 93). The same tendency rips apart suburban sporting associations. Perhaps the most brutal local instance was the fate of Australia's South Melbourne, for many years a working-class, inner-city club in the old Victorian Football League. It was dispatched to Sydney, because live coverage of games there on Sundays would boost ratings back in Melbourne, where professional football was illegal on "the Sabbath" (Stoddart 1986: 105). The return on this cultural loss was the emergence of new markets, such as the search for the "pink dollar" which initially brought a significant gay male following to the Sydney Australian Football League side.

Such commodification reached its symbolic apogee at the 1992 Olympics in Barcelona. After winning the gold medal for basketball, the US "Dream Team" staged a protest on the victory podium because Reebok, an official Olympic sponsor, had supplied the team with warm-up suits that must be worn to display its logo. But some players were Nike clients, and threatened to boycott proceedings. At the ceremony, two team members wrapped themselves in the national flag to cover the Reebok emblem, while the others unzipped their jackets to obscure it (Miller *et al.* 2001).

The 1988 Seoul Olympics were known colloquially as "the Breakfast Games," because NBC paid the organizers US$300 million to conduct most events before two in the afternoon, in order to coincide with prime time in the US. This shifting of time is not new; an early notorious instance being the 1967 US Open golf and All-Star baseball game, which started late to accommodate TV, to the players' annoyance. In fact, baseball moved from being an entirely daytime sport, and golf gave up match-play conditions for major tournaments, under ratings pressures, while Australian tennis scheduled night games at the request of Channel 7. Nowadays NBC uses a "plausibly live" policy, pretending that the Olympic events it carries are taking place naturally during prime time when they are in fact recorded and edited hours before. Time is manipulated in concert with the interests of global capital to suit narrative drive, audience targeting, and commercial spacing. At a less public site of interference, Channel 10 endeavored to influence the election of Australian Olympic officials by using its leverage as an Olympics broadcaster (Harmond 1979: 90–1, Edgerton and Ostroff 1985: 271; Boylen 1988; Jeffery 1989).

The whole question of television lighting has seen lamp makers around the world use the Olympics as their test-case and showroom; not because of the light required for spectators or competitors, but to provide the illumination craved by TV to highlight advertising hoardings and logos. This amounts to perhaps three times the illumination expected by people in the stands ("Lighting Assignment of Olympic Proportions" 1988: 50). By the early-twenty-first century, an "eye-in-the sky" held up football games in the US and Test Matches and tennis tournaments around the world, to permit TV-mediated advice to officials on refereeing and umpiring decisions. The idea of the body as an untrammeled expression of humanness is overdetermined by this technocratic discourse, which requires that bodies and their intersection are depicted beyond the ability of the naked umpiring or spectating eye.

The political economies of sport and television are now so closely intertwined that it is difficult to imagine life otherwise. One-third of English Premier League club revenue comes from TV, with wages increasing at a fast rate – much more than anywhere else – in step with the value of these rights. In the decade from 1990, European football rights costs grew by 800 percent, during a period of minimal macroeconomic inflation (Ofcom and Human Capital 2006: i–11; Papathanassopoulos 2002: 197). India's explosion of television in the twenty-first century made billions of dollars flow into cricket worldwide, as the country became the major economic power of the sport worldwide (though always struggling with the political hegemony of England and its white-settler sporting satellite, Australia). The advent of fifty news networks across fourteen languages saw cricket become India's lingua franca, a means of distributing stories nationally that displaced other news from the headlines due to its replicability (Mehta 2007). As per a struggle over TV rights to cover the game that led to a cricket revolution in 1970s Australia, when new money supplanted old boys' clubs, South Asian television finance was transforming the sport. The local Indian cricket administration denied rights sales in 2007 to the highest media bidder, as per its Sydney equivalent thirty years earlier. The response was to set up a rival league. But that provocation was of minor moment next to the Indian Board's own rebellious intervention. The Board took the recent English invention of Twenty20, whereby the game is even quicker – and much more fun – than baseball, and set up new urban franchises across the nation via the Indian Premier League (IPL). In 2008, ESPN Star Sports, a joint Disney–News Corporation venture (Mickey meets Rupert), invested a billion US dollars over a decade in the new Twenty20 cricket world championships, while the IPL used a draft system whereby players are bid for as per the US – but as established stars rather than rookies. People flocked from across the globe to sign up for unprecedented sums. What are the implications in terms of the nursery for young players provided by the longer, less-profitable version of the game? What will happen to national identification (Gibson 2009b; Hutton 2009)? Meanwhile, powerful teams and leagues were establishing their own televisual networks. Manchester United, Benfica, Barcelona, Middlesbrough, Olympique de

Marseille, Real Madrid, AC and Inter Milan, and Chelsea boast channels, as does the New York Yankees, while Major League Baseball started a network in 2009, and the National Hockey and National Football Leagues expanded theirs. The NFL Network won the ratings among US cable stations in December 2008, for the first time (Schwartz 2008; Papathanassopoulos 2002: 189; Reynolds 2008).

Some sports are virtually owned by TV. Consider boxing. We often think of the premium-cable station HBO as a by-word for quality, based on its critically lauded, globally successful dramas. But sport lies at the heart of the station's viability. At the time of HBO's formation in the 1970s, broadcast networks had deserted boxing, which mostly circulated through closed-circuit arena screenings. The station approached the leading promoters and offered to pay a fee to co-screen events, arguing that it posed no threat to the existing model because of its tiny size. The satellite telecast of the world-heavyweight bout between Joe Frazier and Muhammad Ali in 1975 in Manila established HBO as a household acronym. Its average monthly increase of 15,000 subscribers quickly doubled. By the end of the year, 300,000 homes had signed up through hundreds of wee cable companies; the network could boost a system's subscriber rolls by as much as 20 percent. A 1981 survey disclosed that the Marvin Hagler–Mustafa Hansho and Mike Weaver–James Tillis fights out-rated commercial network shows (Mair 1988).

This increase in subscriptions inspired senior management to "claim some ownership in the sport," in the network's words. It built up likely contenders as stars, then signed them to long-term contracts (Gottlieb 2006). HBO spent tens of millions of dollars marketing Mike Tyson during his heyday; its corporate parent, Time Warner, fetishistically referred to him as "a walking billboard for HBO." In 1991, boxing became the most successful pay-per-view genre, with a-million-and-a-half sales for a contest between George Foreman and Evander Holyfield, in an era when pay-per-view was available in fifteen million homes, and the decision to buy necessitated a physical visit to rent a converter box – all for an event the network itself helped to organize. Today, boxing is the second or third reason customers give for subscribing. Fresh from US$126 million in receipts from pay-per-view in 2005, in 2006 the network advised that its boxing centerpiece was "as big as any commitment that we've ever made ... the anchor and foundation of our efforts" (quoted in Umstead 2006).

YouTube has featured unauthorized uploads of the network's bouts. A few hours after Fernando Vargas was knocked out by Shane Moley in 2006, the last thirty-five seconds of the fight as narrowcast by HBO on pay-per-view were available at the site. Within less than a week, 180,000 watchers had seen it, compared with 350,000 HBO subscribers who had paid close to US$50 each for live access. The network was exasperated, in part because this compromised plans for free replays to regular subscribers. HBO lobbied to restrict what its subscribers may do with what they have paid for, arguing before the FCC that its programs should not be subject to the same reuse rights as free-to-air material. Many critics worry that it wants to criminalize copying programming to boost profits, rather than as a necessity to remain afloat. This is a question of commodifying new forms of content and delivery, not surviving: HBO's sporting offerings have been very popular since becoming part of digital on-demand services in 2006, as corporate parent Time Warner seeks to restrain any audience gallop to satellite (Ourand 2006).

Despite these successes, the idea of an endlessly expanding universe of TV sport, a recession-proof genre that keeps going and going, may be a fantasy. Morgan Stanley says the major US television networks lost US$1.3 billion on sports between 2002 and 2006. The NFL suffered a 13 percent decrease in TV ratings in the five seasons to 2002; symptomatically, Disney dispatched *Monday Night Football* from ABC to ESPN in 2006 due to falling audience numbers, where it was a success at that much lower ratings threshold. This has led to an expected US$3 billion dollar write-down in the value of rights to sport paid by US media companies. Even India has seen risks to IPL's advertising base (Miller *et al.* 2003; Hiestand 2005; Goetzl 2008; "IPL Loses Sponsors" 2009).

In the UK, it's not clear how much sport will be *too* much. During the first five years of the Premier League, sixty matches were screened per season; by 2006, the number was 138. Games remained popular with viewers, but there were few competitors for the franchise, and the European Commission expressed major concerns about the prospects for new bidders, due to the price. That opened the way to Setanta, a global satellite channel that was moving from an original home in Irish pubs around the world to homes around the globe. Between them, Setanta and Sky paid £2.7 billion for national and international rights between 2007 and 2010. Half the revenue went to the teams themselves. With the major rights-holders through 2013 being a subsidiary of News Corp, which has manifold debts, and Setanta, which operates under serious financial strictures, and many teams themselves owned by debtors, the bubble looked tighter yet more tumescent by 2009. Setanta and ITV raced to renegotiate rights deals as the recession deepened, in addition to deferring some payments. More and more mavens and pundits thought that football would trip, stumble, and perhaps even fall as its owners, players, and broadcasters lost capitalization because advertising revenue was diminishing. The implications were much more dire for other sports that were covered by TV, in part due to the popularity of football, which allowed less-popular pastimes to be cross-subsidized (Thiel 2009; Ofcom and Human Capital 2006: ii; Gough 2009; Gibson 2009b, c). Television and sport still went together very successfully, but the idea that they would grow into an even larger behemoth was uncertain for the first time since the 1960s.

QUESTIONS FOR DISCUSSION

(1) What does flow mean in television?
(2) What is a genre?
(3) What is the controversy about *24* – and what do you make of the debate?
(4) How has TV changed sport – and sport changed TV?

NOTE

(1) In fairness to the fuddy-duddy, even postmodern novelists are susceptible to flow (Wallace 1997: 31–2). It was a concept within the professional discourse of TV advertising well before Williams made his Atlantic crossing – his description even reads rather like Professor Houghland's demonstration in *Murder by Television*. Flow is used to gauge viewer loyalty to program, station, genre and so on, to work with the "hammock" effect, whereby two popular shows are slung at either end of a less successful program to guard viewers' attention. For debates on these questions, see Miller (2002).

FURTHER READING

Brookes, Rod. (2002). *Representing Sport*. London: Arnold.

Newcomb, Horace. (1974). *TV: The Most Popular Art*. Garden City: Anchor Press/Doubleday.

Tulloch, John. (1990). *Television Drama: Agency, Audience and Myth*. London: Routledge.

Williams, Raymond. (1978). *Television: Technology and Cultural Form*. Glasgow: Fontana/Collins.

4

AUDIENCES

In most societies in which supernatural elements are important in attaining success, some form of divination is practiced, because fore-knowledge is one way of control. In parts of East Africa, the entrails of chickens are used for divining the future, while among the Karen of Burma it is the gall bladder of a pig; in Hollywood polls are used to determine the mysterious tastes of the audience.

(Hortense Powdermaker 1950: 285)

I was around when television started, and nobody can deny that when television started it was more peaceful and more friendly. I think we have used the competition within television … to edge ourselves and others towards the presentation in ever greater volume of things that were better not presented … television people … must be made aware that if things go as they are now, they will – unwittingly because of competition and such factors – destroy civilization.

(Karl Popper, quoted in Wedell and Luckman 2001: 195–6)

We all know the power of television to make us laugh, cry, hide behind the sofa or forget our worries, particularly as we spend more time at home trying to escape the doom and gloom of the credit crunch. To help the nation seek some solace in February, one of the most depress-ing months, psychologist Donna Dawson has put together her pick of the month's programmes on Sky+HD to help lift your spirits.

(Donna Dawson 2009)

Babette had made it a rule. She seemed to think that if kids watched television one night a week with parents or stepparents, the effect would be to de-glamorize the medium in their eyes, make it whole-some domestic sport.

(Don DeLillo 1986: 16)

My television. My rules.

Rule #2:
Turn it off and go out and play.

CHAMPIONS
for CHANGE
Network for a Healthy California

Source: California State Department of Public Health (2007).

The masses are the opium of television. The quotations above from Don DeLillo and Karl Popper encapsulate the anxiety over the influence of TV that bedevils households, while Sky's in-house program adviser allegedly uses the psy-function to direct viewers toward uplifting and self-improving shows (on Sky). For its part, the image from "Champions for Change" was a 2007 billboard campaign by the California State Department of Public Health that placed women as the governesses of the home, with responsibility for family health in terms of increased biking, swimming, fruit, vegetables, walking, dancing, raking, running, football, and basketball – and decreased television-watching.

For their part, TV producers want to *make audiences*, not simply *attract viewers*. Audiences are not already-extant entities participating in a relationship of supply and demand, in the sense that a person who goes to the supermarket is a consumer. Most of the time, television is not directly selling anything to its audience, and the audience is not buying anything from it. Rather, the TV "industry has always defined itself at the intersection of time and real estate" (Maggio 2008). Fifty years ago, Smythe explained that audience attention – presumed or measured – was sold by stations to advertisers (2004: 319–20). TV texts are therefore not so much consumer commodities but "symbols for time" (Hartley 1987: 133).

Hartley suggests that "the energy with which audiences are pursued in academic and industry research" is "larger and more powerful than the quest for mere data," because it seeks "knowledge of the *species*" (1992: 84; also see Ang 1991). Effects and ratings research traverses the industry, the state, and criticism.

Academic, commercial, and regulatory approaches to television focus most expansively and expensively on audiences as citizens and consumers. Audiences tend to characterize discussions about TV, far more than its technology, law, or even content.

The fear that television impresses "the same stamp on everything" is exemplified in the critical-theory/political-economy wing of TV Studies 1.0. Theodor Adorno and Max Horkheimer's account of production-line culture (1977) argues that because demand is dispersed and supply centralized, television operates via an administrative logic. Far from reflecting already-established and -revealed preferences of consumers in reaction to their tastes and desires, it manipulates them from the economic apex of production. Coercion is mistaken for free will. The only element that might stand against this leveling sameness is individual consciousness. But that consciousness has been customized to the requirements of economical media production. Television is one more industrial process subordinated to dominant economic forces within society that are always seeking efficient standardization. TV and its associated industries "employ the characteristic modes of production and organization of industrial corporations to produce and disseminate symbols in the form of cultural goods and services, generally, although not exclusively, as commodities" (Garnham 1987: 25).

For Horkheimer, media technologies promise deliverance from drudgery and suffering, but deliver control over individuals and minimal spontaneity. In place of "the joy of making personal decisions, of cultural development, and of the free exercise of imagination," we have "technological expertise, presence of mind, pleasure in the mastery of machinery, [and] the need to be part of and to agree with the majority of some group." The capacity to engage in "personal cultivation" is disabled because the "record player, radio, [and] television" diminish conversation between people. This "machinery of mass opinion" makes leisure decisions for people who are exhausted by their jobs, becoming "more and more like machines" themselves. The sovereignty of the consumer is really about a new mastery and a new servitude, for those who labor to serve – and shape – that consumer; people who might in turn be consumers in another role. Despite having invented technology "correlative with the development of the autonomous individual," the logic of industrial uniformity tailors consciousness "to ever more precisely prescribed tasks," set by the technology itself (Horkheimer 1996). In Alexander Kluge's words, capitalism seeks "to designate the spectators themselves as entrepreneurs. The spectator must sit ... in front of the TV set like a commodity owner: like a miser grasping every detail and collecting surplus on everything" (1981–2: 210–11).

Frankfurt School critics, as per the drama and sports traditionalists we encountered in Chapter 3, argue that entertainment TV appeals to base instincts and lowest common denominators, instilling either quietude or hysteria. The opulence of media technology is matched only by its barren civilization. Such criticisms come from both left and right, agreeing that a surfeit of signage and a deficit of understanding cheapen public culture, as kitsch overruns quality (Martín-Barbero and Rey 1999: 15–16, 22, 24). Here is an everyday-life exemplum of such anxieties, detailing television's advent in Australia:

In September 1956 many Sydney residents had their first opportunity to experience first-hand contact with the new mechanical "monster" – TV – that had for the last seven or eight years been dominating the lounges of English and American homes. Speculation on its effects had run high. On the one hand it was claimed: it would eventually destroy the human race since young couples would prefer viewing to good honest courting; children would arrive at school and either go to sleep or disgorge half-baked concepts about the Wild West and the "gals" who inspired or confused the upholders of law; it would breed a generation of youngsters with curved spines, defective eyesight, American vocabulary but no initiative; it would result in a fragmentation of life whereby contact among, and even within, families would be reduced to the barest minimum. On the other hand, supporters claimed that it would initiate a moral regeneration of the nation by enticing straying husbands home to see "Wagon Train" and "The Perry Como Show"; it would encourage dead-end kids to explore the richness of books and of life in general; and it would unite the family by offering common goals and common interests.

(Campbell assisted by Keogh 1962: 9)

Television and the Australian Adolescent (the 1962 source of this quotation) finds its authors concerned about "habits of passivity" that television might induce, and the power of particular genres to "instill certain emotions, attitudes and values." The upshot of all this, they feared, might be "a generation of people who are content to be fed by others" (Campbell assisted by Keogh 1962: 23). Today's version claims that niche cable-TV stations focus viewers "on our own little segment of reality" to the point where "we lose all touch with the larger reality that matters to us" (Andersen 2005: 14); esteemed participants at the Peabody/Loveless Seminar on the industry worry that audiences "avoid content, styles, values, or commitments that counter or contradict their own" ("Television in an Era of Fundamental Change" 2007). These critiques contrast an allegedly active public with a putatively passive audience:

> we are not happy when we are watching television, even though most of us spend many hours a week doing so, because we feel we are "on hold" rather than really living during that time. We are happiest when we are successfully meeting challenges at work, in our private lives, and in our communities.
>
> (Bellah *et al.* 1992: 49)

Happiness has become a major research object in the US, as economics, marketing, and the psy-function merrily merge to divine that TV viewers are less happy than others (Robinson and Martin 2008).

Organizations like Adbusters, with their "Mental Detox Week," loathe TV and work assiduously toward its demise (adbusters.org). They are touching on themes that recur throughout popular culture itself – mistrust of the apparatus. David Cronenberg's 1983 film *Videodrome* famously sees "Professor Brian O'Blivion," a criminal parody of Marshall McLuhan, proposing that "television is reality and reality is less than television." And it's certainly true that when newspapers start noting that more Britons vote in *Big Brother* than the European elections, panic about television is in full flight, even though US data show the number of children watching news is on the increase (Lewis *et al.* 2005: 2; "Saturday Morning Network News" 2009).

Cary Bazalgette, writing as Head of Education Projects at the British Film Institute, argued for the necessity of expecting and imparting aesthetic discrimination among students, given the nature of much TV. She tells the following tale:

> I showed the Odessa Steps sequence from *Battleship Potemkin* [Sergei Eisenstein 1925] to a class of very large and frightening dockers' daughters in south-east London, at the end of which the biggest and scariest of them all hammered on the desk with her not inconsiderable fist and said "Why don't they show things like that on television instead of some of the fucking rubbish we do get?"
>
> (Bazalgette 1999)

So aesthetic critiques of TV cross classes.

Television continues to provide both measures of, and stimuli to, social change in its dual function as an index and an incarnation of the social world. Worries over this indexical and incarnate power underpin a wealth of Television Studies 1.0 research that questions, tests, and measures the number and the conduct of people seated before the apparatus. The most socially significant part of TV Studies 1.0, as measured by psy-function funding, publication, influence, and community concern, is the search to comprehend, to capture, the audience. Why? Because television audiences participate in the most global (but local), communal (yet individual), and time-consuming practice of making meaning in the history of the world. The concept and the occasion of being an audience link the society and the person, even though watching and listening involve solitary interpretation as much as collective action. In the US, despite the fact that so many houses have several TV sets, 80 percent of homes have just one on during prime time. Viewing remains a collective act as well as an individual one (Collins 2009). Production executives invoke the audience to measure success and claim knowledge of what people want, regulators to organize administration, psychologists to produce proofs, lobby-groups to change content, and advertisers to promote products. Hence the link to panics about education, violence, and apathy supposedly engendered by TV, and routinely investigated by the state, psychology, Marxism, conservatism, the church, liberal feminism, marketers, anti-racists, and others. The television audience as consumer, student, felon, bigot, citizen, voter, and idiot engages such groups.

THE DEM/GEM

Two accounts of the audience are dominant in TV Studies 1.0, public policy, and social activism. In their different ways, each is an effects model, in that they assume the media *do* things *to* people, with the citizen understood as an audience member at risk of abjuring either interpersonal responsibility or national culture: the *domestic* effects model (or DEM) and the *global* effects model (or GEM).

The DEM is dominant in the US and exported around the world. It is typically applied without consideration of place or time, and is nestled within the psy-function (see Comstock and Scharrer 1999; Cooper 1996; Surgeon General's Scientific Advisory Committee on Television and Social Behavior 1971). The DEM offers analysis and critique of education and civic order. It views television as a force that can either direct or pervert the citizen-consumer. Entering young minds hypodermically, TV both enables and imperils learning. It may even drive the citizen to violence through aggressive and misogynistic images and narratives. The DEM is found at a variety of sites, including laboratories, clinics, prisons, schools, newspapers, psy-function journals, media organizations' research and publicity departments, everyday talk, program-classification regulations, conference papers, parliamentary debates, advertising agencies, and state-of-our-youth or state-of-our-civil-society moral panics. The DEM is routinely embodied in the claims made by marketers about the efficacy of their work; and spectacularly embodied in the nation-wide US media theatrics that ensue after mass school shootings, questioning the role of violent screen images (not religion, race, masculinity, a risk society, or firearms) in creating violent people. For instance, following a referral from Bill Clinton after the 1999 Columbine school shootings, the Federal Trade Commission (FTC) surveyed studies of "exposure to violence in entertainment," concluding that consuming violent texts was only one "factor contributing to youth aggression, anti-social attitudes and violence. Nevertheless, there is widespread agreement that it is a cause for concern." The FTC noted that high levels of exposure to violent texts generated "an exaggerated perception of the amount of violence in society" (2000: i–ii). Whiteness? Gender? Gun laws? Protestantism? These are subordinate topics – when they are deemed relevant.

Smythe wrote of the DEM in 1951: "Everybody seems to be doing it, especially those who are best qualified by virtue of the fact that 'they wouldn't have a television set in the house'" (2004: 319). Recalling the 1960s in Greenwich Village, Bob Dylan put it this way: "sociologists were saying that TV had deadly intentions and was destroying the minds and imaginations of the young – that their attention span was being dragged down." The other dominant site of knowledge was the "psychology professor, a good performer, but originality not his long suit" (2004: 55, 67). The psy-function still casts a shadow across that village, and many others.

Dorothy G. Singer and Jerome L. Singer call for centering media effects within the study of child development:

> [C]ritical analyses and careful research on social learning ... and literally scores of psychophysiological and behavioral empirical studies beginning in the 1960s have pointed much more to aggression as a learned response.... [C]an we ignore the impact on children of their exposure through television and films or, more recently, to computer games and arcade video games that involve vast amounts of violent actions?
>
> (2001: xv)

To take two small samples of the DEM's proclivities and prominence, between mid-2004 and mid-2005, US psy-function studies found television responsible for "childhood obesity, the early onset of puberty, a propensity towards bullying, and a net gain in intelligence" (Attallah 2007: 339). In the first three months of 2009, psy-function research was promoted in the bourgeois media for its claims that children watching TV were the most likely to develop asthma and mental illness and engage in violent and sexual conduct (Sample 2009; Doughty 2009). Quite a record. How do they keep breathing through it all? In Argentina, parents remain more convinced of the perils of TV than they are of video games or the Internet – it remains the demon of choice (Morduchowicz 2008: 115). The nation's alarmingly-named Liga de Armas de Casa, Consumidores y Usuarios [League of Household Warriors, Consumers and Users] (ligadeamasdecasa.com.ar) conducts a "Cruzada a favor de la familia y en contra de la TV basura" [Crusade for the Family and Against TV

Rubbish], targeting programs that are said to undermine morality, foment violence, glamorize drugs, and distort the minds of the young (Galli 2005).

Ego psychology engages in experimentation as part of its contribution to the DEM. Another element of the psy-function, psychoanalysis, reads audience responses from texts. It doesn't feel the need to talk to or observe anyone in order to announce that, for example, women enjoy soap operas because their lives are fragmented as per soap storylines since they spend so much time waiting and subordinating their needs to others. As a consequence, women supposedly identify with maternal concerns in soap characters, and are uninterested in more teleological narratives about unerringly seeking and ultimately attaining a goal (Modleski 1984). This fraction of TV Studies 1.0 holds that certain universal struggles are enacted through images. They form "a pathway to our deepest psychic levels," exercising a "potent resonance with the unconscious" through TV (Nelson 1992: 22). A somewhat less mechanistic, behavioral approach to TV effects emerged in the 1980s via cultivation analysis. Rather than looking for these hypodermic-like impacts, either through experimental or textual methods, it seeks correlations between how much and what kind of television people watch and their views of social life. Interesting information has been uncovered, for example, about correspondences between the distorted representation on the racial background of victims and perpetrators of crime in US TV news and drama versus criminological data and the apparent impact on popular knowledge as disclosed in opinion polls (Shanahan and Morgan 1999).

The GEM, primarily utilized in non-US discourse, is spatial and historical rather than psychological. Whereas the DEM focuses on the cognition and emotion of individual human subjects via observation and experimentation, the GEM looks to the customs and patriotic feelings exhibited by collective human subjects, the grout of national culture. In place of psychology, the GEM is concerned with politics. Television does not make you a well-educated or ill-educated person, a wild or self-controlled one. Rather, it makes you a knowledgeable and loyal national subject, or a *naïf* who is ignorant of local tradition and history. Cultural belonging, not psychic wholeness, is the touchstone of the global effects model.

Instead of measuring responses electronically or behaviorally, as its domestic counterpart does, the GEM interrogates the geopolitical origin of TV texts, and the themes and styles they embody, with particular attention to the putatively nation-building genres of drama, news, sport, and current affairs. GEM adherents hold that local citizens should control television, because they can be counted on in the event of war. This model is found in the discourses of cultural imperialism, everyday talk, broadcast and telecommunications policy, unions, international organizations, newspapers, heritage, cultural diplomacy, and post-industrial service-sector planning, as per the NWICO and globalization issues described in Chapter 2 (see Schiller 1976; Beltrán and Fox 1980; Dorfman and Mattelart 2000).

The GEM favors "creativity, not consumerism," in the words of UNESCO's "Screens Without Frontiers" initiative (Tricot 2000). It is exemplified in Armand Mattelart's stinging denunciation of First-World TV's influence on the Third World:

> In order to camouflage the counter-revolutionary function which it has assigned to communications technology and, in the final analysis, to all the messages of mass culture, imperialism has elevated the mass media to the status of revolutionary agents, and the modern phenomenon of communications to that of revolution itself[,] …
>
> … an element in a total system answering to the imperialist metropolis's conception of the role of the superstructure in the counter-revolutionary struggle in Third World countries, i.e. that of smuggling in its models of development and social relations.
>
> (1980: 9, 17)

Néstor García-Canclini notes in this context that: "We Latin Americans presumably learned to be citizens through our relationship to Europe; our relationship to the United States will, however, reduce us to consumers" (2001: 1). Transcending the old NWICO critiques of imperial and corporate power, vigorous critiques of imported television have come from Islamists, with religious leaders and researchers leading the way. They have focused on secular, pro-Western elites dominating the airwaves to the exclusion of faith-based TV and governance. Spirituality and ethics have displaced technological transfer and capitalism as sites of struggle, and exerted great influence on Arab states and diasporas (Mowlana 2000: 112–14). In Nigeria, concern is expressed that violent gangs have formed in the twenty-first century in emulation of US versions seen on TV (Onwumechili 2007: 138). In Canada, the Aboriginal Peoples Television Network targets viewers who are spread across a massive nation, often in small clusters, to enable the maintenance of their culture. The network broadcasts in several languages. The only way it could survive in this form is thanks to a GEM mandate from regulators – market economics would probably see the spectrum space go to a US-programmed network (Beaty and Sullivan 2006: 62).

How should we evaluate these models? The DEM suffers from all the disadvantages of ideal-typical psychological reasoning. The psy-function claims the status of a science, and goes guarantor of both happiness and productivity. Its histories praise famous forefathers and their "findings," rarely problematizing the production of data in any meaningful way (Danziger 1998). It assumes "anything that is important in its history will have been absorbed into the ongoing research tradition." This very sanguine model connects to the essentialist conceit "of an a-historical human nature" (Brock 1995). The DEM relies on methodological individualism, failing to account for cultural norms and politics, let alone the arcs of history that establish patterns of text and response inside politics, war, ideology, and discourse. Each massively costly laboratory test of television's impact on audiences, based on, as the refrain goes, "a large university in the mid-West," is countered by a similar experiment, with conflicting results. Prudish politicians, generous grant-givers, and jeremiad-wielding pundits call for more and more research to prove that TV makes you stupid, violent, and apathetic – or the opposite. Television Studies 1.0 academics line up at the trough to indulge their contempt for the apparatus and their rent-seeking urge for public money. The DEM never interrogates its own conditions of existence – namely, that governments, religious groups, and the media themselves use it to account for social problems, and that TV's capacity for private viewing troubles those authorities who desire surveillance of popular culture. And it trends to focus on life in the First World, from which endless, effortless extrapolations are magically made to account for all of humanity

(Osei-Hwere and Pecora 2008: 15). When the audience is invoked by critics and regulators, the assumption is often that "[c]hildren are sitting victims; television bites them" (Schramm *et al.* 1961: 1). Television is blamed for "sapping IQs and compromising SAT scores, while we all sit there on ever fatter bottoms with little mesmerized spirals revolving in our eyes," an "innocent populace" set upon by a nasty toy (Wallace 1997: 36).

As for the GEM, its concentration on national or sectarian culture denies the potentially liberatory and pleasurable nature of varying takes on the popular, forgets the internal differentiation of publics, valorizes frequently oppressive and/or unrepresentative local bourgeoisies in the name of maintaining and developing national culture, and ignores the demographic realities of its "own" terrain. In Australia, networks that are statutorily obliged to show many hours of local production (which may be popular but are often costly) often argue for special provisions to protect their businesses, raising barriers to new competitors entering markets (Manning 2006). In Britain, much of the BBC's mission has been about elevating an often unwilling and unwitting audience (Brunsdon 2004). In Jordan and Saudi Arabia, reality television is the object of fatwas from the Muslim Brotherhood in Jordan and Saudi Arabia, because it is deemed to aid globalization and Yanqui interests (Kraidy 2007: 191). The GEM also animates the ordinary science of policy research into ownership and control that downplays the power of audience interpretation. The GEM irresistibly "imagines audiences as imperiled," bewitched, or horrified by foreign content (Attallah 2007: 343). But they may watch imported television ironically as well as pleasurably, like Peter Corris' hardbitten Sydney private eye, Cliff Hardy, for whom the US TV he happily sits in front of is "appalling" (Corris 2009: 12).

Studies of the image of US TV in the Middle East in 2004 reveal that it provides almost the only sources of positive feeling engendered by that great, tumultuous, destructive, productive country. There is also, of course, massive variation across the region. The US-enabled and US-allied society of Saudi Arabia is much more opposed to US popular culture than Morocco or Jordan. Everywhere, the much-feared youth of each country are more positive about US television than their elders. The Saudis receive almost no US TV drama for public screening, but are determined haters, whereas those most-exposed to Hollywood are most positive about the country. Across the board, reactions to US television imports are effectively unrelated to what angers people: Washington's policies on Iraq and Palestine (Zogby International 2004). When an exported series such as *The West Wing* (1999–2006) touches in depth on US–Middle East relations, it becomes a useful debating point for Arab audiences, not a cause of anti-US feeling (Cass 2007). Similarly, do Canadians fail to maintain a sense of distinctiveness because their preferred entertainment programs in the early-twenty-first century were *CSI*, *CSI: Miami*, *American Idol* (2002–), and *Survivor* (2000–) (Beaty and Sullivan 2006: 68)? After all, during the waning days of apartheid, the favorite program among white Afrikaners was *The Cosby Show* (1984–92) (Glenn 2008: 69). In the Indian case, the deregulation of the 1990s that brought new forms of TV also brought new producers and audiences, with non-resident Indians acting as affluent audience targets and makers of programs, mostly in Britain and the US (Moorti 2007). Were these vulnerable audiences, and if so, vulnerable to which influences?

The DEM/GEM complex has been "devoted to showing how TV affected *other* people's behavior (the masses, women, children, and so forth) … by those who pathologized, feared or opposed TV" (Hartley 2005: 102; also see Hartley 2008: 70–1). Hence David Foster Wallace's critique of "TV-scholars who mock and revile the very phenomenon they've chosen as vocation" because they are like people who despise "their spouses or jobs, but won't split up or quit" (1997: 29). The DEM/GEM operates in contradistinction to the more populist, qualitative theories of Television Studies 2.0.

Harold Garfinkel responded to the DEM/GEM's condescending attitude to the populace by developing the notion of the "cultural dope," a mythic figure who supposedly "produces the stable features of the society by acting in compliance with pre-established and legitimate alternatives of action that the common culture provides." The "common sense rationalities … of here and now situations" actually used by people can be obscured by such categorizations (1992: 68). As Foucault said, "On se plaint toujours que les médias bourrent la tête des gens. Il y a de la misanthropie dans cette idée. Je crois au contraire que les gens réagissent; plus on veut les convaincre, plus ils s'interrogent" ["Some complain that the media brainwash people. This seems misanthropic to me. I believe that people resist; the more one tries to convince them, the more they ask questions"][1] (2001: 927).

Such critiques have generated an entire paradigm of research. Marshall McLuhan declared television to be a "cool" medium, because it left so much up to the viewer to sort out (1974: 31). Umberto Eco's mid-1960s development of a notion of encoding–decoding, open texts, and aberrant readings – developed as a consultancy on audiences for Italian public broadcasting – was crucial (Eco 1972). Eco looked at the ways that meanings were put into programs by producers and extracted from programs by viewers, and the differences between these protocols. His insights were picked up by Frank Parkin (1971) then Stuart Hall (1980), David Morley (1992), and Ien Ang (1982) on the left, and Elihu Katz (1990) on the right. Much valuable work of this kind has been done to counter the *données* of TV Studies 1.0 and the GEM. In the case of children and television – perhaps the most contentious and loaded area of audience study – anxieties from the effects tradition about turning Edenic innocents into rabid monsters have been challenged by research into how young people distinguish between fact and fiction; the particular generic features and intertexts of children's news, drama, action-adventure, education, cartooning, and play; and how talking about TV makes for social interaction (Buckingham 2005: 474–5).

The active-audience perspective has spawned a research paradigm that fabulates two other model audiences: the all-powerful consumer (invented and loved by neoliberal policy-makers, desired and feared by oligopolistic corporations) and the all-powerful interpreter (invented and loved by Television Studies 2.0 narcissographers, tolerated and used by cynical corporations). These models have a common origin. In lieu of the DEM/GEM's citizen-building, their logic is to construct and control consumers and activists. Drawing on Garfinkel's cultural-dope insight to adopt the reverse position from rat-catching psy-doomsayers, they claim that the audience, like neoclassical economics' consumers, makes its own meanings, outwitting institutions of the state, academia, and capitalism that seek to measure and control it.

There have been two principal iterations of this approach: uses and gratifications (U&G) and ethnography/cultural studies. Uses and gratifications operates from a psychological model of needs and pleasures; cultural studies from a political one of needs and pleasures. U&G focuses on what are regarded as fundamental psychological drives that define how people use the media to gratify themselves. A strong sense of normativity underpins the theory. Like people in general, audiences are viewed as individual organisms who adapt to prevailing social systems, rather than as politically and economically active agents who can transform their environment through organizing for progressive change, or even as collective subjects influenced by ritual as much as individuated needs (Staiger 2005: 54–5). The method sits well with the prevailing, slightly guilty logic of many TV watchers, exemplified in journalist Lucy Mangan embracing "the passivity that lies at the heart of all happy television viewing" (2008). It celebrates the used and the gratified.

Conversely, cultural studies' ethnographic work has shown some of the limitations to, for example, psychoanalytic and GEM claims that viewers are stitched into certain perspectives by the interplay of narrative, dialog, and image. *Contra* speculation that soap operas see women identify with maternal, policing functions and US images of power and happiness, this research suggests that actual viewers may identify with villainous characters because of their power. The genre appeals because it offers a world of glamour and joy in contradistinction to the workaday world of patriarchy (Ang 1982; Seiter *et al.* 1989). This position has been elevated to a virtual *nostrum* in some later research into fans, who are thought to construct parasocial or imagined social connections to celebrities and actants in ways that either fulfill the function of friendship, or serve as spaces for projecting and evaluating schemas to make sense of human interaction. TV Studies 2.0's counter-critique attacks TV Studies 1.0's opposition to television for failing to allot the people's machine its due as a populist apparatus that subverts patriarchy, capitalism, and other forms of oppression (or diminishes the tension of such social divisions, depending on your politics). Popular television is held to be decoded by viewers in keeping with their social situations, hence empowering the powerless (Horton and Wohl 1956; Jenkins 1992). Sometimes, such faith in the active audience reaches cosmic proportions. It has been a *donnée* of Television

Studies 2.0 that television is not responsible for – well, anything. This position is a virtual *nostrum* in some research into, for instance, fans of drama, who are thought to construct connections with celebrities and actants in ways that mimic friendship, make sense of human interaction, and ignite cultural politics. Interestingly, neo-liberal economists concur, associating Brazilian increases in divorce and decreases in fertility with the spread of TV and *telenovelas*, which portray happy independent women and happy small families (Chong and La Ferrara 2009; La Ferrara *et al.* 2008).

The active audience is said to be weak at the level of cultural production, but strong as an interpretative community, especially via imagined links to stars. Eco suggests that viewers can "own" a program, psychologically if not legally, by quoting characters' escapades and proclivities "as if they were aspects of the fan's private sectarian world" (1987: 198). This world is then opened up to other followers through shared experiences such as conventions, Web pages, discussion groups, quizzes, and rankings. TV has a unique hold here. Whereas just 38 percent of US residents talk about their favorite websites, 79 percent chat about preferred television programs (Deloitte Media & Entertainment 2007). References to segments of an episode, or the typical behavior of an actant, may become "catalyzers of collective memories," regardless of their significance for individual plot-lines (Leets *et al.* 1995: 102–4). As Joanne Woodward once remarked of the difference between film and TV: "When I was in the movies I heard people say, 'There goes Joanne Woodward.' Now they say, 'There goes somebody I think I know'" (quoted in McLuhan 1974: 339). This level of identification is assumed by Jane Wyman's children in *All That Heaven Allows* (Douglas Sirk 1955) when they buy her a TV set to cathect onto in place of her hunky gardener, Rock Hudson.[2]

Consider televised sport. Broadly based magazine formats such as *Grandstand* (1958–2007) or *SportsCenter* combine an omnibus approach to a variety of sports with talk segments. The gossip format of such programs is far from incidental. It fits Eco's concept of sport cubed, or sport chatter, where sport becomes multiplied first by TV coverage and then by TV talk, putting us still one further remove from the point of supposed origin (1987: 162–4). University tests have shown an inverse relationship between the time programs devote to actual live sporting activity and their ratings. Spectator numbers and interest often increase with stop-pages, discussions, replays, advertisements, and diversions (Meier 1984: 274).

Talking about television may, as Eco says, be phatic, providing a bridge between people. For example, continuous serials mirror the time that viewers have passed since each previous episode through an intertextual merging of television drama and life. This encourages a view of the TV text as neither a mirror nor a window, but rather as part-generator of the manufacture of experience by the viewer. The complexity of drama is said to lead audiences to engage in very subtle and complex practices, such as writing slash fiction that turns *Star Trek* characters into lovers, or interrogating the science in *House* (2004–) and *Fringe* (2008–) for accuracy (Penley 1997: 116–25; Pickard 2008).

Researchers in this tradition frequently described themselves as optimistic versus pessimistic, deriding Television Studies 1.0 as in denial of the agency that audiences exercise. Audience resistance to the way programs are encoded by producers is supposedly evident to 2.0 scholars from narcissography: perusing audience paratexts or watching with their children (Fiske 1987). Very droll. But can fans be said to resist labor exploitation, patriarchy, racism, and US neo-imperialism, or in some specifiable way make a difference to politics beyond their own selves, when they interpret texts unusually, dress up in public as men from outer space, or chat about their romantic frustrations? And why have such practices become so popular in the First World at a moment when media policy fetishizes consumption, deregulation, and self-governance? Why is this not about an active audience in the spirit of Stuart Hall: "I speak and talk to the radio and the TV all the time. I say, 'that is not true' and 'you are lying through your teeth' and 'that cannot be so'. I keep up a running dialogue" (Taylor 2006)?

The idea that audiences using several different communications technologies while watching TV makes them more independent of, for example, commercials is laughable. No fewer than one-third of sports audiences who send instant or text messages while viewing refer to the commercials they have been watching, and almost two-thirds have greater recognition of those commercials than people who simply watch television without reaching out in these other ways to friends/fellow-spectators (Loechner 2007). The

Internet provides cheap market testing, so TV producers leak information or request input about planned changes to programming in order to drum up opinion without paying for it, and they keep weather eyes open on televisionwithoutpity.com, tvsquad. com, and thefutoncritic.com. Over half the people visiting such sites, supposedly the bailiwick of liberated viewers, are professionals in the TV industry, and televisionwithoutpity.com was even bought by NBC (Kushner 2007). This is, ironically, a replay of the earliest forms of TV Studies 1.0. In the early 1940s, NBC would mail a program schedule to all 6,000 people who owned television sets in the United States with a questionnaire inviting viewers to respond to the shows in terms of their likes and dislikes (Kersta 1942: 120). Once more, the new media are faithful retreads.

It is often alleged that the political economists of TV Studies 1.0 did not account for the ability of audiences to interpret what they receive. This accusation is unsustainable. Unlike their psy-function stable-mates, the writings of the principal scholars from that tradition show they were all aware of this capacity. In the 1950s, Smythe wrote: "it is important to understand that audience members act on the program content. They take it and mold it in the image of their individual needs and values." He took it as read that soap-opera *habituées* sometimes viewed the genre as fictitious and sometimes as a guide for dealing with problems (1954: 143, 148). Smythe saw no necessary contradiction between this perspective and political economy. Similarly, in his classic 1960s text *Mass Communications and American Empire*, Schiller (1969) stressed the need to build on the creativity of audiences by offering them entertaining and informative media. And at the height of Armand Mattelart's 1970s policy interventions in revolutionary societies, from Latin America to Africa, he recognized the relative autonomy of audiences and their capacity and desire to generate cultural meanings (1980). Even Horkheimer derided "[t]he stereotyped rejection of television" by those who considered themselves above it; their arrogance "highlights with special clarity the impossibility of turning the clock back," because "flight into the past is no help to the freedom that is being threatened" (1996: 140). And Adorno recognized that the best way to draw mass acclaim was to attack the mass media – that manipulating one's audience by denouncing audiences as vulnerable to demagoguery is itself an old demagogic trick (1972: 72).

USES OF THE DEM/GEM

Of course, these theoretical and conceptual limitations have not undermined the substantive, material bases to the two principal effects models: how to explain and control conduct and how to sell things to people (the DEM) versus how to strengthen national, regional, and sectarian culture (the GEM). So we need to be aware how the models are deployed, regardless of our skepticism about them. Some uses of the DEM and GEM offer interesting critiques rather than being common-or-garden, normal-science displacements of social problems onto television. The two models may even mix interestingly. Consider Mexican *telenovelas*, many of which are researched, produced, and revised by TV Azteca via a blend of genre study and *análisis semántico basado en imagines* [semantic analysis based on the imaginary], using viewer interviews that detail responses to stories as they unfold on screen. This research helps to determine future plots (Clifford 2005; Slade and Beckenham 2005: 341 n. 1). The process involves an interesting application of textual and audience analysis, and is open to progressive politics. The DEM and the GEM can merge over young people, in protocols like the UN's Convention on the Rights of the Child. Children's television has inspired such agreements and manifestoes as the Africa Charter on Children's Broadcasting, which criticizes the exploitation of young audiences through hyper-commercialism, and scholarly studies that disclose the dominance of US cartoons across the world. The DEM/GEM nexus also leads to investigations of decoding the Hollywood image and its investment in commodities by contrast with quotidian life in import cultures – classics being the way that the expansion of US TV in Korea and India this century generates dissatisfaction with the everyday (Osei-Hwere and Pecora 2008: 15, 18; Götz *et al.* 2008; Yang *et al.* 2008). Progressive politics can animate the mixture of content analysis and examination of audience numbers by health researchers within the DEM/GEM, such as research into smoking in TV drama – so *A Case for Two* (1985–2004) favorably portrayed smoking throughout its run on German TV, leading to public-health anxieties. This was not just a national issue, because the program was exported to fifty-nine countries (Hanewinkel and Wiborg 2008). Similarly, researchers have exposed attempts by US firms to circumvent Singapore's pioneering prohibition of cigarette advertising through product placements on television that associate smoking with Europe and the US (Assunta and Chapman 2004).

The DEM on its own is rarely progressive, because it is dominated by the psy-function. Consider potentially valuable recent studies into food advertising aimed at children on commercial US TV. Drawing on samples of successful programs, this research evaluated 50,000 commercials for nutritional content and found that nine-tenths were for foodstuffs associated with high health risks. In a country where one-fifth of pre-schoolers are clinically obese, the effects of such advertising on audiences are not really in much doubt (Powell *et al.* 2007). Responding to these studies, Nickelodeon, the children's network clearly keenest to exploit children as consumers, and Bill Clinton, a binge eater of fast food, entered into a partnership in 2005 to encourage young people toward healthy diets (Banet-Weiser 2007: 1). But one needs to take the next step. A reductive, television-centric, nation-based response to this research would be to petition the state, the networks, or the advertisers to regulate commercials. Realistically, however, an entire revision of food production, distribution, and use is required that transcends the wee box in the corner – an easy target for exploitation by capital and blame by science. Instead we must engage US corporate agriculture, state protectionism, and the fact that 4 percent of the world's population (Yanquis) consumes 25 percent of its food (Miller 2007: 112–43).

Censorship is a core and regressive aspect of the DEM/GEM. Ofcom polices Britain's "9 pm Watershed," which means some nudity, sex, drugs, and violence can be shown from then until six the next morning, when it is assumed that children are asleep (2008c). Similar watersheds are popular around the world: in Argentina it's 10 pm–8 am; Germany 10 pm–530 am; Canada 9 pm–6 am; and the US 10 pm–6 am (with the embarrassing term "safe harbor" being used in place of the quaintly euphemistic "watershed"). Throughout most of Asia, audiences are deemed by censors to be too bigoted and fragile to deal with queerness, so Murdoch's STAR network muted the words "gay" and "lesbian" in fifty-three countries during the 2009 Academy Awards, while Chinese TV eliminated two same-sex kisses shown during coverage (Flumenbaum 2009). In the US, the First Amendment to the

Constitution supposedly guarantees freedom of speech against government censorship. But the hyper-religious sexual obsessions of the US population – or its very vocal Christians, at least – give the FCC an incentive to stop people watching and listening to what they want. Front organizations for the Republican Party and right-wing Protestants gleefully orchestrate rote email campaigns to protest on behalf of supposedly vulnerable youth whose morals are corruptible by the loose lips and looser limbs of liberals. The Internet makes signing such petitions easy. It has seen the number of indecency complaints to the FCC grow from under fifty in 2000 to almost a million and a half in 2004. While cable channels cannot be censored, broadcast ones are subject to the "Safe Harbor" rule, which restricts materials screened before 10 pm if they are deemed "indecent" by the magically endowed Commission. Programs censored include the award-winning *9/11* documentary (2002) (heroes never say "fuck," apparently – though they did in the telecast of *Saving Private Ryan* (Steven Spielberg 1998)) while the accidental display of a breast during the 2004 Superbowl at half-time resulted in a gigantic fine for the host broadcaster, and *America's Funniest Home Videos* (1989–) became the object of critique (though not, ultimately, a fine) for depicting a naked infant reclining on top of its pacifier or dummy in what the FCC embarrassingly named the "butt plug" video. There are numerous other cases. Apart from holding the Commission and the nation up to deserved ridicule for their prurient prudishness, these laughable interventions chill program-makers, who have to guess which artistic or factual materials may draw the opprobrium of nutty religionists (Rintels 2006). The US used to have self-regulation to protect young livers from advertisements for spirituous liquors, but the 2009 economic crisis put an end to them (Semuels 2009). In the UK, the Advertising Standards Authority can order companies to withdraw commercials that appeal to risky conduct such as gambling (Blitz and Bradshaw 2009) and Ofcom presides over a Broadcasting Code that viewers can refer to when they complain about programs (Ofcom 2008c).

The American Psychological Association's Task Force on the Sexualization of Girls produced a report evaluating TV from a DEM perspective. While its feminist concerns about the restricted repertoire of female subjectivities were important, terror in the face of young people and sex seemed to be the true animators of a remarkably conventional document. It was dedicated in faithful Yanqui DEM style to reiterating the *nostra* of just one approach, ego psychology, ignoring linguistic and other cultural differences plus the lessons of ethnography. The report's reactionary politics were paradoxically underlined by its faith in superstition, via recommendations that churches mobilize – for the umpteenth time in human history – to restrict young women's sexuality (2007). If they had been less insular in geographical and disciplinary terms, the report's authors might have been pleased that just 5 percent of commercials in the US feature women doing housework, when the percentage is closer to 25 percent in Latin countries (Valls-Fernández and Martínez-Vicente 2007) – but that would have required transcending the psy-function's universalism and heeding developments elsewhere.

We see a similar panic informing the Kaiser Family Foundation's *Sex on TV* series of reports, a seemingly endless stream of studies into US television's sexual imagery aimed at the young that draws on such wonderful psy-function neologisms as the notion that TV is a "sexual super-peer," and each viewer has a "Sexual Media Diet" – as measured by a profoundly Puritanical and odiously anxious form of content analysis (Kunkel *et al.* 2005). The rather ominously-named Common Sense Media coalition rails at commercials that reference the body during US "football": "sex, violence, and erectile-dysfunction drugs marketed during pro football games create an environment that makes millions of parents squirm – and gives kids way too much information way too soon" (2009). It may well make parents squirm. And your point is?

Bodies like the FCC and their moralistic *confrères* also obsess about violence. But like their anxieties over sexuality, they never connect these questions to corporate methods of selling and advertising's role in cultural politics, so beholden are they to capitalist ideology and its principal guardian, individualistic models of responsibility as represented by the psy-function. It's telling to read the FCC's 2007 report on the subject for the way in which supposedly learned, responsible servants of the public invoke their own, unexciting parenting experiences to validate their feelings of panic about childhood (an instance of narcissography crossing over from Television Studies 2.0 to 1.0). Noting that one to two-thirds of children have TV sets in their rooms, and will have spent three school years in front of them before commencing first grade, the Commissioners examined audience effects for the umpteenth time, hoping for Constitutional means of restricting speech. Thank you, thousands of overemployed behavioral scientists since the 1960s. Can we move on now? Actually, no, because other theocratic regimes, such as Sudan's, are even more frightened about exposing their audiences to unpleasant truths such as desire and violence. Sudanese television proscribes all footage of sex, violence, and war, instead using soap operas, poetry, and cartoons to ensure Islamic familial moral uplift (Howard 2008: 58–9).

That said, I think there is room for a new (type of) effects study. It seems to me that a major research program is needed that looks at the viewing patterns since early childhood of US congressional representatives, Defense Department officials, and state politicians and judges who preside over capital punishment. This might allow us to understand their bloodthirsty roles in world affairs and domestic executions – in short, their violent tendencies. Put another way, and following Laura Nader's (1972) imprecation to her fellow anthropologists that they "study up," let's investigate hegemony through effects studies. Here are some threshold issues. The Bush Administration (like Obama) supported the death penalty, despite the welter of evidence that it fails to deter criminals and arguments against its constitutionality (Sarat 2001). When George W. Bush sent a record number of people to be executed during his time as Governor of Texas, which TV programs and movies had he been watching? On the foreign-policy front, the Bush Administration opposed international law's attempt to provide democratically-generated norms of conduct. It asserted that threats to US society existed, where rigorous scrutiny by academic and policy experts doubted the fact, and proceeded to engage in massive programs of destruction that disrupted the lives and livelihoods of millions of people. How many war films had Donald Rumsfeld seen before and during his period as Secretary of Defense? Which movies espousing anti-Palestinian positions had Bush's various press secretaries been exposed to? Did Secretary of State Colin Powell respond positively to violence in wartime cinema? Did Vice President Dick Cheney have a special relationship to the vigilante films that might be correlated with his policy advice? Could he in any sense be said to 'cycle' with these texts?

When the Bush Cabinet was shown graphics referring to "collateral damage" from proposed military intervention, were members' heartbeats and other signs of excitation regularly measured? When the Administration offered or witnessed military PowerPoint presentations, were any studies done of their genital responses to the material? Which members of the 2001–9 administration were exposed to criminological studies of the costliness and ineffectiveness of capital punishment, and what have their responses been to this research? Similar questions could be asked of the Blair Cabinet in the UK and the Howard government in Australia. Why did these administrations feel able to endorse mass violent conduct? The project I am proposing would use the DEM to explain how world leaders endorsed monumental violence. It is unlikely to happen. It doesn't suit the model. And it doesn't suit politics. The old-style DEM, based on individuals or gangs and their private lives, will continue in its time-honored way.

SURVEILLANCE

Another key applied area of audience research relevant to the DEM/GEM is surveillance to satisfy the desire of marketing and advertising to know what audiences watch (Maxwell 1996, 2000). The euphemism for constant surveillance in the industry is "accountability." That term *should* refer to corporations and governments being accountable to popular representation under a democracy, but in TV, it signifies the amount of information about audiences that networks hand to advertisers – what people watched, when, and where, and what that then urged them to purchase. Audience surveillance starts with focus groups, which are conducted to see what potential audiences will think of potential new shows. Focus groups sample the population to find small numbers of people whose identities represent the social formations desired by advertisers. They are shown pilots of programs to judge the likelihood that their cohorts will watch. Focus groups are part of the great unstudied lacuna of television studies, apart from earnest methodologists (Morrison 1998). These groups are neglected because they don't interest the textualists, narcissographers, political economists, and psy-function mavens of TV Studies 1.0 and 2.0. Only a few businesses undertake focus groups, which are crucial to the life and demise of every US show. The firms are very small; they routinely work for both producers and networks, thereby creating an outrageous conflict of interest; none of them are Spanish-speaking, unlike public relations or advertising itself; and they veer between being influential and of no significance whatsoever. But they are vital sources of surveillance before programs have begun.

Ratings of broadcast shows are the key to determining success in TV – how many people watched and who they were. The US networks attained their peak viewing numbers in 1976, with 92 percent of the national audience; by 2005, they had 45 percent of it. US cable stations have grown at their expense. More people watched CNN that any network on election night in 2008, and no fewer than thirty-seven cable stations that carry commercials reported their best prime-time viewing figures that year, while CBS, ABC, NBC, and Fox dropped by an average of 11 percent. The numbers are not about raw humans, though – their social identities and consuming practices also matter. Three basic systems of fantasizing about consumers dominate marketing: individual, regional, and global. The first is animated by classifications of race, class, gender, age, and psyche; the second by geopolitical clusters; and the third by a growing cosmopolitanism. In the area of sport, Fox Soccer Channel succeeds not because it commands huge audiences, but because of their composition – men aged 18–34 with household income over US$75,000. A show like *Alias* (2001–6), which did not rate well, remained on the air due to the youthfulness of its fans and because it promoted high DVD sales. In the US, low-rating situation comedies that are about elites, like *30 Rock* (2006–) and *The Office* (2005–), are much-loved by affluent viewers. This can enable unpopular series to survive, because advertisers of costly merchandise are promised ruling-class audiences. At the same time, with overall declines in ratings, broadcast networks are being forced to offer free commercial time to advertisers who have paid for programs that do not attract the right people in terms of commercial desires. Then there is very specific, local targeting, which is seeing broadcast stations following the lead of radio and the airlines, via credit and debit cards articulated to frequent viewing, and a rewards system with local advertisers for redeeming points (Attallah 2007: 330; Flaherty 2008; Hassan *et al.*

2003: 446–7; Morris 2007; "Fox Soccer Channel" 2008; Downey 2007b; Consoli 2008; Greenwald 2009).

In the case of Australia, where cable came very late and the networks were dominant for five decades, ratings eventually changed to disclose that only half of TV viewing occurred exclusively during prime time, and people under fifty-five were abandoning television in ways that were quite unusual internationally, even amongst other privileged white-settler imperialist colonies/US–UK satellites. The DEM/GEM nexus has also been used against its own politics, by industry exponents of the psy-function, when intercultural communications research helps to exploit children's purchasing power across nations in the face of the pesky refusal of young boys to consume as assiduously as young girls. Hence Disney's concerted international focus on boys in the new millennium and surveillance of them by a team of ethnographers led by an executive (Kelly Peña) known in Hollywood as "the kid whisperer" ("Subscription TV" 2009; Young 2008; Barnes 2009a, b).

Audience numbers have massive effects, but they are not pure, unvarnished accounts of popularity. For example, ratings apartheid was practiced for decades in the US until 2007, initially because Spanish-language networks thought their viewers were being lost in the Anglo mass. When Spanish-language networks were finally measured alongside Anglo ones, the results shocked Anglo executives: Univision won the ratings amongst advertising's most desired age group – eighteen-to-forty-nine – no fewer than fourteen times in 2008; Latin@s were not departing network TV for cable or the Internet, due to their economic situation (Bauder 2008; Goodwin 2009). This prompted one more tedious but nasty turn in a perverse GEM-like national debate over assimilation that made ludicrous accusations to the effect that young Latin@s were not learning English or patriotic identification, as a consequence of watching shows in another tongue (Arnoldy 2007). But empirical studies of minority groups using TV to solidify their culture and remain in touch with places of origin, such as Turks in Greece or Arabs in the US, counter the notion that this precludes integration. Latin@s move easily between languages, code-switching both inter-sententially and between phrases, in keeping with their use of both Anglo and Spanish television channels (Madianou 2005: 55; Rizkallah and Razzouk 2006; "Bi-lingual Hispanics" 2009). The belated recognition of Univision's importance also emphasized the limitations of ratings. Measurement of bilingual audiences to Anglo networks was so incompetent that it was wrongly used to downplay the appeal of ethnically inclusive English-language material, misreading viewers' desires and hence diminishing work prospects for minority talent. Numerous multicultural shows were prematurely canceled, such as *Greetings from Tucson* (2002–3), *Kingpin* (2003), and *Luis* (2003), because their audiences were underestimated – in every sense. What else were Spanish speakers to do but turn to Univision, when Anglo networks systematically ignored, distorted, and/or misunderstood them, as decades of content analysis in the *National Brownout Report* has illustrated (National Association of Hispanic Journalists 2006; Rincón & Associates 2004; James 2007)? This connects not only to the intellectual narrowness of Anglo executives, but also attempts by traditional networks to minimize the power of cable stations by stressing prime time as the centerpiece of measuring audience size. This suits their heavy investments in marquee drama programming shown at that time, and their cozy relationships with the companies that research viewers.

There was massive anxiety in the 1980s when video-cassette recorders and pay cable seemed to take control of the audience away from TV networks and toward film studios, cable companies, and viewers. These concerns were heightened when Digital Video Recorders (DVRs)/Personal Video Recorders permitted viewers to elude the clutches of capital by avoiding commercials in real time. DVRs were even advertised for these qualities, supposedly making viewers into schedulers. Initially, the major versions of these devices only worked when subscribers hooked them up to the Internet to allow service providers, TiVo and ReplayTV, to collect information. In addition to amassing a huge database of consumer information, they pinpointed the identities and actions of television viewers. By 2009, almost one-third of US homes had one (Lewis 2001: 40; Rose 2001; Attallah 2007: 330; "The Revolution That Wasn't" 2009). Time-shifting became common for a while. The initial upshot was a dramatic loss of confidence in TV's efficacy amongst major advertisers, despite this additional intelligence about viewers out of fear that "[l]e pouvoir de programmer passe des mains de l'éditeur à celles du télépectateur"

["the power to program is shifting from the editor to the spectator"] (Cristiani and Missika 2007). But the data don't support this
view. In the US, where the DVR is much more popular than anywhere else, just 5 percent of TV is time-shifted, and people skip
3 percent of commercials ("The Revolution That Wasn't" 2009).

Ratings firms develop ever-more-impressive-sounding methods
of investigating audiences – 10,000 US viewers are under surveillance through People Meters nowadays, to add to the 15,000
examined by other means, such as measuring DVR records and
using the Anytime Anywhere Media Measurement across technologies ("Nielsen Media Research" 2006). Again, the elemental
desire that drives advertisers is not absolute numbers of viewers.
They want information about, and surveillance of, those audiences
in terms of identity, wealth, and taste, so highly targeted networks
with original programming seek a signature in the public mind
(Richardson and Figueroa 2005). The latest methods focus on cor-
relating consumption with viewing (Collins 2009). New online
sites replaying network television and movies, such as Hulu, are
predicated on "geo-filtered access logs." These are measured each
day, alongside confessional testimonies by potential viewers – if
you tell us about your life and your practices of consumption, we'll
tell you the programs that may interest you (Mermigas 2008).
Cable, which used to be in the vanguard calling for more finely
grained ratings to prove that they had taken audience numbers
away from the networks, opposes such innovations, because leading
companies like MTV have young audiences who are less inclined
to sit through commercials than their elders. Some research suggests their attitude is about altering the TV schedule to suit viewers'
own schedules, rather than an effort to avoid advertising. So now
there are more and more ideas about interactive commercials,
where viewers use their remote controls to respond to pitches for
products – and offer more data about themselves. In addition, capitalist lackeys in neuroscience argue that they scan audience brains
to see which segments activate purchasing desires while viewing
(Helm 2007; Downey 2007c; Reynolds 2008; Edgecliffe-Johnson
2007; Bürgi 2007).

For many decades, advertisers, marketers, and stations, both
private and public, have been obsessed with young viewers. I recall
being invited by BBC Three, whose motto is "accessible news," to

talk about media coverage of executions in the Middle East. I agreed to go to the Corporation's New York studios uptown. Then I got follow-up emails: how old was I (forty-three at the time), and given the answer, would I mind directing the producers to an online photo of me? They explained there was a "requirement" to vet my looks to see whether I would appeal to their youth audience at my advanced years. What is this obsession about? For the BBC, it demonstrates ongoing relevance and secures faithful viewers for the future (Ofcom 2007: 29). For commercial stations, it is because the young are thought to be still deciding on their favorite commodities – toothpaste, transport, and so on. To quote 1970s ABC executive Leonard Goldstein, they are "the most curious, who would seek out the new." The advent of the People Meter in 1987 strengthened this obsession, because it permitted more authoritative information on viewing than from people keeping diaries, the previous method. So the success of *Friends* (1994–2004) encouraged networks to find comedies that would appeal to people in their twenties and thirties for the next decade. Other age groups got the message that they were not a priority and did the sensible things of turning to cable networks. Ironically, when CBS reverted to the idea of appealing to a mass audience in 2008, it won the ratings both overall *and* among young people (Collins 2009).

Lest it be assumed that ratings and so on are purely the stuff of TV Studies 1.0, marketers like nothing better than the 2.0 fetish of active audiences full of knowledge about programs; nothing better than diverse groups with easily identified cultural politics and practices; nothing better than fine-grained ethnographic and focus-group work in addition to large-scale surveys that provide broad-based demographic data. The supposedly resistive individual or group is just one more category for their delectation. Training students to analyze TV texts is in no way threatening to commerce: "Advertisers think media education is great" (Bazalgette 1999). The industry's own research on marketing's efficacy is guarded as proprietary information. It is publicly disseminated via journalistic reports about the constant monitoring of marketing activities and their routinely urgent modification, ironically indicating a lack of confidence in applied research that is echoed in the executive mantra, "Marketing is just a tool." Marketers know that respondents are not candid; that they are silent about viewing pleasures that embarrass them; and that resistance to audience surveys is too high to justify confident findings (Klady 1998: 9).

None of this deters the desire for surveillance of viewers, with the goal of selling information about them to advertisers. ESPN uses interactive TV fora such as "My Vote" and "My Bottom Line." They uncover more and more data about audience drives in the name of enabling participation and pleasure in watching. Internationally, ESPN has sought to purchase broadband portals that ensure global dominance, and now owns Cricinfo, Scrum.com, and Racing-Live (Nordyke 2008; Hampp 2008; Spangler 2009; Gibson 2009b). How do such techniques work? Visitors to HBO's website on boxing encounter a section entitled "COMMUNITY," which invites readers to participate in polls, subscribe to a newsletter, and express their views on bulletin boards. Of course, this "COMMUNITY" is also and equally a system of surveillance that allows the network to monitor viewers for ideas without paying them for their intellectual property.

Marketers use both TV Studies 1.0 and 2.0, avowing their powerlessness over audiences when challenged in the public sphere (2.0), but boasting omnipotence over them in the private world (1.0): the essay that won the oleaginous "Best New Thinking Award at the 2003 Market Research Society Conference" acknowledged that successful marketing does not "view ... the consumer as an individual" but "part of the herd" (Earls 2003). And producers who hide behind the rhetoric of sovereign consumption frequently have contempt for audiences. Tim Kring, the creator of *Heroes* (2006–), refers to people who view his show on network TV as "saps and dipshits who can't figure out how to watch it in a superior way" (quoted in Hirschorn 2009).

Networks are forever announcing new, failsafe schemes for captivating and capturing the audience. In 2006, NBC unveiled "Television 2.0," which was meant to be the end of drama in prime time. In 2008, it declared the return of the "8 o'clock Family Hour" with serial drama throughout the year – this was called "The New Paradigm." Then 2009 ushered in "The NBCUniversal2.0," a "New, New Paradigm" with less original programming and more reality and talk shows, described in the idiotic vocabulary of managerialism as a "margin enhancer." It's hard to believe that these people inhabit the same world as us when they continue to use inelegant and aggressive metaphors to describe the surveillance and management of viewers. The industry turns the manifold, manifest failures of these managerial–warlockcraft follies into assertions that audiences are their masters. Consider this embarrassing quotation from the head of NBC-Universal's TV and movie interests in 2009: "We have a sniper focus on 8 p.m. to 10 p.m. to drive a power audience flow" (de Moraes 2008; Friedman 2009c). The translation is that the network had given up on creating high-quality drama other than during those two hours.

Audiences are also targeted through product placement, which began seventy years ago in the movies with autos, diamonds, alcohol, cosmetics, and tobacco, *inter alia* (Wasko 1994; Wenner 2004; del Pino and Olivares 2006). Product placement now has the capacity to tailor placements to specific audiences via digital insertion into specific platforms and regions. "Major distributors employ placement companies or brokers to ensure that virtually everything you see, other than background stuff, is a negotiated deal" (Herman 2000: 48) through logos, advertising, or actual use of products. The latter is the most costly, because objects are animated within shows (DeLorme and Reid 1999).

There are about thirty-five product-placement companies in the US. The Entertainment Resources and Marketing Association links manufacturers to members' placement operations; visitors to erma. org receive a primer on the wonders of making consumer goods integral to scenery. Retailers and consumer-goods producers pay placement companies annual retainer fees of US$50,000 or more to scan hundreds of scripts a year for scenes in which to place their brand names and products. One placement company boasts that this is "legitimately the only way to pay one time for an 'ad' that appears forever" (Herman 2000: 48).

Televisa's Mexican *telenovelas* have product placements that change with each foreign sale (Wenner 2004). Industry insiders boast that the process will soon operate in reverse: "program content may be finding its way inside TV commercials" (Friedman 2009d). Britain outlaws this cynical, covert practice, but more and more countries are opening up to its clandestine methods of selling: globally, television product placement grew 37 percent in 2006 (European Union 2007). The US comedy *Trust Me* (2009), set in a fictitious advertising agency, even featured the program's sponsors as clients of the on-screen firm (Stasi 2009). Car companies in the US continued to spend untold amounts on commercials up to the point of their public disgrace, and NBC's loss of 13 percent in the 2008 ratings was matched by a jump in profit – of 50 percent (Friedman 2008a, b, c). How? Because massive automobile product placement successfully amortized the costs of unpopular shows. With the huge economic downturn of 2008–9, product placement also became an increasingly key element of US TV journalism, with the traditional barrier between advertising and editorial functions blown apart: McDonald's pays to appear on Fox News programs, and local medical centers pay for stories to feature their achievements (Hart 2009a).

CONCLUSION

As Susan J. Douglas explains, audiences today are addressed as "ironic, knowing, media-savvy" – and that can include the notion of being both a victim to media effects and a manipulator of media messages. From pessimistic political economists and psy-function mavens through optimistic narcissographers and the used and gratified, and finally on to anxious regulators and producers, there is a recognition that debates about audiences have become part of public discussion, from lamenting the quality of TV to celebrating its populism, from deriding its mind control to parading its resistance. Many shows now address the viewer by implying: "'We know that you know that we know that you know that this is excessive and kitschy, that you're too savvy to read this straight and not laugh at it'" (Douglas 2009: 49). In 1997, ABC sought to lift itself from third in the ratings via the US$40 million "TV Is Good" campaign, which saw buses emblazoned with ironic invocations of TV-viewing as ludicrous, such as "It's a beautiful day; what are you doing outside?," "Scientists say we use 10% of our brain. That's way too much," "You can talk to your wife anytime," "8 hours a day. That's all we ask," and "Don't worry, you've got billions of brain cells." ABC's campaign remained in use for many years (Einstein 2002). It fitted Eco's sly exemplification of postmodernity:

> For me the postmodern attitude is that of a man who loves a woman who is intelligent and well-read: he knows that she

knows he cannot tell her, "I love you desperately," because he knows (and she knows that he knows) that that is a line out of Barbara Cartland. Yet there is a solution. He can say, "As Barbara Cartland would say, I love you desperately."

(Eco 1983: 2–3)

John T. Caldwell (2008a) confirms that reflexivity *about* TV *on* TV is an ordinary part of the industry and its assumptions about viewers. Resistive interpretations by active audiences? Perhaps, but a more accurate account might be what IBM has dubbed, in an ugly and revealing neologism, "consumer bimodality." This is the discourse of both corporations and the self-appointed prelates of the new media that decries people who watch TV as their principal electronic medium. IBM, as arrogant as it is sub-literate, disparages "Massive Passives" as people "in the living room," while valorizing and desiring "Gadgetiers and Kool Kids" who "force radical change" because they demand "anywhere, anytime content." This bloated corporation diminishes "the historical and still predominant passive experience" as "a 'lean back' mode in which consumers do little more than flip on the remote and scan programming" (2006: 1, 10).

As ever, these trite binaries are entirely misleading, as Table 4.1 below illustrates; for the two groups are often composed of the same people. Quite apart from the question of how passive audiences are when they use remotes to interpret long-form drama versus how active they are while typing on keyboards to look at temperature forecasts, the fact is that people move inexorably, inevitably, between screens, using TV as a reliable source of information about the Web. This applies to the young most of all, those fabled early adopters of new technology who are so desired by corporate lizards.

Every year, every season, every week, pundits celebrate or lament the passing of what is divined as the era of the mass audience. The mysterious disappearance of this group is understood variously as the demise, or at least the decline, of terrestrial, broadcast TV and the rise of these alternative technologies and occasions of viewing.

Things *are* changing. For example, Christmas Day, December 25th, is a traditional occasion for collective, familial television in the UK, marked for some by the Queen's Message (1957–), an Olympian

Table 4.1 US children visiting websites after watching commercials for them, December 2008

Children aged 6–11	46.3%
Boys	50.6%
Girls	49.4%
Age 6–7 years old	26.5%
Age 8–9 years old	33.3%
Age 10–11 years old	40.2%

Source: Mediamark Research & Intelligence, 2008.

pronouncement on the year passed and the year to come by the head of state. In 2008, the Director of BBC Future Media and Technology drew a shift in age terms: "Mum and dad are watching linear television in the living room but kids are watching ... on the iPhone, iPod Touch or laptop" (quoted in Clark 2008). Britain's most popular TV website is iPlayer, the BBC's online platform. iPlayer viewership grew fourteen times in the first year of service, mostly on computers (85 percent) but with some limited access via game consoles and cellphones. The major television networks in Britain have equivalent services: Sky Anytime, 4oD, and ITV Player. Only iPlayer is *gratis* (Clark 2008). In the US, within three weeks in 2005, iTune's new offer to download TV from ABC and Disney saw a million shows purchased at US$1.99 per episode, inspiring CBS, Time Warner, and NBC to follow suit (IBM 2006: 8).

But wiser heads/those who read books as well as blogs, numbers as well as narcissography, have heard revolutionary refrains before. Two decades ago, it was asserted that ITV was about to expire because its advertising model would collapse with the advent of multichannel broadcasting via satellite. Buying agencies and advertisers predicted doom. The result of more advertising-supported channels? Rather than a problem for ITV, it was a goldmine, as the splintering of audiences meant advertisers paid a premium for any service that could deliver what approximated to a mass (Dyke 2005). The problem for commercial broadcast networks today is satellite, cable, and the recession, not the loss of an audience for television.

People who watch TV on different devices and via different services are watching more, not less, television. Even IBM gets it: "TV content is more popular than ever" (2006: 3). Consider NBC's 2008 numbers for its situation comedy *The Office* (not the UK original, but a remake): a typical episode had 15.5 million viewing on television, 6.9 million streaming and 37,000 downloading to computers, 33,000 watching on demand, and 37,000 peering at their cells (Friedman 2008b). Television still dominated as the mode of production, distribution, and reception. Time-shifting amounted to a more mobile version of what had long been the dominant norm – watching from afar. For public-sector broadcasters, the fragmentation of audiences offers some paradoxical pleasures. They welcome "more intense interaction, giving up some control and becoming less of an institution and more of a 'space'" (Simons 2008). For private-sector rent-seekers, what matters continues to be not "people who actually watch television" but "the commodity audience," the one whose attention and consumption profile can be sold (Meehan 2002: 217). It would be odd to assume that control of audiences has ever been total; and equally odd to assume that the resistance of audiences is either absolute or novel (Juluri 2003: 13).

QUESTIONS FOR DISCUSSION

(1) How has the psy-function engaged TV viewing?
(2) What is the DEM?
(3) What is the GEM?
(4) How does TV engage in surveillance of audiences?
(5) What is product placement?

NOTES

(1) Thanks to Dana Polan and Dominic Thomas for endorsing my translation of this sequence, which differs from the usual version.
(2) Thanks to Manuel Alvarado for reminding me of this sequence.

FURTHER READING

Ang, Ien. (1991). *Desperately Seeking the Audience*. London: Routledge.
Butsch, Richard. (2000). *The Making of American Audiences: From Stage to Television, 1750–1990*. Cambridge: Cambridge University Press.
Garfinkel, Harold. (1992). *Studies in Ethnomethodology*. Cambridge: Polity Press.
Hartley, John. (1992). *The Politics of Pictures: The Creation of the Public in the Age of Popular Media*. London: Routledge.

HOW TO DO TV STUDIES 3.0

"My" television is gone. It began to disappear (disintegrate? Dissolve? Die?) in the early 1980s, but I didn't notice. I was too busy figuring out what had intrigued me for so long (and what became a career [job security? identity? burden?]).

(Horace Newcomb 2009: 117)

[I]t is one of the great ironies of the project to challenge cultural paternalism and celebrate audience diversity that by undermining one bit of the ruling class, it appeared to endorse the ambitions of another. Thus did post-Marxist academia give a progressive seal of approval to letting the multicultural market rip; and if, as the Austrian economist Ludwig von Mises said, the ultimate socialist institution is the post office, then postmodernism and poststructuralism have persuaded post-socialists to abandon playing post offices and take up playing shop.

(David Edgar 2000: 73)

Nothing shocks me except reality television and house prices.

(Cliff Hardy, in Corris 2009: 105)

Remember the problems of TV Studies 1.0 and 2.0 described in Chapter 1? How might we go beyond that stage to account for new social relations and technologies? As we have seen, television has become an alembic for understanding society. In both Television Studies 1.0 and 2.0, TV is privileged because "it speaks *about* us" (Attallah 2003: 485). But it seems as if old moves are being repeated, rather than a dynamic new agenda appearing. This chapter suggests how to construct Television Studies 3.0, then provides three case studies to illuminate infrastructures, texts, and themes. The first is about policy, the second about programming, and the third about a topic. The resources described in the first case study are germane to conducting the analyses essayed in the second and third segments.

Studying TV today requires interrogating the commodification of textuality, the global exchange of cultural and communications infrastructure and content, the suburbanization of First-World politics, and the interplay between physical and visual power (Hartley 1999: 13). A new formation, a hybrid, critical Television Studies 3.0, cannot accept the old shibboleths that separate political economy and cultural studies. It must realize that "programs [do] not fall out of the sky" – so we must understand their material conditions of production – and equally, that their meanings are far from "explicit and unambiguous" – so we must understand their malleable materiality as texts (J. Lewis 1991: 23, 25). John D.H. Downing has criticized hegemonic traditions of media research because "politics and power ... are often missing, presumed dead" (1996: x). The absence of politics and power in the study of TV is no longer sustainable. Nor is the time-honored automatic extrapolation from US or UK research to understand the rest of the world, which dogs the GEM *and* the DEM, cultural imperialism as much as textual analysis, and political economy as well as the psy-function (Sreberny 2008: 9–10). Television texts and institutions are not just signs to be read; they are not just coefficients of political and economic power; and they are not just innovations. Rather, they are all these things. TV is a hybrid monster, coevally subject to textuality, power, and science – all at once, but in contingent ways (Latour 1993).

So comprehending television requires a more comprehensive interdisciplinarity than is on offer from TV Studies 1.0 and 2.0. If your background is in the social sciences, try moving beyond your own experiences and methods to look at what history and textual analysis have to say. If you come from the humanities, take a peek at the law and content analysis. If you're an ethnographer, try out uses and gratifications and effects studies. If you're an audience researcher, see what political economy and environmental science have to say. If you generally work alone, try teamwork. If you only read scholarly and primary materials in one language, learn another and work with native speakers. If your thing is drama, try covering politics. If you like to focus on reality, how about looking at sport? If you want to understand TV, you can't just engage approaches and genres that you like. That's giving up without even *trying* to do the hard work. And never reduce television to TV itself or the social relations surrounding it. We need to acknowledge the specificity of television as a cultural, economic, and technological apparatus, even as we recognize that it has only a relative autonomy from its social setting.

TV Studies 3.0 necessitates a radical contextualization that acknowledges the shifts and shocks that characterize the existence of institutions and programs: their ongoing renewal as the temporary property of productive workers and publics, and their stasis as the abiding property of unproductive businesspeople. It must combine political economy, ethnography, and textual analysis. A model derives from Roger Chartier's tripartite historicization of books. He aims to reconstruct "the diversity of older readings from their sparse and multiple traces," focusing on "the text itself, the object that conveys it, and the act that grasps it," and identifying "the strategies by which authors and publishers tried to impose an orthodoxy or a prescribed reading" of it (1989: 157, 161–3, 166). This grid turns away from reflectionism, which argues that a text's key meaning lies in its overt or covert capacity to capture the Zeitgeist. It also rejects formalism's claim that close readings of sound and image can secure definitive meanings, because texts accrete and attenuate meanings on their travels as they rub up against, trope, and are troped by other fictional and social texts and interpreted by viewers (Attallah 2007). At the same time, we need to comprehend that television is situated alongside "corporations, advertising, government, subsidies, corruption, financial speculation, and oligopoly" (McChesney 2009: 109). As an example, the international transfer of texts needs to address sites (from trade conventions to small meetings); business models; industry actors (from independent or studio producers to buyers); texts themselves; and such contextual features as audiences, legal frameworks, and economies (Bielby and Harrington 2008: 47).

That approach fruitfully connects text to performance, in what Ian Hunter calls an "occasion … the practical circumstances governing the composition and reception of a piece" (1988: 215). Those circumstances may reflect, refract, or ignore social tendencies. Televisual texts are part of a multi-form network of entertainment, via commercial-free and commercial-driven stations, video,

CD-ROMs, the Web, DVDs, electronic games, telephones, radio, and multiplexes. Engagements with audiences and texts must be supplemented by an account of the conditions under which these materials are made, circulated, received, interpreted, and criticized. "The produced program is ... more than the sum of the program ingredients" because it is encrusted with "contextual and explicit layers of meaning" that are generated at moments of creation and consumption (Smythe 1954: 143). Television represents a space beyond the worlds of work, school, and family, even as it overlaps with them as a forum for ideas that may challenge those institutions (Newcomb and Hirsch 1983). The life of any TV text is a passage across space and time, a life remade again and again by institutions, discourses, and practices of distribution and reception – in short, all the shifts and shocks of a commodity. To understand a program or genre we require an amalgam of interviewing people involved in production and circulation, from writers and editors to critics and audiences; content and textual analyses of shows over time, and of especially significant episodes; interpretations of knowledge about the social issues touched on; and an account of programs' national and international political economy.

Core resources for undertaking Television Studies 3.0 include:

- policy documents from public bureaucracies (international, national, regional, state, and municipal governments) and private bureaucracies (corporations, lobby groups, research firms, non-government organizations, religions, and unions);
- debates (Congressional/parliamentary, press, lobby-group, activist, and academic);
- budgets (where do producers and stations draw their money from?);
- laws (is there enabling legislation, and are there legal cases about labor, copyright, environmental impact, importation, or censorship?);
- history (what came before and what is new?);
- places (can analysts in dominant nations contextualize their experiences as partial, not universal, by examining other examples?);
- people (who is included and who is excluded from making TV?);

- pollution (what are the environmental costs of television?);
- genres (what is being made and screened?);
- scripts (are they written before or after production, as in drama versus reality shows respectively?); and
- reception (how are people making sense of what they hear and see on various technologies?).

POLICY

Statistics are at the core of analyzing any industry: how many people there are, what they make, what it sells for, who buys it, and so on. In very large countries with wealthy populations, it's tempting to look to domestic numbers, laws, and trends and effortlessly extrapolate from them to divine what television is, what people like, and so on. This makes it all the more important for analysts in the Global North to relativize their own experience rather than universalize it, even as they recognize that it often forms policy blueprints elsewhere. In this instance, I'll suggest some good overall sources, then show how they can be drawn on to comprehend how US TV drama is funded.

More and more major organizations are putting together policy information on TV. UNESCO promulgated a *Framework for Cultural Statistics* in 1986. Periodically revised on a piecemeal basis, it was scheduled for replacement in 2009. The UN's *International Flows of Selected Cultural Goods, 1994–2003* and Latinobarómetro, Eurostat, and Eurobarometer are helpful, along with the European Commission's 2006 *White Paper on a European Communication Policy* and 2007 *Communication for a European Agenda for Culture in a Globalizing World.* Other valuable resources include the Motion Picture Association of America (mpaa.org), the World Intellectual Property Organization (wipo.int) (which has its own Creative Industries Division and a 2003 *Guide on Surveying the Economic Contribution of the Copyright-Based Industries*), the National Association of Television Program Executives (natpe.org), and the Convenio Andrés Bello (www.cab.int.co). Good ways of staying current include subscribing to online digests, such as the Benton Foundation's service (Benton.org) and daily headlines from the Free Press (freepress.net), mediauk.com, Indiantelevision. com, mediaguardian.co.uk, Center for Media Research and *Media Daily News* (mediapost.com), TVNewsday.com, pressgazette.co.uk,

NatpeVideoNuze Report, mediabistro.com, smartbrief.com, contenti-nople.com, creative.org.au, tvbythenumbers.com, digitaltveurope.net, variety.com, and telecoms.com. Be sure to look at non-English-language and international sources as well as the dominant ones, or your analysis will betray its provincialism. Gossip sites are frequently helpful for disclosing scandalous business practices – not just celebrity gallivanting. Consider tmz.com, archives of the much-lamented fuckedcompany.com, thesmokinggun.com, and jossip.com. Some excellent podcasts are *The Listening Post* – Al Jazeera English; *On the Media* – WNYC; *Digital Planet* – BBC World Service; *Media Matters* – WILL; *Media Show* – BBC Radio Four; and *Media Talk* – the *Guardian*. You can find the podcasts *gratis* on iTunes.

Sadly, in the case of the United States, which forms this case study, most television–industry information is proprietary: tiny but informative research reports sell for vast amounts (I'd love to have summarized the latest research on people streaming TV, but the document sells for almost US$2,995 – if you'd like to buy it, contact InStat). A further problem is that in the US, unlike most other nations, the fantastical claim is repeatedly made that there is no such thing as cultural policy, or that it exists in live performance and the plastic arts but not television. Of all the places seeking gen-eration or regeneration through state strategy designed to stimulate industries, California should be the last on the list, given its claims to being at the very heart of laissez-faire. Yanquis take this as an article of faith, and pour scorn on European media subvention in favor of a mythology that says Hollywood was created because of the desire to tell stories that bound the nation together and, less altruistically, to make money by fleeing the militant unions and shadowed frosts of New York's Lower East Side for the South-land's unorganized labor and bountiful sun.

The industry's laissez-faire rhetoric is so powerful that even those who directly benefit from the way that public–private part-nerships drive Californian screen drama willfully deny that corpor-ate capital and state aid animate the industry. One needs to be inventive to find out the truth when investigating Hollywood, a veritable citadel of cultural policy secreted behind an illuminated sign of private enterprise. To transcend that rhetoric, we must follow the money, asking how television is actually financed. Where is the evidence? In TV credits, trade magazines, legal disputes that go to court and necessitate disclosure, balance sheets and annual reports of public authorities, industry analyses by for-profit research firms (if you can afford them), books about how-to-shoot offshore or finance shows with taxpayers' money, and occasional papers or protests from unions and activists. Hollywood relies on the state in a myriad ways, some of them barely visible. It uses foreign sources of government money, about 200 publicly-funded film commissions across the US, Pentagon services, and ambassadorial labor from the departments of State and Commerce. The State Department undertakes market research and shares business intelligence. The Commerce Department pressures other countries to import screen texts with favorable terms of trade. Negotiations on so-called video piracy have seen Chinese offenders face severe penalties, even as the US claims to monitor human rights there. And the US pressures South Korea to drop screen quotas (Miller 2005).

If it's German money from the 1990s or the early-twenty-first century funding Hollywood, the chances are that it came from tax breaks for lawyers, doctors, and dentists. If it's French money, it might be from firms with state subvention in other areas, such as cable or plumbing. If a TV show is shot in Canada, public welfare to attract US producers is a given. If it is filmed in any particular state of the US, the credits generally thank regional and municipal film commissions for subsidizing everything from hotels to hamburgers. State, regional, and municipal commissions reduce local taxes, provide police services, and block public way-fares. Accommodation and sales-tax rebates are available to Hollywood producers almost universally across the country. The California Film Commission, for example, reimburses public personnel costs and permit and equipment fees, while the state government's "Film California First Program" has covered everything from free services through to wage tax credits (Miller 2005).

On the war front, Steven Spielberg is a recipient of the Defense Department's Medal for Distinguished Public Service, Silicon Graphics designs material for military and cultural uses, and virtual-reality research veers between soldierly and audience applications, much of it subsidized by the Federal Technology Reinvestment Project and Advanced Technology Program. The University of Southern California's Institute for Creative Technologies uses military money and Hollywood directors to test out homicidal technologies and narrative scenarios. The governmental–screen industry link is clearly evident in the way that studios sprang into militaristic action in concert with Pentagon preferences after September 11, 2001, and became consultants on possible attacks via the "White House–Hollywood Committee," which ensures coordination between the nations the US bombs and the messages it exports. The industry even argues before Congress that preventing copyright infringements is a key initiative against terrorism, since unauthorized copying funds transnational extra-political violence. And with the National Aeronautics and Space Administration struggling to renovate its image, who better to invite to lunch than Hollywood producers, so they will script new texts featuring the agency as a benign, exciting entity (Miller *et al.* 2005)?

Finally, it is worth seeing how closely the fiscal fortunes of Hollywood are linked to the complexion of the government. After the 2000 election, Wall Street transferred money away from Silicon Valley/Alley and Hollywood and toward manufacturing and defense as punishments and rewards for these industries' respective attitudes during the campaign and subsequent coup. Energy, tobacco, and military companies, 80 percent of whose financial contributions had gone to George Bush Minor in the 2000 elections, suddenly received unparalleled transfers of confidence. Money fled the cultural sector, where 66 percent of campaign contributions had gone to Al Gore Minor. There was a dramatic shift toward aligning finance capital with the new Administration – a victory for oil, cigarettes, and guns over drama, music, and wires. The former saw their market value rise by an average of 80 percent in a year, while the latter's declined by between 12 and 80 percent (Schwartz and Hozic 2001). Thinking about policy in this way is outside the methods and concerns of TV Studies 1.0 and 2.0, but central if we want to comprehend the industry.

PROGRAMMING

To illustrate how to imagine TV Studies 3.0 in order to analyze a particular program rather than a policy, let's examine a 1960s drama – *The Avengers* (1961–9) – and a contemporary reality show – *Queer Eye for the Straight Guy* (2003–7). In the case of *The Aveng-*

ers, I try to reconstruct a historic show via original sources and rec-
ollections from an era when paratexts *about* TV were far less
numerous than is the case of *Queer Eye*, which has a superabun-
dance of information and critique that is instantly available.

The Avengers entered an established field of prime-time TV
drama and made it look very different. The late 1950s and early
1960s on UK and US television had been characterized by male
action adventure, frequently in dyadic form. In the mid-1960s,
situation comedies began to dominate schedules, because they were
cheap to make. That changed in 1965–6, when eight espionage
programs appeared across the three principal US networks, capital-
izing on James Bond's popularity. The longest-lasting show,
Mission: Impossible (1966–73, 1988–9) rose and fell with the high
moment of covert action by US spy agencies, before Watergate
deglamorized breaking the law in the name of security. It returned
in the 1980s during a lengthy writers' strike, when offshore
remakes appealed to the networks and Australia offered cheap locations and personnel. Another success, *Get Smart* (1965–70, 1993)
embodied both the 1960s popularity of stylish espionage and TV's
taste for parodying its own genres (Miller 2001b; Miller *et al.*
2005).

Stereotypes about women proliferated in action adventure of the
day, as they did in most other genres. Exhaustive content analysis
of US network television from the 1950s to the 1970s reveals that
women comprised just 20 percent of working characters. Action
series had especially strict segregation, with few heterosocial part-
nerships. The genre was basically a male world of crime. Barbara
Tuchman summarizes the situation thus: "Symbolically subservient,
policewomen who have been knocked to the floor by a bad guy
are pulled from the floor by a good guy; in both cases, women are
on the floor in relationship to men" (1979: 531). The situation
continues to trouble critics, as the extensive content analyses cited
by the American Psychological Association Task Force on the Sexualization of Girls (2007) clarify.

But something different happened in the ITV's UK drama series
The Avengers, at a time when casting a woman in an adventure
series, and then *not* having her romantically involved with the male
lead, shocked network executives. A huge hit around the world,
for decades it was the only import shown in prime time on the US

broadcast networks during ratings periods. To study the show, we must first of all deal with the extraordinary ephemerality of television before producers realized how long their texts could thrive as money-making opportunities and archivists recognized the medium's importance as cultural history. For example, just 15 percent of 1960s British TV still exists. In the case of *The Avengers*, its massive overseas sales saw the series with different titles and voices depending on the territory, while it also spawned adaptations for radio, theater, film, and literature, in addition to inspiring clothes, music, fanzines, board games, websites, coffee-table books, memoirs, and other paratexts that are part of its heritage (Miller 1997, 2003a; for later academic work on this series, see Black 2004; Britton and Barker 2003; Chapman 2002; Freeman 1999; O'Day 2001; Redmon Wright 2007). To comprehend the twists and turns of this complex cultural commodity, we need a wide array of tools in our kitbags: archival study of the series' paratexts and episodes, accounts of the production process and how it drew both on established generic narrative codes and on fantasies about audiences, through to actually existing fragments of critique and reception (Henderson 2007).

When I wrote a book about *The Avengers* (Miller 1997), the series was not yet available on DVD and only spottily on VHS, so I spent many hours viewing programs on film at the British Film Institute. My other sources included press books, scrapbooks, production stills, cultural histories of the era, fan sites and discussion groups on the World Wide Web, and email correspondence. The Web had only just become publicly available when I was doing my research, in 1995 and 1996. I wasn't aware of any earlier book-length studies of programs that extensively drew on it, so I lacked a how-to guide. I located numerous online fan groups and used what I now know to call a snowballing sample to contact people who remembered the program, drawing on my own international networks and these nascent fan sites. This allowed me to find out what viewers around the world made of the show, and I followed up on their memories in search of other sorts of verification whenever possible. This produced some dissonance. For example, my recollection before I wrote the book was that I had watched *The Avengers* in 1965–6 in London each Thursday, along with *The Man From U.N.C.L.E.* This was not true, as I learnt from consulting newspapers for British TV schedules of the day. But my faulty memory disclosed something interesting, in that I had collocated similar texts in order to understand them. Similarly, when one of my informants recalled watching the show in the US in 1963, this couldn't have happened, because it had not been sold there at that time; but when further interrogated, that memory led the viewer to talk about how *The Avengers* struck her in the context of family dynamics and viewing practices in the physical space of her early childhood.

Since then, of course, many other studies of texts have been done that draw on the Web to learn about audience interpretations, and get feedback (in my case, a site is dedicated to my errors and pomposities in the book – theavengers.tv/forever/bloop-1. htm). I assume I am not alone in receiving a letter from the copyright holder of *The Avengers* threatening legal action due to my publisher's reproducing stills from the series. This was *only* a threat, because the company – the French cable giant Canal Plus – liked the publicity offered by my work, perhaps because it was reviewed by *Playboy*, the *New York Times*, *Entertainment Week*, the *International Herald Tribune*, and the *Globe & Mail*, *inter alia*.

Spy-theme storylines often clearly bifurcated good from evil in *The Avengers*, thereby recreating the structural opposition of West versus East, of capitalism versus state socialism. The Soviet Union was an enemy, but a familiar one that in certain ways was a mirror image of oneself; the real villains were frequently frustrated British ex-imperialists or craven capitalists. Once an accomplice to straight, unstylish, empiricist but ideological policing, screen espionage in the 1960s re-focused on a hip modernity that privileged individuation and pleasure over uniformity and politics. *The Avengers* was part of a wider movement of stylish commodity/sex motifs. Technology, fashion, and fun fused in its stories and its look. Storylines allegorized, cars and clothes diverted, and satire displaced didacticism. Once more, one can see the influence of Bond.

The Avengers' first lead female character was Mrs Catherine Gale (Honor Blackman). She was planned as a mixture of actress and princess Grace Kelly, visual anthropologist and sex theorist Margaret Mead, and *Life* magazine photojournalist Margaret Bourke-White. Press releases described Mrs Gale as a "cool blonde, with a degree in anthropology, who married a farmer in Kenya and became adept with a gun during the Mau–Mau troubles." When her husband was killed in that struggle, she moved to Cuba to aid Fidel Castro until he became a Marxist, then worked for the British Museum. A strikingly acute thinker and boldly active character, the French fan magazine of the 1990s *Génération Séries* described Mrs Gale as "féministe (un peu) avant l'heure … et vaguement lesbienne" ["a bit of a feminist before her time … and vaguely lesbian"], a summary based on her black motorcycle and icy attitude. The *Observer* called her a "leather fetishist's pin-up" (quoted in Miller 1997).

"The Gilded Cage" episode finds Cathy explaining the finer points of the global trade in gold to her work partner John Steed (Patrick Macnee). In "The Undertakers," Steed fantasizes aloud about taking a trip together on an ocean liner. She is cleaning a rifle and shows no interest in his suggestion. An array of guns on the wall of her apartment provides a backdrop to her reprimand of him in "Death of a Great Dane": "Must you be so callous?" she asks as they look over x-rays of a sick man. She labels him a "cynic." But this is to forget the treasured moment that finds them listening to music at her place. She is lying on a couch, wearing a serious lift-and-separate plus form-hugging clothes. Steed sits on the floor below her. Standing up, she lets a silken scarf fall on his head. He is enchanted. Then there is the wonderfully ambiguous moment in "Death of a Batman" when Steed removes Mrs Gale's boots by standing with his back to her, the boots held between his legs as he pulls, hard and pleasurably.

Writers for the series worked with a set of gendered pointers on the two characters. Cathy is straightforward, virtuous, and sensual. Steed is slightly untrustworthy, willful, and exciting. Her beauty, her sexuality, her power, and her look out at the male form and back at the male gaze are foregrounded. Blackman says she "half-killed" some extras: her skills put her on a front cover of *Judo Illustrated*. The program was hardly free from prevailing modes of representing women: the video slick to a "pirated" North American release is a color studio shot of Macnee fully clothed and Blackman in bra and panties. Blackman has said she "got quite hysterical" over policies that limited her character's conduct, and both Mrs Gale and her successor, Mrs Emma Peel (Diana Rigg), were frequently trapped by sadistic men who wanted to cause them harm. (The need to balance the series' shooting schedule with Macnee's contractual deals for vacation time provided some of the stimulus to this focus on his partner.) Such set-ups troped conventional horror-film methods of demeaning women, such as the evocation of panic, and point-of-view shooting from the perspective of assailants. The idea of disfigurement as a gendered punishment, taking away woman's principal currency in a patriarchal cultural economy, is referenced in unknown men cutting up pictures of Mrs Gale or Mrs Peel. That opening sequence is frequently followed by an invitation to an isolated country estate, psychological torture, and powerlessness, until there is a turnaround. The women always prevail, sometimes with assistance from Steed, in ways that show how resourceful and rational they are. He provides a top-and-tail presence to mark equilibrium, but his partner is often the agent of change (Miller 2003a).

When Rigg replaced Blackman in 1965, the show was shot on film in order to satisfy US network deals, which required high production values in return for purchasing the series. Publicity for the new lead said she was "a younger and gayer girl and there is more warmth and humour in the partnership" with Steed. The person who wrote that material, Marie Donaldson, was also responsible for the new character's name: writing down in a meeting the producers' requirements – for additional "Man Appeal" – she shortened this to "M Appeal," then sounded it out. There have been criticisms of Rigg and the other heroines on the grounds that abilities are linked to traditional beauty, and that realism was sacrificed in the interests of style and passion. But the face, body, vehicle, clothing, and apartment must be as they are if the diegesis is to cohere and the joke about the implausibility of it all to emerge (Miller 1997).

The indeterminacy of Mrs Peel's connection to Steed – have they or haven't they? – is added to by the reversed styles of gender. In 1965, executive producer Brian Clemens said the producers made Steed "fight like a woman," with his umbrella or a honey jar, to differentiate him from Mrs Peel's martial artistry. "The Town of No Return," Rigg's debut, stages a fencing duel between them. When it's over, she mentions having just finished writing an article for *Science Daily*. The episode ends with her on a motorbike and Steed riding side-saddle. Rigg remarked that "I identify with the new woman in our society who is evolving. Emma is totally equal to Steed. The fighting is the most obvious quality." As the series was about to commence in the US, Rigg said of her character that "the widow part shows that she knows what it's all about." Publicity made much of "A Touch of Brimstone," an episode that was not shown in the States because of her "sin queen" attire: a black whalebone corset, laced boots, whip, and spiky dog-collar. A thirty-eight-second sequence (why are these always timed when other segments commented on are not?) even offended British officials. The program clearly referenced subcultural codes from 1950s porn. Perhaps that was why it drew more viewers than any other episode screened there. "The Danger Makers" has a telling scene in which Mrs Peel approaches Steed from behind. Their physical positioning conditions the dialog that follows. She draws very close, neck to neck, asking him how to "play it" with a person she must quiz. Steed turns to look at her, his face close to her breasts: "Show him your bumps." The alibi for this remark is that the character in question is interested in phrenology. What reads as a sexist remark is transformed by the banter in their delivery, her approach from his rear, and the set-up of the two-shots (Miller 1997).

The sense of changing eras is beautifully captured during "Escape in Time." Apparently dispatched via time travel back to the eighteenth century, Emma tells the villains: "I'm thoroughly emancipated." When the controls are reset to 1570, she is put in the stocks. A brutal man accuses her of being "a heretic, a bawd, a witch − designed to drive a man to lust." Her reply, from this somewhat undignified and powerless place, is to look up, toss back her hair, and offer the following: "You should see me in four hundred years." Back in the twentieth century, and the battle won, she looks at a woman she has just fought with, now in chains: "Didn't we get the vote?" The stereotype of a woman tied down whilst evil men taunt her is also overdetermined in "The Positive Negative Man" by a gaze back at her tormentors. Told she is dealing with "a superman," Mrs Peel replies: "His pectorals are far from perfect." Frustrated, her opponents counter that 100 such men, generated from the force of electricity, will destroy the government and take over society. "What if there's a power cut?" is her riposte. "The Cybernauts" episode sees Emma researching the holdings of murdered industrialists in the import–export, automation, and electrical businesses. When Steed describes the victims as "all in the top bracket," she adds "where the vultures gather." This skepticism about the patriarchal domain of capital is shown to be very apposite as the story develops. Mrs Peel directly encounters sexism at a karate school where the chief instructor says: "It is difficult for a woman to compete in such company." Her counter is good-humored but with an edge: "It's the idea of competition that appeals to me." Then she defeats an opponent and makes her point. The ironic deployment of strong female sexuality in concert with physical force is exemplified in "The Gravediggers." Mrs Peel is on the ground. Steed, standing, holds a villain between her legs. She closes them around the man's head, scissoring him into a nearby pond. Years later, Rigg looked back on the era like this: "kinky. I always seemed to be strapped into a dentist's chair with my feet in the air," while Macnee tried to scotch rumors that his early-childhood spankings at prep school and Eton had left him with a life-long taste for sado-masochistic sex (Miller 1997). Textually, the program represented a Britain that was passing as an imperial, manufacturing power and regenerating as a cultural, service power, and a renewed moment of struggle in gender relations. Economically, it stood for global success across a wide variety of places, formats, interpretations, and fans. It plays a starring role in the history of popular television by any measure.

The online application to appear on *Extreme Makeover* (2002–7) performed dual tasks. At one level, it was a recruitment device. As such, it was unreliable and rapidly becoming outmoded. In its second, covert, role – surveillance – it was a neatly targeted way of securing data about viewers that could be sold to advertisers, achieved under the demotic sign of outreach and public participation, via plastic surgery for the soldier who thinks his career is being held back by ugliness, or Botox shots for the fast-food manager who wants to advance his job prospects (Heyes 2007: 25). Which is where we meet *Extreme Makeover*'s cousin in surveillance, commodification, and governmentality – *Queer Eye for the Straight Guy* (*QESG*).[1] It began on the Bravo network and became the station's highest-rated hour ever; 3.35 million were viewing by the third episode. Parodies followed on *Saturday Night Live* (1975–) and *MAD TV* (1995–), while Comedy Central offered *Straight Plan for the Gay Man* (2004–5) (Nutter 2004; Heller 2006b: 3; Westerfelhaus and Lacroix 2006: 429). Mark Simpson (2004) dubbed it *Metrosexuality: The Reality TV Show*, and the program avowed that it taught "the finer points of being a 'metrosexual'" (bravotv.com/Queer_Eye_for_the_Straight_Guy/Episodes/207/).

What are its origins, beyond unfurling commodity interest in the queer dollar? *QESG* is part of the wider reality-television phenomenon, a strange hybrid of cost-cutting devices, game shows taken into the community, *cinéma-vérité* conceits, scripts written in post-production, and *ethoi* of Social Darwinism, surveillance, and gossip – bizarre blends of "tabloid journalism, documentary television, and popular entertainment." No wonder Ofcom embarrassedly and embarrassingly distinguishes between "Serious Factual" programs – by which it means news, current affairs, and documentary – and reality, which it euphemizes as "Other Factual." In 2006, "Other Factual" comprised 44 percent of peak-hour Channel 4 shows and 36 percent on BBC Two (Ofcom 2007: 38).

Makeover, programs such as *QESG* take economically underprivileged people and offer them a style they cannot afford to sustain, promoting the responsibility of people to get better jobs, homes, looks, and families. Reality TV is suffused with deregulatory *nostra* of avarice, possessive individualism, hyper-competitiveness, and commodification, played out in the domestic sphere rather than the public world. The genre represents a moment in US television's ongoing struggle with other media for the attention of young people, something that began in the late 1960s, when popular magazines were locked in a contest with color TV for audiences. Both sides reacted by addressing young people as readers (through stories on popular culture) and as problems (through generational stereotyping). This practice continued as the cultural industries promoted the existence of catchy-sounding generational cohorts to advertisers ("the Greatest Generation," "Baby Boomers," "Generation X," "Generation Y," and "Generation Rx") with supposedly universal tendencies and failings. Reality shows poached young people back from alternative activities, and bound themselves to the Internet as a means of audience participation/surveillance, melding numerous technologies and techniques of surveillance/participation (Ouellette and Murray 2008: 8–10; Hill 2005: 15; Banet-Weiser and Portwood-Spacer 2006; Heller 2006a; Bennett 2006: 408; Deery 2006: 161; Fraiman 2006; Miller 2008; Attallah 2007: 332; Ouellette and Hay 2008: 123).

Between 2001 and 2008, reality shows proliferated to the point where they occupied 20 percent of prime-time US network programming. So the writers' unions, which include over 3,000 people, sought to gain coverage of the genre, though program owners insisted that their work did not amount to creating scripts as per drama. This counter-claim was ludicrous. Reality television relies as much as ever on writers, but engages the labor process in reverse: a logger notes scenes of interest from raw footage, which are then resurrected as a show by five to ten writers working for a supervising story producer. Like all TV, reality programs are written; people create scripts with dialog and drama, even though they don't invent characters as per action or comedy. For example, on *Survivor* (2000–), story editors interview contestants on-site then influence their subsequent conversations. *Big Brother* leaves the script to post-production (Higgins and Benson 2005; Ross 2009; Writers Guild 2008). A study of US cable networks at the height of *QESG* found that reality shows accounted for 39 percent of writing jobs – this for a putatively natural, unscripted genre, that is actually created again and again in highly competitive environments that work against collective bargaining and the expression of collective interests on the production side, even as the texts themselves fetishize individual transcendence. The result for employees? Eighteen-hour days, no healthcare, no meal breaks, no overtime, and poor wages. The genre features infinitely greater insecurity of every kind than other television. Writers on *America's Next Top Model* (2003–) were fired when they sought to unionize, while two class-action lawsuits were settled in 2009 for US$4 million. Meanwhile, editors and other workers filed a similar action that year against FremantleMedia North America, which owns *American Idol* (2002–), in protest at up to twenty-hour work days, seven days a week, without meal breaks (Richardson and Figueroa 2005; "In Focus" 2006; Friedman 2009g).

The common view is that reality television proliferated simply because it met audience desires: Michael Grade, head of Britain's ITV, claims that drama fails to match the genre's "emotional drain" (quoted in Billington and Hare 2009); John Birt, the BBC's former Director-General, says it has "liberated Britons to express themselves imaginatively and individually" (2005). Nevertheless, although it is fixed upon by cultural critics who either mourn it as representative of a decline in journalistic standards or celebrate it as the sign of a newly feminized public sphere, reality should frankly be understood as a cost-cutting measure and an instance of niche marketing. Stuart Hall notes the failure of attempts to use *Celebrity Big Brother* (2001–) for political purposes. They derive from the mistaken belief that "this was an authentic site of the popular and that one could go into it and pass a message to the outside in an untransformed way" (Taylor 2006).

The origins of reality television lie in the activities of the Propaganda Ministry of the Nazi Party in the 1930s. *Die Kriminalpolizei Warnt!* [*The Criminal Investigation Department Warns!*] was the Party's centerpiece of TV programming. Fritz Schiegk spoke live with police officers about unsolved cases and invited audiences to cooperate in catching opponents of the state. When television returned to Germany after the war, the genre quickly became popular. For forty years, that show's successor, *Aktenzeichen XY ... ungelöst* [*File Sign XY ... Unsolved*] (1967–), has been a model for police–civilian collaboration series around the world, such as *Crimewatch* (1984–) and *America's Most Wanted* (1988–). The key contemporary source of the reality-TV phenomenon has been Italy, where public television pioneered the modern genre due to competition from new private concerns (Bourdon *et al.* 2008: 113–20).

A second key genealogy situates reality from the same period and the home of the DEM, namely the psy-function. During the 1930s, the psychology department at Columbia University hired Allen Funt as a research assistant. Funt drew on the psy-function sadisms he learnt there to create a radio show called *Candid Microphone* (1947–8, 1950), which migrated to television in 1947 as *Candid Camera* and traversed five decades of television history (1948–53, 1960–7, 1974–9, 1991–2, 1998–2001). *Candid Camera* pioneered the notion of surveillance as a source of fun, information, and narcissism – Funt would hail his audience with "You are the star!" (Simon 2005: 180–1).

The makeover varietal of reality TV focuses on dramatic aesthetic transformations (Heyes 2007). Its emphasis on spectacle and cost – transformations are very personal and hence cheap for broadcasters – has made the genre appealing. The Kaiser Foundation's 2006 study of US reality television drew on encounters with TV producers and healthcare critics and professionals to get at the dynamics of how the genre represents medicine and related fields. The research found that, for all its populist alibis, reality television constructs professional medical expertise as a kind of magic beyond the ken of ordinary people – and certainly beyond their informed critique. Again and again, whether it's plastic surgeons or paediatricians, miraculous feats are achieved by heroic men who deliver ignorant and ugly people from the dross of the everyday, transcending what off-screen primary-care physicians have been able to do for them. For all the world channeling *Ben Casey* (1961–6), these daring young men make astonishing breakthroughs. The Foundation's study could find nothing in the genre even remotely critical of this model of what "*they* can do." The representation of medical expertise deemed it ungovernable other than by its own caste (Christenson and Ivancin 2006). Such a landscape is not about powerful citizen-viewers, as per TV Studies 2.0; it's about deities in scrubs. The use of the commodity form to promise transcendence through the national healthcare system, as embodied in patriarchal medicine, is sickening. And as with makeovers of houses and personal style, it offers a transcendence of the putatively grubby working and lower-middle classes that viewers cannot afford to emulate. Helpless and ugly, patient bodies testify to the surgeons' skill just as fashion consultants might confront a lack of savoir-faire (Heyes 2007: 19). Enter *Queer Eye*.

With excellent ratings, a soundtrack album that topped the electronic-music sales charts, and revenue from many parts of the world via both export and format sales, *QESG* won an award from the Gay & Lesbian Alliance Against Defamation (GLAAD) and an Emmy for Outstanding Reality Program in 2004. It was variously heralded as a mainstream breakthrough text for queers, an exemplification of male vulnerability, a virtuous exemplar of progressive popular culture in an era of conservatism, *and* the epitome of cultural imperialism – the encapsulation of the "ambivalent text" thanks to an allegedly carnivalesque instantiation of "*Commodity and Difference*" (Rogers 2003; Hart 2004; Fraiman 2006; Di Mattia 2007; Allatson 2006; Pullen 2007: 194, 207, 210). Bravo paired *QESG* with *Boy Meets Boy* (2003), another gay reality show, on Tuesday evenings, thereby branding itself as an alternative to its corporate parent (Cohan 2007: 177). This endowed Bravo with a certain chic quality, "as the unofficial gay network." *Metrosource* places *QESG* in the pantheon of greatest moments of gay television: "it catapulted gay culture into the mainstream" (DeJesus 2008: 46). The American Film Institute nominated *Queer Eye* as its major cultural development for 2003, alongside copyright (Cohan 2007: 178).

Some inevitably criticized the show for stereotyping, including out Congressman Barney Frank, while from the other side of politics, the Family Television Council thundered that it appealed to an "element in our culture already earning an advanced degree in Sin Acceptance."[2] Media Research Center maven L. Brent Bozell III (as improbable as his name) called it "The Gay Supremacy Hour" and said "I want to vomit." When NBC, Bravo's network parent, first screened the show in 2003, it drew 6.7 million watchers despite some affiliates declining to screen the show until the middle of the night because of its queerness, leading to a write-in campaign orchestrated by GLAAD. Meanwhile, adherents of straightacting.com opposed the program, because it didn't suit their preference for sport-loving, macho gay men, while others were sly in their mix of endorsement and critique. Boston Red Sox baseballers who participated insisted they did so only to aid charity, even as they subjected themselves to floral footbaths, waxing, and other procedures. Taboos were under erasure, as per unwanted hair (Berila and Choudhuri 2005; Council quoted in Sender 2006: 132; Dossi 2005; Bozell 2003; "Tell Your Local NBC Affiliate" 2003; Rocchio and Rogers 2007; Clarkson 2005; Skinner 2003; Cometta 2005; Westerfelhaus and Lacroix 2006: 427; Allen 2006).

QESG embodied the ethos of reality TV: originating on cable, an under-unionized sector of the industry, with small numbers of workers required for short periods, and production funds derived in part from the producer's credit-card award points (later turned into a marketing point by the card company). These flexible arrangements quickly led to a lawsuit on behalf of a queer star who was dispensed with after two episodes, while those left recognized that "we could be fired at any moment" ("Dave Collins" 2004; participants quoted in Giltz 2003). There was a furor when thesmokinggun.com disclosed that the Fab Five were receiving just US$3,000 each per episode, with tiny raises and none of the typical perks of celebrity – they got mere fractions of the tens of thousands of dollars available to minor but unionized characters in broadcast drama.

This contingent, flexible labor is textualized in the service-industry world of the genre, which creates "a parallel universe" for viewers (Lewis *et al.* 2005: 17) in a show that "generates huge ratings ... [and] manufactures celebrities with no clout." Fame is produced, but without the ability to use it to gain economic and artistic power, because the celebrity derives from ordinariness and a tie to the everyday (Attallah 2007: 332). *QESG* looked for loser-male makeover targets in the suburban reaches of the tri-state area (New York, New Jersey, and Connecticut) who needed to be transformed from ordinary folk into hipsters. Cosmopolitan queers descended on these hapless bridge-and-tunnel people, charged with increasing their marketability as husbands, fathers, and (more silently and saliently) employees. This seems to compromise claims for the program's "ideological edginess" in favor of one that turns "straight men into straight men with better shoes." Change was predicated on affluence (Allen 2006).

The program's success can be understood in four ways. First, it incarnated a trend in US television: a sanitary, light-skinned, middle-class queer urban world of fun, where gays and lesbians are to be laughed with, not at. Their difference is a new commodity of pleasure – safely different from, but compatible with, heteronorma-tivity. Second, it is a sign that queerness is a lifestyle that can be adopted, discarded, and redisposed promiscuously. Third, it signi-fies the professionalization of queerness as a form of management consultancy for conventional masculinity, brought in to improve efficiency and effectiveness, like time-and-motion expertise, total-quality management, or just-in-time techniques. And finally, it indicates the spread of self-fashioning as a requirement of personal and professional achievement through the US middle-class labor force. Even the queer language games of the show became systems of translation across cultures, while their camp ways showed the power of mainstream containment and a bias toward urban living that offended the self-regard of those who repeatedly lay noisy claim to being "the Heartland" of the nation (Weiss 2005; Lacroix and Westerfelhaus 2005).

Commodities were central to the secular transcendence of *QESG*. Viewers were gently led toward a makeover that would meld suburban heteronormativity with urban hipness. A virtual gay parachute corps solved a dilemma for capital; namely, that "white, heterosexual men have been hard to train as consumers" (Sender 2006: 133). *QESG* undertook "a full-scale humanitarian relief mission: Queers Without Borders" that reached "a virgin makeover-market niche in basic cable" (Chocano 2003). They did so in accordance with US self-help literature for men, which focuses on augmenting capital, rather than the women's version, which seeks emotional resolution to private–public dilemmas (McGee 2005). The *QESG* website offered the following:

> FIND IT, GET IT, LOVE IT, USE IT. You've seen us work wonders for straight guys in need of some serious help. Get the same results at home with the same great products, services and suppliers that put the fairy dust in our Fab Five magic wands at "QUEER EYE'S DESIGN FOR LIFE PRODUCT GUIDE."
>
> (www.bravotv.com/Queer_Eye_for_the_Straight_Guy/ Shopping_Guide)

Sales were immense (Redden 2007: 150). "Q[*ueer*]E[*ye*] isn't really about mutual understanding between homos and heteros. It's about mutual understanding between Bravo/NBC and Diesel … and Roberto Cavallia and Ralph Lauren and Via Spiga and Persol and Baskit Underwear" said *New York Magazine*, while the *Village Voice* announced that the "agenda is about tempting guys who have managed to get by without facials and instant tans to become consumers of same," distilling yet concealing "the essence of the info-mercial: It meets a need you didn't know you had" (Dumenco 2003; Goldstein 2003). No wonder Terry Sawyer worries that this implies the status of minstrelsy for queers, via their incarnation as "materialistic vamps" (2003). In that sense, a reactionary like Bozell is correct to call the program "almost a parody of product placement, a veritable plug-a-minute infomercial." The problem is that he also derides it for being "drenched in references to raw, perverted homosexual sex" (2003). TV Studies 1.0 can create odd fellow-travelers.

The wholesale commodification of male subjectivity witnessed in *QESG* is actually about re-asserting, re-solidifying very conventional masculinity. The latter has long relied on women's work and queer work, or gay work at least, for its style: there has always been a contribution by women and gay men to straight men's looks and professionalism. The question is, has that ever led to a feminization of the public sphere, or recognition of the legitimacy and centrality of queerness, as per the utopics of TV Studies 2.0? This program was the ultimate in the commodification and governmentalisation of queerness as a set of techniques that could be applied and then cast aside. When that is done in the service of retaining conventional straight masculinity, one has to ask how progressive it actually is. And of course the show did not last forever, with a huge 2004 ratings slump prior to the inevitable detours of a failing program. It tried focusing on weight issues as well as personal style in an attempt to reinvigorate itself in 2006, before being cashiered the following year. Bravo asserted, in true TV Studies 2.0 fashion, that *Queer Eye* had "really helped open the closet doors on gays and their presence on television and in popular culture," and claimed corporate credit for featuring queer leads ("Bravo's 'Queer Eye'" 2006; Dossi 2005; Bravo, quoted in Rocchio and Rogers 2007; Pullen 2007: 207).

TOPIC

News and current affairs is a crucial element of a vibrant and informed citizenry, both in terms of domestic and foreign affairs. Citizens rely on independent information in order to make judgments about their governments, employers, and organizations, and international relations. As we saw in earlier chapters, television has become the crucial source of such knowledge. And despite the success of the Internet in drawing people away from newspapers as sources of information, TV remains the key to public knowledge of current affairs. My focus here is on the US. In the pre-remote-control era, networks around the world used nightly news as a loss leader. News was "an audience builder," designed to hold attention through the evening's programs that followed it. Since that time, it has been a crucial means of endowing stations with a cover of corporate citizenship (de Leeuw *et al.* 2008: 131).

Competent journalism should focus on: domestic political affairs defined through law-makers' deliberations and judicial review; policy issues defined by social movements and parliamentary parties; election coverage; cultural politics; science; and international relations, understood in terms of local and global security. The intent must be to draw citizens into the policy process – informed public comment, dissent, and consent. But around the world, tough domestic and foreign stories are being frozen out. Since the 1990s, news agencies, which provide the vast majority of data behind stories, have shifted their focus to sport, fashion, and the media. These topics are cheap, because they tie in to promotional strategies for firms that offer raw material free of cost and controversy, so that it can be sold globally (Sreberny and Patterson 2004: 5).

In the US, this tendency is twinned with a close link between the state and TV. I was extremely troubled in 2003 by the way that television news and current affairs fell into step with the transparently problematic interpretations of military threat claimed by the government, so I sought to establish both the backdrop to this failing and its current contours. I knew that the supposedly independent, critical television coverage of the American war in Vietnam had mostly been lockstep propaganda until elite opinion more generally shifted (Hallin 1989). This was a repeat, as we can see by borrowing from political economy and textual and content analysis.

Given the expansion of US power over the last quarter of a century, it is noteworthy that TV coverage of governmental, military, and international affairs dropped from 70 percent of English-language network news in 1977, to 60 percent in 1987, and 40 percent in 1997. In 1988, each network dedicated about 2,000 minutes to international news. A decade later, the figure had halved, with about 9 percent of the average newscast covering anything "foreign." Between May 2000 and August 2001, 22 percent of network news was international – ten points below, for example, its British and South African equivalents, and twenty points below Germany. Just 3 percent of US coverage addressed foreign policy. In 2000, three stories from beyond the US (apart from the Olympics) made it into the networks' twenty most-covered items. And all three were tightly linked with domestic issues: the Miami–Cuba custody dispute over Élian Gonzales, the second Intifada, and the bombing of the USS *Cole* off Yemen. The main broadcast networks have closed most investigative sections and foreign bureaux, other than in Israel. ABC News once maintained seventeen offices overseas. Now it has seven. CBS has one journalist covering Asia, and seven others for the rest of the world (Miller 2006; Thussu 2004: 47).

How did this come to pass? When GE purchased NBC in 1986, and tobacco beneficiary Lawrence Tisch bought CBS the following year, they commenced programs of disinvestment and disemployment, with news divisions subjected to similar profit expectations as entertainment sectors. Hundreds were fired from the news service, following a budget cut of millions. NBC eliminated 30 percent of its news employees in the five years to 1992. The impact on programming was obvious. Consider ABC's *20/20* (1978–). This program takes audience interest as the alibi for its trivia, but the reality lies in its drive for a Tayloristic control of input, such that topics are tested in advance with advertisers, rather than being spontaneous reactions to stories of import (Barkin 2003: 89). The celebrity aspects of contemporary newsgathering derive from decisions to program such shows as *Inside Edition* (1989–) and *Entertainment Tonight* (1981–) against network news in the late 1980s. By 1990, news shows had responded by doubling their own coverage of star gossip (Calabrese 2005: 271–2). This has not been a success in attracting audiences; ratings have plummeted during the era of "soft" news (Boyd-Barrett 2005). These innovations are designed to cut production costs, not satisfy viewers.

It should come as no surprise, then, that from September 2001 to December 2002, network-news coverage of the September 11 attacks and their aftermath basically ignored a stream of relevant topics: Zionism, Afghanistan after the invasion, and US foreign policy and business interests in the Middle East (McDonald and Lawrence 2004: 336–7; Traugott and Brader 2003: 183–4, 186–7; *Tyndall Report* 2003). And that corporate influence pushed hard to distort the US public's knowledge of the geopolitical situation. Viacom, CNN, Fox, and Comedy Central refused to feature paid billboards and commercials against the invasion of Iraq (Hastings 2003). During the occupation, General Motors – the country's biggest advertiser at the time – and other major corporations announced that they "would not advertise on a TV program about atrocities in Iraq" (quoted in McCarthy 2004). UN activities in the region, including weapons inspections, were the least-covered relevant items on network news (Huff 2003). And when US authorities finally admitted in January 2005 that no weapons of mass destruction had been found in Iraq, only ABC made that a lead story. Fox News barely touched on it, and CBS and NBC relegated it to a minor item – fewer than sixty words on the nightly news (Whiten 2005).

And consider the coverage of civilian casualties in US imperialist conflicts since 2001. Lawrence Eagleburger, a former Secretary of State, who was called in to comment by CNN after the attacks on the US, said: "There is only one way to begin to deal with people like this, and that is you have to kill some of them even if they are not immediately directly involved," while Republican-Party house intellectual Anne Coulter told a disabled Vietnam veteran: "People like you caused us to lose that war." She proceeded to propose that the right "physically intimidate liberals, by making them realize that they can be killed too" as well as informing Fox News watchers and magazine readers that liberals desire "lots of 9/11s" and "Arabs lie" (quoted in Alterman 2003: 3–5). Coulter's reward for such hyperbolic ignorance was frequent appearances on NBC, CNN, MSNBC, ABC, and HBO, *inter alia* (Alterman 2003: 5; FAIR 2005).

When US retaliation commenced, desperate Afghans in refugee camps were filmed by the BBC, which then sold the footage on to the US ABC network. But the soundtrack to the two broadcast versions gave them incompatible meanings.

> British media presented the camps as consisting of refugees from U.S. bombing who said that fear of the daily bombing attacks had driven them out of the city, whereas U.S. media presented the camps as containing refugees from Taliban oppression and the dangers of civil war.
>
> (Kellner 2003: 125)

CNN instructed presenters to mention September 11 each time Afghan suffering was discussed. Walter Isaacson, the network's President, decreed that it was "perverse to focus too much on the casualties or hardship" (quoted in Kellner 2003: 107).

As the 2003 Iraq War loomed, Rupert Murdoch said: "there is going to be collateral damage … if you really want to be brutal about it, better we get it done now" (quoted in Pilger 2003). The human impact of the invasion was dismissed by PBS *News Hour* Executive Producer Lester Crystal as not "central at the moment" (quoted in Sharkey 2003). Fox News Managing Editor Brit Hume said that civilian casualties may not belong on television, as they are "historically, by definition, a part of war." In the fortnight prior to the invasion, none of the three major commercial networks examined the humanitarian impact of such an action. Human Rights Watch's briefing paper, and a UN Undersecretary-General's warning on the topic, lay uncovered. Viewers were treated to a carnival of *matériel* that privileged the technological sublime and oscillated between glorifying and denying death. Thirty-eight percent of CNN's coverage of the bombardment emphasized technology, while 62 percent focused on military activity, without referring to history or politics. In the rest of the world's media coverage of the Afghan and Iraqi crises, invasions, and occupations, such military maneuvers and masculinist odes took second place to civilian suffering. The Qatar-owned TV news network Al Jazeera, for example, dedicated only one-third of its stories to war footage, emphasizing human distress over electronic effectiveness, vernacular reportage rather than patriotic euphemism. Thousands of civilian Afghan and Iraqi deaths reported by it and South Asian, South-East Asian, Western European, and other Middle Eastern news services were taboo topics on US television for years. Empathy for non-combatants was essentially banned by NBC, while CNN and PBS discouraged commentators from referring to torture (FAIR 2003a; Lewis *et al.* 2004: 14; Rich 2003; Jasperson and El-Kikhia 2003: 119, 126–7; Herold 2001; Flanders 2001; Kellner 2004: 334; della Cava 2003; Greenberg 2003; Hart 2009b).

More than half the US TV-studio guests talking about the impending action in Iraq in 2003 were superannuated white-male pundits (FAIR 2003b), "ex-military men, terrorism experts, and Middle Eastern policy analysts who know none of the relevant languages, may never have seen any part of the Middle East, and are too poorly educated to be expert at anything" (Said 2003). During the war, news effectively diminished the dominant discourse to technical efficiency and state propaganda. Of 319 people giving "analysis" on ABC, CBS, and NBC in October 2003, 76 percent were current or previous officials. Of the civilians, 79 percent were Republican-Party mavens. And all in all, 81 percent of sources were Yanquis (Whiten 2005; Rendall and Butterworth 2004; Grand Rapids Institute for Information Democracy 2005). The *New York Times* refers to these has–been and never–were interviewees like this:

"part experts and part reporters, they're marketing tools, as well" (Jensen 2003). Their virtually universal links to arms-trading were rarely divulged, and never discussed as relevant. Retired Lieutenant General Barry McCaffrey, employed in this capacity by NBC News, points to the cadre's "lifetime of experience and objectivity." In his case, this involved membership of the Committee for the Liberation of Iraq, a lobby group dedicated to influencing the media, and the boards of three munitions companies that make ordnance he had praised on MSNBC. Even amongst the thoroughly ideologized US public, 36 percent believed the media over-emphasized the opinions of these retirees (T. Miller 2007). Perhaps the most relevant number to consider is that the company that owns MSNBC and NBC, General Electric, is one of the largest defense contractors in the world. It receives billions of dollars from the Pentagon each year. Disney (which owns ABC) is also a beneficiary of largesse from the Department of Defense (Turse 2008: 3).

In addition to these complex domestic imbrications of private and public, the US government attempts to limit the expression of alternative positions on world television. To hide the carnage of its 2001 invasion, the Pentagon bought exclusive rights to satellite photos of Afghanistan. And consider its treatment of Al Jazeera. The US State Department tried to disrupt the network via pressure on Qatar's Emir Sheikh Hamid bin Khalifa al-Thaniof. Its Washington correspondent was "detained" en route to a US–Russia summit in November 2001, and its offices were assaulted by US munitions in Afghanistan in 2001 (where it was the sole broadcast news outlet in Kabul) and Iraq in 2003. The network was subject to then-Secretary of Defense Rumsfeld's denunciation of it as "Iraqi propaganda" and the Bush regime's ignorant and insulting moniker: "All Osama All the Time." Throughout the early US occupation of Iraq, Al Jazeera workers were assaulted by US soldiers, culminating in murders. Rear Admiral Craig Quigley, then US deputy assistant defense secretary for public affairs, justified the attack on the network's Kabul operations with the claim that Al Qaeda interests were being aided by activities going on there. Quigley's nutty proof was that Al Jazeera was using a satellite uplink and was in contact with Taliban officials – pretty normal activities for a news service (T. Miller 2006; 2007).

When I appeared on New York 1, a local cable news channel, shortly after the 2001 attacks on the US, I was asked to comment on the psychology of terrorists via trans-historical queries, "What makes people do these things?" "Are they maladjusted?" I endeavored to direct the conversation toward US foreign policy and its support of totalitarian regimes in the Middle East that restricted access to politics, hence turning religion into a zone of resistance. And I spoke of US TV journalists' sparse and prejudicial narrative frames and background knowledge. The production staff later told me that the board lit up with supportive reaction when the program accepted phone calls from the public. Those I spoke with thanked me for saying the *non dit*. The staff said I would be invited back. I was not. And when CBS News contacted me in 2005 to discuss the admission that the White House had acted contrary to law by directing the National Security Agency to spy on US citizens without judicial review, the producer asked me if I could contextualize this in terms of the history of the media during wartime. I replied that I could. Then he asked me about the limits to publicizing information. I indicated that whilst most critics would agree that the precise timing and location of an event such as D-Day could legitimately be kept secret, extra-juridical contravention of civil liberties would generally be considered another matter. The producer thanked me for my time, and noted that my services would not be required. He already had a lawyer to support the revelation, and needed someone who would attack the *New York Times* for having broken the story and forced the President to tell the truth. He didn't want the history of the media during wartime. He wanted jingoism.

In order to understand the rabid nationalism of US television journalism, one needs to become acquainted with the alternatives that exist – journalists who do not merely report government statements with faith; journalists who do not believe that being at war embargoes the truth; journalists who are encouraged to learn other languages than their own; journalists who ask independent academics rather than dependent, coin-operated think-tanks and soldiers for opinions; journalists who work for peaceful communication and against imperial censorship; and journalists who do not believe there are always and everywhere two binarized positions on a topic in addition to a putatively decent, middle-American mid-point that acts as cover for nationalistic blood-letting. TV Studies 3.0 must always go beyond the spatial and temporal coordinates of here and now to ask how things might be otherwise, elsewhere or in another time. We must contextualize texts at the same time as we textualize contexts.

QUESTIONS FOR DISCUSSION

(1) What should Television Studies 3.0 look like?
(2) How can we use more global material to learn about TV?
(3) How does the state help in making US TV?
(4) What should be television's role in foreign-affairs reporting?

NOTES

(1) The title was changed to *Queer Eye* in its third season, when targeted makeovers expanded to include queers and women.
(2) Sign me up.

FURTHER READING

Downing, John and Charles Husband. (2005). *Representing "Race": Racisms, Ethnicities and Media*. London: Sage.

Hesmondhalgh, David and Jason Toynbee, eds. (2008). *The Media and Social Theory*. London: Routledge.

"My Media Studies." (2009). *Television & New Media* 10, no. 1.

Spigel, Lynn. (2008). *TV by Design: Modern Art and the Rise of Network Television*. Chicago: University of Chicago Press.

CONCLUSION

The TV is Dead. Long Live the TV.

> (*Wired*, quoted in Borland and Hansen 2007)

Television has made billions based on how many people watch a show at its regular time. That idea may already be obsolete.

> (*Washington Post*, quoted in Bauder 2007)

TV is far from dead.

> (Verizon, quoted in Buckley 2008)

TV used to be a one-way pipe.... Now the audience is being completely heard on every aspect of the show. That has changed the nature of television and the kind of shows that get programmed.

> (Carlton Cruse, co-creator of *Lost*, quoted in Kushner 2007)

Television is dying.

> (Damon Lindelof, co-creator of *Lost* 2007)

The end of television as we know it.

> (IBM Business Consulting Services 2006)

Americans are watching more traditional television than ever.

> (Nielsen 2008)

Long Live Traditional Media.

> (Deloitte Media & Entertainment 2007)

American representations of television in India often offer a stereotypically prosaic image: a huddled mass seated on the floor, transfixed by the television set jammed between articles of everyday living. Incommensurability is the defining feature of these images; the television set becomes sign and symbol of modernity and the West, while the cluttered room with its bags, calendars, utensils, crude objects of everyday life encapsulates the lack of development characteristic of the East.

(Sujata Moorti 2007: 1)

There's a world where life is lively, where nobody spends six hours a day unwinding before a piece of furniture … your best and only access to this world is TV.

(David Foster Wallace 1997: 39)

There's something ironic in the eight epigraphs collected together above. *Wired* magazine, self-anointed sacerdotal prophet of new media, says TV is finished yet reborn. The *Washington Post*, scion of traditional newspapers, thinks it's obsolete. Verizon, a US$100 billion-dollar-a-year telephone company, sees the device adapting to new circumstances. And the men who made millions from the successful prestige drama *Lost* (created because of the success of the down-market reality program *Survivor*) can't agree on the future of the medium that feeds their appetites (Torres 2008). IBM, the pioneer of computing that now earns vast sums consulting on communications, and Nielsen, the biggest audience-measurement company in the world, take diametrically opposed positions on where TV is today, while Deloitte, a major accounting and consultancy multinational, comes down on the same side as Nielsen. Meanwhile, Mike Griffith, chief of Activision, which makes *Guitar Hero* (2005–) and the *Tony Hawk* series (1999–), has announced that "Video games are poised to eclipse all other forms of entertainment" because TV is "stagnating or contracting" (quoted in "Games Will 'Eclipse' Other Media" 2009). By contrast with these ideas, which so carelessly conjure up beginnings and endings in easily activated slogans, Moorti localizes and engages these categories through a dialectical process where opposites intersect without neat resolution or universal application, and Wallace shows the way the medium offers us a life on screen that its very existence seems to preclude.

The debate over the so-called decline of TV brings me to a struggle I had in 1998 to begin a new academic journal about television. I discussed the idea with three publishing houses, each of which was interested. One quickly proceeded to test the market, and duly reported almost universal acclaim for the proposal. Then, I was told, the managing director of the firm held a cocktail party on his yacht and asked his guests what they thought of this idea. Someone had just been at a conference in the Netherlands that had announced the end of TV. The notion of a new journal devoted to it suddenly seemed anachronistic. The project was put in crisis due to this conversation, and I had to rework the proposal with my editor from the publishing house. *Television* became *Television & New Media*, contracts were exchanged, and we began a productive ten-year collaboration. I tell the story both to record the irrationality of capitalism, and to indicate how long people have been burying TV – as long as they have been buying it.

This much is clear: we are in the midst of a major transformation in television. Shifts are underway in wealthy nations from analogue to digital systems, rendering broadcast TV unwatchable by some existing technology. In the OECD countries, 52 percent of TV households received only broadcast signals in 1995. By 2002, that number had dropped to 37 percent, as cable in particular proliferated. Digital television was in one-fifth of households by 2001, and analogue signals will end there by 2015. Synchronized moving images and sounds can now be sent to and received from public spaces, offices, homes, shops, schools, and transportation. The devices include TVs, computers, telephones, and personal digital assistants. The networks vary between broadcast, satellite, cable, telephone, and Internet. The stations may be public, private, community, or amateur. The time of watching is varied, from live to on-demand. These technologies increasingly transgress the boundaries and policing established by nations. The spread of some transmission systems is very limited – perhaps two-and-a-half-million homes worldwide had Internet television in 2005 – but others are on the move – cable and satellite channels in the OECD almost doubled between 2004 and 2006. At the same time, very few people frequent more than a handful of stations – in the US, the average is fifteen a week. In terms of types of TV, between one-third and one-half of viewers in OECD countries watch public television (this figure is dragged down by the US, where 2 percent of the population watches PBS each day). In terms of technology that permits one to shift time and space, DVRs, which integrate TVs and computers, and Slingboxes, which enable use of digital television anywhere, are fringe toys other than in the US. Internet video advertising remains tiny both in absolute terms and its actual growth. The old, sluggish, supposedly dying US networks received US$9.2 billion in revenue in 2008, up 5 percent from 2007. All the signs during the profound recession of 2009 were that they remained the most-trusted site for advertisers (Organisation for Economic Co-operation and Development 2007: 172–6; Sweney 2008; "Downloading TV" 2008; Fine 2009).

An example of new trends comes from Showtime, a premium US cable and satellite channel that features films, boxing, and original drama and has fifteen million subscribers. The network carries no commercials and receives no government funding. Somewhat slower than others to offer shows online for fear of alienating paying customers, in 2008 it offered the first season's episode of *The Tudors* (2007–) on YouTube with sexual content removed. The next year, the beginning of *The United States of Tara* (2009–) was available to 170 million people through 125 websites, phone services, and film theaters. The same sites began screening its series *The L Word* (2004–9) and *Secret Diary of a Call Girl* (2007–) *gratis*, which encouraged many viewers to subscribe (Stelter 2008; Goetzl 2009; Hein 2009). The Internet was a useful marketing device for television.

In Korea, the future for the rest of us arrived some time ago. Since 2005, Seoul's bus and metro systems have been laden with commuters watching television on their cell-phones – over seven million customers enjoying broadcast TV, not something sent via an individual stream to their apparatus. The service is free as mandated by the government, which also did sensible things like establishing fully-compatible, universal technological standards ("Screen Test" 2007) – policies that are far too rational and anti-neoliberal for countries such as the US or the UK to learn from, sadly. Japanese TV corporations are coping with threats from the Wii, Nintendo's cheap alternative electronic-games console designed for easy-going neophytes and familial and casual users rather than needy obsessives with too much time on their hands. Within two years of its launch, the Wii boasted forty million users. The next move was to start the Wiinoma channel, available through the Wii via the Internet and featuring programming aimed at children and parents in a partnership with the nation's biggest advertising agency, Dentsu. But as its other attempts to make the gaming console the basis for something else – such as music – had failed, it was unclear that the TV set would be subordinated to it (Lewis 2009).

In 2008 there were 1.1 billion TV sets in the world, with 43 percent receiving signals from broadcast and 38 percent from cable ("World Television Market" 2009). Television is more diverse, more diffuse, more popular, more powerful, and more innovative than ever. Our spanking-new flat-screen TVs will soon be tossed cavalierly away if the next generation from Sony, Samsung, LG, Toshiba, Sharp, and Panasonic, with streaming movies and Yahoo!/Intel widgets for Internet connections with information about weather and stock prices, or Blu-ray players that access the Internet, takes off. They are already available in Japan, as screens move from elegant anorexia to bulimic interactivity. But even the cybertarians at MySpace and Jupitermedia, not to mention Sony and Sharp, insist that viewers want TV to remain TV, with a few add-ons – their preference is for watching programs, albeit with some added elements, while flat-screen sets are generally already constructed with connections to computers. This is the fate of a technology that is moving from "an object of denial to [an] *objet d'art*" (Richtel 2009; Garrahan and Taylor 2009; Moses 2009; MacMillan 2009; Attallah 2007: 347 n. 8; Daum 2007). As it undergoes that transition, "TV will be finished only when the population as a whole turns instinctively to another medium just to see what's on" (Ellis 2007: 5). Even hard-edged US viewers in search of business news prefer television as a source of information, with barely one-sixth looking online (Behavior Research Center 2008).

The Internet *is* finally catching up with high-quality services that borrow from TV's resolution standards, thanks to Hulu, TV. com, and Veoh, re-broadcasters of network drama online. In just twelve months, Hulu became the sixth-most viewed video site, as legal online viewing of television shows by adults in the US grew by 141 percent in 2008 (streaming is becoming more popular than downloading, as it is generally free, fast, simple, and legal). TV.com viewers increased by 1,261 percent in January 2009 over the previous month. Of US Internet users aged thirteen to fifty-four, one-fifth now use these services. Many do so to get back in touch with favored series prior to the appearance of new episodes on TV.

They are coming to be known as "Televidualists." Advertisers flock to Hulu by contrast with YouTube: after its first year, Hulu had 70 percent of YouTube's revenue with 1 percent of the users. When CBS streamed coverage of the 2009 college basketball finals online, it sold US$30 million in advertising immediately – much less than the US$400 million for TV, but indicative of the maturity of streaming (when it is articulated to television). And in the UK, by the end of 2008, one-fifth of Britons with broadband were watching TV with it. In Germany, the number increased by 38 percent in 2008 (Mermigas 2008; Collins 2008; "Downloading TV and Watching Video" 2009; Friedman 2008d; Baltrusis 2009; Friedman 2009e; Tancer 2009; "Hulu Who?" 2009; O'Malley 2009; Friedman 2009f; Learmonth 2009a; Richmond 2009a; Franchi 2009; Ofcom 2009: 31; "Internet Radio and TV" 2009).

In some ways, things have not changed as much as the prelates of technological convergence and television's decline predicted – yet these self-anointed sacerdotes continue on their merry way! In other ways, a lot has changed – but through deregulation, cable, and macroeconomic crisis – not technology and cybertarianism. The idea of a comprehensive service offered by a single station still lingers, but niche, specialized, genre-driven stations proliferate. In their cynical way, marketers have dubbed this a "New TV Ecosystem" (Navar 2008). The lesson of new technology remains the same as ever: as per print, radio, and television, each medium is quickly dominated by centralized and centralizing corporations, despite its multi-distributional potential. This centralism is obviously less powerful in the case of the Internet than technologies that are more amenable to being sealed-off. And the cost of producing high-quality work for the electronic media *has* diminished. Cybertarian interpretations emphasize the technical ease of entry for new players on new platforms; but the most influential change derives from the massive increase in political TV advertisements occasioned by this price reduction (Preston 2007). When the recession/depression hit at the end of 2008, US media buyers sought huge cuts in the cost of television commercials both at that moment and for the year to come; but national TV remained the most reliable means of reaching the largest number of people and having the maximal impact on their consumption (Lafayette 2008). And commercials are, in any event, no longer the core of US television. QVC, a shopping network that sells products directly as its source of revenue, makes almost as much profit as the networks, while HBO subscriptions exceed advertising revenue for popular networks (Higgins 2006; James 2009b). Worldwide, 49 percent of TV is advertiser-supported, but 42 percent is paid for through subscriptions, a model that is clearly the future − and much more sophisticated than the Internet has been able to create. Within the advertising-driven sector, although 2008 and 2009 figures show a global drop in expenditure, television's share was increasing because advertisers were cutting their TV budgets last of all the media ("World Television Market" 2009; "TV Advertising" 2009).

Lynn Spigel explains what is happening:

> [I]ncreasing commercialization of public-service/state-run systems, the rise of multichannel cable and global satellite delivery, multinational conglomerates, Internet convergence, changes in regulatory policies and ownership rules, the advent of high-definition TV, technological changes in screen design, digital video recorders, and new forms of media competition − as well as new forms of programming … and scheduling practices … have all transformed the practice we call watching TV. This does not mean all of television is suddenly unrecognizable − indeed, familiarity and habit continue to be central to the TV experience − but it does mean that television's past is recognizably distinct from its present.
>
> (2005b: 83)

The challenge for public broadcasters, for example, is to maintain and develop their strengths as new technology comes along, something the BBC has done better than virtually any other TV network, private or otherwise, in the world (Thompson 2009).

Since its inception, television has principally been a means of profiting and legitimizing its controllers, and entertaining and civilizing its viewers. In the words of the famous BBC executive Huw Wheldon, the Corporation's 1960s mission was "To make the good popular, and the popular good" (quoted in Airey 2004). A nice phrase; but Bourdieu sees these as competing rather than consistent imperatives. He refers to a duel between "populist spontaneism and demagogic capitulation to popular tastes" versus "paternalistic-pedagogic television" (1998: 48). This tension is embodied in the career of the person quoting Weldon, Dawn Airey (who ran Britain's Channel Five as twenty-first-century TV's first out lesbian CEO) with mainstays of, in her words, "football, films and fucking" (quoted in Wells 2003).

Whatever happens to TV in the next few years, we must bear in mind that its history is not a tale of visionary inve(n)(s)tors finding means to satisfy the existing curiosity of audiences – a consumer-driven market – but an uncertain dance of law, the state, capital, labor, performance, and interpretation that reveals complex, shifting power relations. Yet media policy is dominated by neoliberalism, with neoclassical economists saying there should be no governmental barriers to the exchange of programs and no state subvention of entertainment. The market is a site of magic for such true-believers. Neoclassical economic discourse is also of great moment in such areas as cross-sectoral ownership, anti-union activity, control of distribution, hidden public subsidies, the rhetoric of technological determinism, and the New International Division of Cultural Labor. Public understanding of these topics is governed by economists, business journalists, corporate lobbyists, and agents of the state. Research is needed that addresses this hegemony, via a critical engagement with the analytic, financial, and governmental power of the psy-function and neoliberalism. That might provide counter-discourses to the continuing public dominance of TV Studies 1.0, which 2.0 has barely addressed. Such work can draw on what I see as the strengths of a critical Television Studies 3.0. Making a radical–democratic future for TV depends on analysis and activism of this kind. Attaching electrodes to Psychology 100 students to examine their neurons, or asking your friends whether they like reality programs, does something else.

LEFTOVERS

I have left this section for the very end of the book for two reasons. First, it is of immense importance, yet is not addressed within TV Studies 1.0 or 2.0. Second, it really *is* about the life and death of television – namely, the carbon impact created during and after its use as a consumer appliance. For example, the UK's National Grid

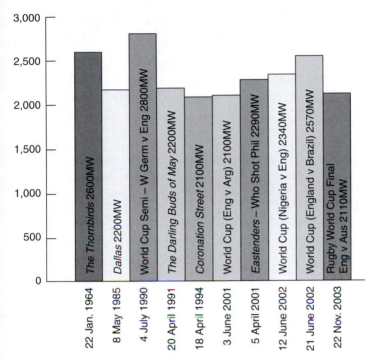

Greatest Impact on UK Electricity Grid Caused by TV Demand (source: National Grid (nationalgrid.com/uk/Media+Centre/worldcup)).

(2006) proudly promotes its relevance to TV by telling consumers how valuable it has been, planning for peak usage based on ebbs and flows based on audience activity. When half-time comes in football matches, and at their end, people race to the kettle. Power use surges by as much as 10 percent in what is known as the "TV pick-up." Is this desirable? What is it telling us?

I remember television sets exploding when I was a child. Some were known as "curtain-burners" because they got so hot (Low 2009). In 2007, 207.5 million sets were sold around the globe, of which 56 percent were old-style, fat-screen TVs. The estimated number for 2011 is 245.5 million, with just one-third being fat-screen and the remainder flat-screen. China and the Asia-Pacific region in general continue to buy old-style sets in much greater numbers than consumers elsewhere ("Samsung Holds Lead" 2007). Marketing for flat-screen televisions stresses the pleasure to be derived from intense use of energy; as the cost of the sets dropped, their uptake increased, with little regard for electricity consumption – up to 250 watts per hour (Crosbie 2008). In Britain, it is estimated that flat-screen televisions will add 700,000 tonnes a year to carbon emissions by 2010, an increase of 70 percent on 2006 levels. They use three-times the electricity required for analog sets (Russell 2006).

And what about when we are finished with television – not in the sense of watching it, but when we throw away our old TV sets? Television is responsible for monumental environmental despoliation, for all the claims that it is part of the "post-smokestack" creative sector, a post-manufacturing utopia for workers, consumers, and residents with by-products of code, not smoke. The Political Economy Research Institute's 2004 *Misfortune 100: Top Corporate Air Polluters in the United States* has media owners at numbers 1, 3, 16, 22, and 39. Media production relies on the exorbitant water-use of computer technology, while making semi-conductors requires the use of hazardous chemicals, including some known carcinogens. Most color televisions have a Cathode-Ray Tube (CRT), which sends electron beams from cesium cathodes into high-voltage electrodes that are projected onto our phosphorescent screens and emit radiation inside tubes to illuminate the phosphors. CRTs are made of zinc, copper, cesium, cadmium, and silver. Viewers are protected from radiation by glass screens forged from strontium, barium, and lead oxide, while neodymium oxide and nickel alloy enhance images. The average tube has four pounds of lead. Major environmental problems occur both when televisions are made and when they are thrown away, when components seep into underground water. Old TVs contribute heavy metals and toxic chemicals when trashed. This worsened with the 2009 transition to digital broadcasting in the US, when 270 million outdated analog sets, considered the hardest device to recycle, were expected to be discarded (Conner and Williams 2004; Puzzanghera 2007).

Dumped TVs from the past go to be recycled offshore, principally in Nigeria and China, because First-World environmental and industrial legislation prohibits the destruction to soil, water, and workers that are caused by the dozens of poisonous chemicals and gases in these dangerous machines (California alone shipped about twenty million pounds of electronic waste in 2006 to Malaysia, Brazil, South Korea, China, Mexico, Vietnam, and India). Much e-cycling is done by pre-teen young girls, ragpickers who work without protection to pull apart outmoded First-World televisions and computers. In China, they pick away without protection of any kind at discarded First-World televisions in order to find precious metals for sale to recyclers. The remains are dumped in landfills; waste from discarded electronics is one of the biggest sources of heavy metals and toxic pollutants in the world's trash piles. The accumulation of electronic hardware causes grave environmental and health concerns, stemming from the potential seepage of noxious chemicals, gases, and metals into landfills, water sources, and e-waste salvage yards (Shiva 2002; Basel Action Network and Silicon Valley Toxics Coalition 2002; Lee 2007; Shabi 2002).

The ragpickers who undertake informal recycling in this way have been important fringe participants in modernity for centuries. They were figures of pathos in the British situation comedy, *Steptoe and Son* (1962–5, 1970–4). The Steptoes and their horse and cart looked for gems amongst the dross of "Swinging London." They represented throwbacks to a time that had not really passed for working people. Steptoe Junior spent his evenings dreaming of transcendence, devouring the works of Karl Marx and George Bernard Shaw; but he could never leave his ragpicker status behind. The Labour Government of the day even invoked the Steptoes to show that it blended old-style workerism with creative innovation (Black 2006: 330–1). The popular Yanqui sitcom *Sanford and Son* (1972–7) about working-class African Americans, and the renowned Nigerian writer Ken Saro-Wiwa's *Basi and Company* (1985–90), were partly based on it. Today's reality is less savory.

There is some hope here. In the US, environmental factors – at least at the production and consumption end of things, if not recycling – are weighing on the minds of consumers, which opens up new corporate power plays: in 2009, Sony announced new liquid-display sets that would require much less power than others, in part by going to sleep when they were not being watched, thanks to motion-sensor surveillance of viewers. The plan was to play environmental politics against economies of scale – to charge a premium for green consumers and hence counter the tendency for HDTV prices to fall ("Sony to Launch Power-Saving TVs" 2009).

So next time you're in class, you might get some discussion going about how to study TV as waste, questioning your fellow-students: how did you get rid of your last set? Where did it go? What happened to it? Don't forget to ask your Television Studies teacher for more information, just as you would on any other topic to do with studying TV.

FINALLY ...

In 1942, NBC executive Noran E. Kersta wrote that: "Television as a communication medium can surpass in speed, accuracy, and security any other communication medium in existence" (1942: 29). He was right then, and he's right now. As *Fortune* business magazine put it recently: "TV is Dying? Long Live TV!" (Colvin 2007). In Hernan Galperin's wise words, there is a shift from "spectrum scarcity, dumb terminals, and one-way services" to "on-demand programming, intelligent terminals, and abundant channels" (2004: 3). The Open Mobile Video Coalition of 850 US stations believes there will be 500 million sets once a universal mobile standard emerges to cover backrests in cars, cell-phones, and MP3s (Kapko 2008). We are experiencing a movement "away from an oligopolistic-based scarcity associated with broadcasting toward a more differentiated abundance or saturation associated with the proliferation of new and old television services, technologies and providers" (Moran with Malbon 2006: 10).

Television's reach is extending, its flexibility is developing, its popularity is increasing, and its capacity to influence and incorporate older and newer media is undimmed. To think otherwise would diminish the material histories of televisual texts and their consumption, reducing commodity signs with complex careers to business-as-usual attempts by the US psy-function to blame them for high national levels of interpersonal violence and low levels of educational attainment, or buying into cybertarian simplifications. Those obsessions should be ever more-troubled by electronic texts' extraordinarily open, malleable, polyphonic qualities – their status as TV texts (Chartier 2005). The psy-function and cybertarianism are both astoundingly solipsistic in the grandiose pronouncements they make, based on absolute ignorance of the role television plays across the world. Each one fails to comprehend the ongoing verity about TV and other devices for audience pleasure and surveillance: that "television is demographic, not democratic" (Nelson 1992: 105).

Television Studies 3.0 must blend ethnographic, political–economic, environmental, and aesthetic analyses in a global and local way, establishing links between the key areas of cultural production around the world (Africa, the Americas, Asia, Europe, and the Middle East) and diasporic/dispossessed communities engaged in their own cultural production (Native peoples, African and Asian diasporas, Latin@s, and Middle-Eastern peoples). TV Studies 3.0 needs to be a politically revised version of area studies, with diasporas as important as regions. It should be animated by collective identity and power, how human subjects are formed, and how they experience cultural and social space. Taking its agenda from social movements as well as intellectual ones, Television Studies 3.0's methods will draw on economics, politics, communications, sociology, literature, law, science, medicine, anthropology, history, environmental science, and art, with a particular focus on gender, race, class, religion, age, region, and sexuality in everyday life across national lines. And it won't privilege pessimism, optimism, audiences, owners, states, technology, or labor – but, rather, stress their mutual imbrication. The same thing goes for debates about TV itself – don't fall for the parlor-game rhetoric of doom and gloom without looking at the numbers. We need "autonomy from the industry and fan logics" (Beaty 2009: 24). TV studies 3.0 must position television "as its subject, but not its center" in order to help build a participatory and democratic polity, economy, and culture (Lewis 2009: 91).

At the beginning of this book, I posed the question: what is television? Here now is my television A-to-Z:

Advertising: Texts that interrupt television, or are the best television, or enable television.
Broadcasting: When television went through the air and was aimed at everyone.
Culture: What television was not.
Drama: Once characterized television, and has *always* characterized its internal workings and debates about it.

Effects: Measuring the impact of worrying about television on Television Studies 1.0 practitioners: politicians, family power dynamics, god-botherers, and the careers of psychology and communication professors.

Flow: The movement of Raymond Williams backwards, forwards, and sideways on a trans-Atlantic liner – *sans soleil*.

Government: The space between television as a vast wasteland and a toaster with pictures.

High Definition: A faster way of making television sets obsolete.

Ideology: What people who live outside plutocracies and militarized states no longer believe in.

Journalism: Endangered species, formerly common in the United States.

Knowledge: Used to disagree with people who refer to an information society.

Liveness: Plausible, in the case of sports coverage.

Media: Subject for corralling undergraduates and teaching them that what they enjoy is also good for them.

News: RIP September 11, 2001.

Ownership: A topic that used to matter but is no longer important, because people allegedly interpret television programs in accordance with their local rituals.

Production: Invisible other than as what media-studies undergraduates must do rather than research and write their essays.

Quality: It's not quality, it's television.

Race: A Grand Prix.

Sex: Only on satellite and cable.

Technology: Sold to the public by offering sport exclusively on latest innovation.

Uses and Gratifications: Jeremy Bentham watching *Survivor*.

Violence: To be derided, other than when done by the state to foreigners.

Women: A market segment.

X-cess: Television Studies 2.0 academics writing about wrestling or their children.

Youth: Spectators learning how to be responsible consumers.

Zworykin: Fabled television inventor from RCA who "liberated" an already-patented invention.

Meanwhile, it's time for me to close this file and look at my second computer screen, the one that uses Slingbox to bring me my satellite subscription wherever I am in the world. I know I'll be watching television as I do so. It's the latest of many incarnations I have experienced since the 1960s.

QUESTIONS FOR DISCUSSION

(1) What does TV's future look like now, versus before you read this book?
(2) Should we *bury* TV, or *buy* it?
(3) What can be done about e-waste and TV?

FURTHER READING

Basel Action Network and Silicon Valley Toxics Coalition. (2002). *Exporting Harm: The High-Tech Trashing of Asia.*

Grossman, Elizabeth. (2006). *High Tech Trash: Digital Devices, Hidden Toxics, and Human Health.* Washington: Island Press.

BIBLIOGRAPHY

"2008: The Top Ten Happenings in Indian TV." (2009, January 2). *Indiantelevision.com*.

Abercrombie, Nicholas. (1996). *Television as Text*. Cambridge: Polity Press.

Abrams, Philip. (1973). "Television and Radio." *Discrimination and Popular Culture*, 2nd edn. Ed. Denys Thompson. Baltimore: Penguin, 102–32.

Abu-Lughod, Lila. (2005). *Dramas of Nationhood: The Politics of Television in Egypt*. Chicago: University of Chicago Press.

AdEx India Analysis. (2008, December 30). "Facts and Figures of Television Advertising in 2008." *Indiantelevision.com*.

Adorno, Theodor W. (1972). *Aspects of Sociology*. Trans. John Viertel. Boston: Beacon Press.

Adorno, Theodor W. and Max Horkheimer. (1977). "The Culture Industry: Enlightenment as Mass Deception." *Mass Communication and Society*. Eds. James Curran, Michael Gurevitch, and Janet Woollacott. London: Edward Arnold, 349–83.

Airey, Dawn. (2004). "RTS Huw Wheldon Memorial Lecture." Royal Television Society.

Airey, Dawn. (2007, July 20). "Is the BBC a Healthy Institution ... or Fundamentally Sick at Heart?" *Independent*: 3.

Aitkenhead, Decca. (2009, February 2). "One Hour with Kiefer Sutherland." *Guardian*.

Alasuutari, Pertti, ed. (1999). *Rethinking the Media Audience: The New Agenda*. London: Sage Publications.

Albornoz, Luis A., ed. (2007). *Al fin solos ... La nueva televisión del MERCOSUR*. Buenos Aires: FUND.

Allam, Samir. (1983). *Fernsehserien, Wertvorstellungen und Zensur in Ägypten*. Munich: Edition Orient.

Allatson, Paul. (2006). "Making Queer for the United States of Empire." *Australian Humanities Review* 28.

Allen, Dennis W. (2006). "Making Over Masculinity: A Queer 'I' for the Straight Guy." *Genders* 44.

Allen, Robert C. (1985). *Speaking of Soap Operas*. Chapel Hill: University of North Carolina Press.

Allen, Robert C., ed. (1992). *Channels of Discourse, Reassembled: Television and Contemporary Television*. Chapel Hill: University of North Carolina Press.

Allen, Robert C., ed. (1995). *to be continued … Soap Operas Around the World*. London: Routledge.

Allen, Robert C. and Annette Hill, eds. (2004). *The Television Studies Reader*. London: Routledge.

Alterman, Eric. (2003). *What Liberal Media? The Truth about* Bias *and the News*. New York: Basic Books.

Alvarado, Manuel and Edward Buscombe. (1978). Hazell*: The Making of a TV Series*. London: British Film Institute/Latimer.

Alvarado, Manuel and John Stewart, eds. (1985). *Made for Television: Euston Films Limited*. London: British Film Institute.

American Psychological Association Task Force on the Sexualization of Girls. (2007). *Report of the APA Task Force on the Sexualization of Girls*.

Ammon, Royce J. (2001). *Global Television and the Shaping of World Politics: CNN, Telediplomacy, and Foreign Policy*. Jefferson: McFarland.

Andersen, Kenneth E. (2005). *Recovering the Civic Culture: The Imperative of Ethical Communication*. Boston: Pearson.

Andersen, Robin. (1995). *Consumer Culture & TV Programming*. Boulder: Westview Press.

Anderson, Harold. (1965). "Exporting TV Know-How – A Case History." *Television Quarterly* 4, no. 1: 19–21.

Ang, Ien. (1982). *Het Geval Dallas*. Amsterdam: Uitgeverij SUA.

Ang, Ien. (1991). *Desperately Seeking the Audience*. London: Routledge.

Aristotle. (1961). *Poetics*. Trans. S.H. Butcher. New York: Hill and Wang.

Armstrong, Paul. (2007, August 28). "How TV Covers the Premier League." *BBC Editor's Blog*.

Arnheim, Rudolf. (1969). *Film as Art*. London: Faber & Faber.

Arnoldy, Ben. (2007, September 17). "Among Networks, Spanish-Language Univision is Now a Top Contender." *Christian Science Monitor*.

Arthurs, Jane. (2004). *Television and Sexuality: Regulation and the Politics of Taste*. Maidenhead: Open University Press.

Asma, Stephen T. (2007, October 12). "Looking Up From the Gutter: Philosophy and Popular Culture." *Chronicle of Higher Education*.

Assunta, Mary and Simon Chapman. (2004). "'The World's Most Hostile Environment': How the Tobacco Industry Circumvented Singapore's Advertising Ban." *Tobacco Control* 13, Suppl. II: ii51–ii57.

Atkinson, Claire. (2005, September 30). "Americans Watch More TV than Ever." *AdvertisingAge*.

Atkinson, Claire. (2008, December 2). "2008 Political Ads Worth $2.5 Billion to $2.7 Billion." *Broadcasting & Cable*.

Atkinson, Claire. (2009, February 7). "Cable Stays Up Amid Big Media Losses." *Broadcasting & Cable*.

Attali, Jacques. (2008, Spring). "This is Not America's Final Crisis." *New Perspectives Quarterly*: 31–3.

Attallah, Paul. (1984). "The Unworthy Discourse: Situation Comedy in Television." *Interpreting Television: Current Research Perspectives*. Eds. Willard Rowland and Bruce Watkins. Beverly Hills: Sage, 222–49.

Attallah, Paul. (2003). Review. *Canadian Journal of Communication* 28, no. 4: 485–7.

Attallah, Paul. (2006). Review. *Canadian Journal of Communication* 31, no. 4.

Attallah, Paul. (2007). "A Usable History for the Study of Television." *Canadian Review of American Studies/Revue canadienne d'études américaines* 37, no. 3: 325–49.

Attwood, Alan. (1990, January 20). "How to Bowl Out the Junk Sport Habit." *Australian Financial Review*: 67.

Bachman, Katy. (2007, October 15). "Candidates Still Favoring Local TV Ads." *MediaWeek*.

Baehr, Helen and Gillian Dyer, eds. (1987). *Boxed-In: Women and Television*. London: Pandora.

Baehr, Helen and Ann Gray, eds. (1996). *Turning it On: A Reader in Women & Media*. London: Arnold.

Balas, Glenda R. (2003). *Recovering a Public Vision for Public Television*. Lanham: Rowman & Littlefield.

Ballard, J.G. (2009, April 25). "The Dying Fall." *Guardian*.

Baltrusis, Sam. (2009, February 12). "Online Views of Full TV Programs Double." *Contentinople*.

Banet-Weiser, Sarah. (2007). *Kids Rule! Nickelodeon and Consumer Citizenship*. Durham: Duke University Press.

Banet-Weiser, Sarah and Laura Portwood-Spacer. (2006). "'I Just Want to Be Me Again!': Beauty Pageants, Reality Television and Post-Feminism." *Feminist Theory* 7, no. 2: 255–72.

Banet-Weiser, Sarah, Cynthia Chris, and Anthony Freitas, eds. (2007). *Cable Visions: Television Beyond Broadcasting*. New York: New York University Press.

Banks, Jack. (1996). *Monopoly Television: MTV's Quest to Control the Music*. Boulder: Westview Press.

Barbrook, Richard and Andy Cameron. (1996). "The Californian Ideology." *Science as Culture* 6, no. 1: 44–72.

Barkin, Steve M. (2003). *American Television News: The Media Marketplace and the Public Interest*. Armonk: ME Sharpe.

Barnes, Brooks. (2009a, February 13). "Disney Aims for the Boy Audience with a Cable Channel and a Web Site." *New York Times*.

Barnes, Brooks. (2009b, April 14). "Disney Expert Uses Science to Draw Boy Viewers." *New York Times*.

Barnett, Steven. (1990). *Games and Sets: The Changing Face of Sport on Television*. London: BFI Publishing.

Barnouw, Erik. (1975). *Tube of Plenty: The Evolution of American Television*. New York: Oxford University Press.

Barnouw, Erik. (1979). *The Sponsor: Notes on a Modern Potentate*. Oxford: Oxford University Press.

Barrett, Michèle and Duncan Barrett. (2001). *Star Trek: The Human Frontier*. Cambridge: Polity Press.

Basel Action Network and Silicon Valley Toxics Coalition. (2002). *Exporting Harm: The High-Tech Trashing of Asia*.

Bauder, David. (2007, May 8). "Data Says 2.5 Million Less Watching TV." *Washington Post*.

Bauder, David. (2008, December 31). "Univision Takes 18–49 Demo Crown." *TVNewsday*.

Bauerlein, Mark. (2006, January 6). "A Very Long Disengagement." *Chronicle of Higher Education*: B6–B8.

Baym, Nancy K. (2000). *Tune In, Log On: Soaps, Fandom, and Online Community*. Thousand Oaks: Sage Publications.

Bazalgette, Cary. (1999). "Sabre-Toothed Tigers and Polar Bears." *Media Education Journal*.

Beaty, Bart. (2009). "My Media Studies: The Failure of Hype." *Television & New Media* 10, no. 1: 23–4.

Beaty, Bart and Rebecca Sullivan. (2006). *Canadian Television Today*. Calgary: University of Calgary Press.

Bechelloni, Giovanni. (1995). *Televisione come cultura: I media italiani tra identità e mercato*. Naples: Liguori Editore.

Becker, Anne. (2005, November 1). "Study Says More Kids' Rooms Have TV." *Broadcasting & Cable*.

Becker, Beatriz and Celeste González de Bustamante. (2009). "The Past and Future of Brazilian Television News." *Journalism: Theory, Practice and Criticism* 10, no. 1: 45–68.

Becker, Christine. (2008). *It's the Pictures That Got Small: Hollywood Film Stars on 1950s Television*. Middletown: Wesleyan University Press.

Beckett, Francis. (2004, January 20). "Bad Press, Good Press." *Guardian*.

Behavior Research Center. (2008). *Business News Impact Study*. Donald W. Reynolds National Center for Business Journalism.

Bell, Philip and Theo van Leeuwen. (1994). *The Media Interview: Confession, Contest, Conversation*. Sydney: University of New South Wales Press.

Bellah, Robert N., Richard Madsen, William M. Sullivan, Ann Swidler, and Steven M. Tipton. (1992). *The Good Society*. New York: Alfred A. Knopf.

Beltrán, Luis Ramiro and Elizabeth Fox. (1980). *Communicacíon dominada: Los Estados Unidos en los medios de América Latina*. Mexico City: ILET/Nueva Imagen.

Benaud, Richie. (1984). *Benaud on Reflection*. Sydney: Collins.

Benhabib, Seyla. (2002). *The Claims of Culture: Equality and Diversity in the Global Era*. Princeton: Princeton University Press.

Benn, Linda. (1990). "White Noise: The Long, Sad Story of TV Criticism." *Voice Literary Supplement* 91: 14–16.

Bennett, Jeffrey A. (2006). "In Defense of Gaydar: Reality Television and the Politics of the Glance." *Critical Studies in Media Communication* 23, no. 5: 408–25.

Bennett, Tony, Susan Boyd-Bowman, Colin Mercer, and Janet Woollacott, eds. (1981). *Popular Television and Film*. London: British Film Institute.

Berger, Teresa. (2002). "Of Clare and Clairol: Imaging Radiance and Resistance." *Journal of Feminist Studies in Religion* 18, no. 1: 53–69.

Berila, Beth and Devika Dibya Choudhuri. (2005). "Metrosexuality the Middle Class Way: Exploring Race, Class, and Gender in *Queer Eye for the Straight Guy*." *Genders* 42.

Bernard, Nancy. (1999). *US Television News and Cold War Propaganda, 1947–60*. New York: Cambridge University Press.

Bhagwati, Jagdish. (2002). "Coping with Antiglobalization: A Trilogy of Discontents." *Foreign Affairs* 81, no. 1: 2–7.

Bielby, Denise D. and C. Lee Harrington. (2008). *Global TV: Exporting Television and Culture in the World Market*. New York: New York University Press.

Bignell, Jonathan. (2004). *An Introduction to Television Studies*. London: Routledge.

Bignell, Jonathan and Andreas Fickers. (2008a). "Introduction: Comparative European Perspectives on Television History." *A European Television History*. Eds. Jonathan Bignell and Andreas Fickers. Malden: Wiley-Blackwell, 1–54.

Bignell, Jonathan and Andreas Fickers, eds. (2008b). *A European Television History*. Malden: Wiley-Blackwell.

Bignell, Jonathan and Jeremy Orlebar. (2005). *The Television Handbook*, 3rd edn. London: Routledge.

Bignell, Jonathan, Stephen Lacey, and Madeleine Macmurraugh-Kavanagh, eds. (2000a). *British Television Drama: Past, Present and Future*. Houndmills: Palgrave.

Bignell, Jonathan, Stephen Lacey, and Madeleine Macmurraugh-Kavanagh. (2000b). "Editors' Introduction to Part II." *British Television Drama: Past, Present and Future*. Eds. Jonathan Bignell, Stephen Lacey, and Madeleine Macmurraugh-Kavanagh. Houndmills: Palgrave, 81–92.

"Bi-lingual Hispanics Live with Ease in Both Worlds." (2009, February 16). Center for Media Research.

Billington, Michael and David Hare. (2009, January 19). "The Lame, the Weak and the Godawful." *Guardian*.

Birt, John. (2005, August 27). "TV Needs More Truth and Beauty." *Guardian*.

Bistane, Luciana and Luciane Bacellar. (2005). *Jornalismo de TV*. São Paolo: Editora Contexto.

Black, David A. (2004). "Charactor; or, The Strange Case of Uma Peel." *Cult*

Television. Eds. Sara Gwenllian-Jones and Roberta Pearson. Minneapolis: University of Minnesota Press, 99–114.

Black, Lawrence. (2006). "'Making Britain a Gayer and More Cultivated Country': Wilson, Lee and the Creative Industries in the 1960s." *Contemporary British History* 20, no. 3: 323–42.

Blake, Adrian D., Nicholas C. Lovegrove, Alexandra Pryde, and Toby Strauss. (1999). "Keeping *Baywatch* at Bay." *McKinsey Quarterly*.

Blind, Sofia and Gerd Hallenberger, eds. (1996). *European Co-Productions in Television and Film*. Heidelberg: C. Winter.

Blitz, Roger and Tim Bradshaw. (2009, January 7). "Ladbrokes Ordered to Pull TV Adverts." *Financial Times*.

Bloxham, Mike. (2008, February 20). "A Recession with a Digital Lining?" *MediaPost's TVBoard*.

Blumler, Jay G., ed. (1992). *Television and the Public Interest: Vulnerable Values in West European Broadcasting*. London: Sage Publications.

Boateng, Beatrice A. (2008). "Television Broadcasting in South Africa: Mandates to Serving the Children." *African Media, African Children*. Ed. Norma Pecora, Enyonam Osei-Hwere, and Ulla Carlsson. Gothenburg: NORDICOM, 193–205.

Boddy, William. (1990). *Fifties Television: The Industry and its Critics*. Urbana: University of Illinois Press.

Boddy, William. (1994). "Archaeologies of Electronic Vision and the Gendered Spectator." *Screen* 35, no. 2: 105–22.

Boddy, William. (2005). "In Focus: The Place of Television Studies." *Cinema Journal* 45, no. 1: 79–82.

Bodroghkozy, Aniko. (2001). *Groove Tube: Sixties Television and the Youth Rebellion*. Durham: Duke University Press.

Boellstorff, Tom. (2003). "I Knew it Was Me: Mass Media, 'Globalization,' and Lesbian and Gay Indonesians." *Mobile Cultures: New Media in Queer Asia*. Eds. Chris Berry, Fran Martin, and Audrey Yue. Durham: Duke University Press, 21–51.

Bogle, Donald. (2001). *Primetime Blues: African Americans on Network Television*. New York: Farrar, Strauss & Giroux.

Boiarsky, Greg. (1997). "The Psychology of New Media Technologies: Lessons from the Past." *Convergence* 3, no. 3: 107–26.

Bolaño, César. (2000). *Indústria cultural informaçao e capitalismo*. São Paulo: Editoria Hucitec.

Bolas, Terry. (2009). *Screen Education: From Film Appreciation to Media Studies*. Bristol: Intellect.

Bolm, Adolph. (1942). "Preface IV." *4000 Years of Television: The Story of Seeing at a Distance*. Richard Whittaker Hubbell. New York: GP Putnam's Sons, xiv–xvi.

Bondebjerg, Ib and F. Bono, eds. (1996). *Television in Scandinavia: History, Politics and Aesthetics*. Luton: University of Luton Press.

Bonner, Frances. (2003). *Ordinary Television*. London: Sage Publications.

Borland, John and Evan Hansen. (2007, April 6). "The TV is Dead. Long Live the TV." *Wired*.

Born, Georgina. (2004). *Uncertain Vision: Birt, Dyke and the Reinvention of the BBC*. London: Secker & Warburg.

Bourdieu, Pierre. (1998). *On Television*. Trans. Priscilla Parkhurst Ferguson. New York: New Press.

Bourdon, Jérôme with Juan Carlos Ibáñez, Catherine Johnson, and Eggo Müller. (2008). "Searching for an Identity for Television: Programmes, Genres, Formats." *A European Television History*. Eds. Jonathan Bignell and Andreas Fickers. Malden: Wiley-Blackwell, 101–26.

Bourne, Stephen. (2005). *Black in the British Frame*. New York: Continuum.

Boyd-Barrett, Oliver. (2005). "Journalism, Media Conglomerates and the Federal Communications Commission." *Journalism: Critical Issues*. Ed. Stuart Allan. Maidenhead: Open University Press, 342–56.

Boyle, Raymond and Richard Haynes. (2000). *Power Play: Sport, the Media & Popular Culture*. Harlow: Longman.

Boylen, Louise. (1988, November 22). "Seven Calls Telecast Shots." *Australian Financial Review*. 68.

Bozell, L. Brent. (2003, July 18). "'Queer Eye' for the Straight Girl." *MediaResearch.org*.

Brandt, George W., ed. (1981). *British Television Drama*. Cambridge: Cambridge University Press.

"Bravo's 'Queer Eye' Taking on Weight Issues as well as Style Problems." (2006, August 21). *Reality TV World*.

"Brief *Amici Curiae* of Thirty-Three Media Scholars in Interactive Digital Software Association, *et al*. v. St. Louis County, *et al*." (2003). *Particip@tions: International Journal of Audience Research* 1, no. 1.

Briggs, Asa. (1979). *Sound & Vision*. Oxford: Oxford University Press.

Briggs, Asa. (1980). *The BBC: The First Fifty Years*. Oxford: Oxford University Press.

Briggs, Asa. (1995). *A History of Broadcasting in the United Kingdom Volumes 1–5*. Oxford: Oxford University Press.

Briggs, Asa and Peter Burke. (2003). *A Social History of the Media: From Gutenberg to the Internet*. Cambridge: Polity Press.

British Council. (2009). *Media Studies*.

British Film Institute. (1986). *Open The Box: Take the Money and Run*. Director Mike Dibb. Writer Jane Root.

Britton, Piers D.G. and Simon J. Barker. (2003). *Reading between Designs: Visual Imagery and the Generation of Meaning in* The Avengers, The Prisoner, *and* Doctor Who. Austin: University of Texas Press.

Brock, Adrian. (1995). "An Interview with Kurt Danziger." *Cheiron Newsletter* 13: 4–9.

Brody, Samuel. (1988). "Television: A New Weapon for the New Imperialist War." *Jump Cut* 33: 105–6.

Brookes, Rod. (2002). *Representing Sport*. London: Arnold.

Brown, Mary Ellen, ed. (1990). *Television and Women's Culture: The Politics of the Popular*. Sydney: Currency Press.

Browne, Donald B. (1996). *Electronic Media and Indigenous Peoples: A Voice of Our Own*. Ames: Iowa State University Press.

Brunsdon, Charlotte. (1996). *Screen Tastes: Soap Opera to Satellite Dishes*. London: Routledge.

Brunsdon, Charlotte. (2004). "Lifestyling Britain: The 8–9 Slot on British Television." *Television After TV: Essays on a Medium in Transition*. Eds. Lynn Spigel and Jan Olsson. Durham: Duke University Press, 75–92.

Brunsdon, Charlotte, Julia D'Acci, and Lynn Spigel, eds. (1997). *Feminist Television Criticism: A Reader*. New York: Oxford University Press.

Bryant, Jennings, Paul Comisky, and Dolf Zillmann. (1977). "Drama in Sports Commentary." *Journal of Communication* 26, no. 3: 140–9.

Buckingham, David. (2000). *The Making of Citizens: Young People, News and Politics*. London: Routledge.

Buckingham, David. (2005). "A Special Audience? Children and Television." *A Companion to Television*. Ed. Janet Wasko. Malden: Blackwell, 468–86.

Buckingham, David, Hannah Davies, Ken Jones, and Peter Kelley. (1999). *Chidlren's Television in Britain*. London: British Film Institute.

Buckley, Sean. (2008, November 17). "TelcoTV: TV is Far From Dead." *Telecommunications Online*.

Buonanno, Milly. (1994). *Narrami o diva: Studi sull'immaginario televisivo*. Naples: Liguori.

Buonanno, Milly. (2008). *The Age of Television: Experiences and Theories*. Bristol: Intellect.

Bureau of Labor Statistics. (2008). *Career Guide to Industries – Broadcasting*.

Bürgi, Michael. (2007, September 24). "Leveraging Brain Power." *MediaWeek*: 9.

Burke, David. (2000). *Spy TV*. Hove: Slab-O-Concrete.

Burns, Gary and Robert J. Thompson, eds. (1989). *Television Studies: Textual Analysis*. New York: Praeger.

Burns, Tom. (1977). *The BBC: Public Institution and Private World*. London: Macmillan.

Burrell, Ian. (2008, March 17). "Greg Dyke's Back: The Former BBC Director General on His New Job – And What's Wrong with Britain's Media." *Independent*.

Burton, Graeme. (2000). *Talking Television: An Introduction to the Study of Television*. London: Arnold.

Buscombe, Edward, ed. (1975). *Football on Television*. London: British Film Institute.

Butcher, Melissa. (2003). *Transnational Television, Cultural Identity and Change: When STAR Came to India*. New Delhi: Sage Publications.

Butler, Jeremy G. (2002). *Television: Critical Methods and Applications*, 2nd edn. Mahwah: Lawrence Erlbaum.

Butsch, Richard. (2000). *The Making of American Audiences: From Stage to Television, 1750–1990*. Cambridge: Cambridge University Press.

Buxton, David. (1990). *From* The Avengers *to* Miami Vice: *Form and Ideology in Television Series*. Manchester: Manchester University Press.

Cabletelevision Advertising Bureau. (2007). *Power of the Young*. New York: CAB.

Cairns, Barbara and Helen Martin. (1996). *Shortland Street: Production, Text and Audience*. Auckland: Macmillan.

Cajueiro, Marcelo. (2009, January 16). "TV Globo Novela Heads to India." *Variety*.

Calabrese, Andrew. (2005). "The Trade in Television News." *A Companion to Television*. Ed. Janet Wasko. Malden: Blackwell, 270–88.

Caldwell, John T. (1995). *Televisuality: Style, Crisis, and Authority in American Television*. New Brunswick: Rutgers University Press.

Caldwell, John T. (2008a). *Production Culture: Industrial Reflexivity and Critical Practice in Film and Television*. Durham: Duke University Press.

Caldwell, John T. (2008b). "Screen Practice and Conglomeration: How Reflexivity and Conglomeration Fuel Each Other." *The Oxford Handbook of Film and Media Studies*. Ed. Robert Kolker. New York: Oxford University Press, 327–64.

Campbell, W.J. assisted by Rosemary Keogh. (1962). *Television and the Australian Adolescent: A Sydney Survey*. Sydney: Angus and Robertson.

Cantor, Muriel G. (1971). *The Hollywood TV Producer: His Work and His Audience*. New York: Basic Books.

Cantor, Muriel G. and Joel M. Cantor. (1992). *Prime-Time Television: Content and Control*, 2nd edn. Newbury Park: Sage Publications.

Cantor, Muriel G. and Suzanne Pingree. (1983). *The Soap Opera*. Beverly Hills: Sage Publications.

Carboni, Ornela and Soledad López. (2008, October 29). "¿Un mundo digital, multiples voces?" *Página 12*.

Cardwell, Sarah. (2002). *Adaptation Revisited: Television and the Classic Novel*. Manchester: Manchester University Press.

Carson, Tom. (1983, April 19). "Homage to Catatonia." *Village Voice*: 58.

Casey, Bernadette, Neil Casey, Ben Calvert, Liam French, and Justin Lewis. (2002). *Television Studies: The Key Concepts*. London: Routledge.

Cass, Philip. (2007). "The Never-Ending Story: Palestine, Israel and *The West Wing*." *Journal of Arab and Muslim Media Research* 1, no. 1: 31–46.

Cassidy, Marsha F. (2005). *What Women Watched: Daytime Television in the 1950s*. Austin: University of Texas Press.

Caswell, Lee. (2008). "*CSI* Influence on Video Surveillance." *Law and Order* 56, no. 10: 135–7.

Caughie, John. (1984). "Television Criticism." *Screen* 25, no. 4: 109–21.

Caughie, John. (1991). "Adorno's Reproach: Repetition, Difference and Television Genre." *Screen* 32, no. 2: 127–53.

Caughie, John. (2000). *Television Drama: Realism, Modernism and British Culture.* Oxford: Clarendon Press.

Cavanagh, Richard P. (1992). "The Development of Canadian Sports Broadcasting 1920–78." *Canadian Journal of Communication* 17, no. 3: 301–17.

Celot, Paolo and Fausto Gualtieri. (2007). "TV Viewers' Rights in the European Union." *Broadcasters and Citizens in Europe: Trends in Media Accountability and Viewer Participation.* Eds. Paolo Baldi and Uwe Hasebrink. Bristol: Intellect.

Central Intelligence Agency. (2007). "The *World Factbook* Page on Field Listing, Television Broadcast Stations." cia.gov/libraries/publications/the-world-factbook.

Cervantes, Abel. (2008). "El hospital sin dogmas." *La Tempestad* 59: 70–1.

Chairs, Robert and Bradley Chilton. (2005). *Star Trek Visions of Law & Justice.* Dallas: Adios Press.

Chakravartty, Paula and Katharine Sarikakis. (2006). *Media Policy and Globalization.* Edinburgh: Edinburgh University Press.

Chalaby, Jean K., ed. (2005). *Transnational Television Worldwide: Towards a New Media Order.* London: IB Tauris.

Chang, Yu-li. (2007). "The Role of the Nation-State: Evolution of STAR TV in China and India." *Global Media Journal* 6, no. 10.

Chaplin, Tamara. (2007). *Turning on the Mind: French Philosophers on Television.* Chicago: University of Chicago Press.

Chapman, James. (2002). *Saints & Avengers: British Adventure Series of the 1960s.* London: IB Tauris.

Charters, W. W. (1935). *Motion Pictures and Youth.* New York: Macmillan.

Chartier, Roger. (1989). "Texts, Printings, Readings." *The New Cultural History.* Ed. Lynn Hunt. Berkeley: University of California Press, 154–75.

Chartier, Roger. (2005, December 17). "Le droit d'auteur est-il une parenthèse dans l'histoire?" *Le Monde.*

Chen, Xi. (2007). "Media Lens Revisited: Television and Socio-Political Changes in China." *Journal of Chinese Political Science* 12, no. 2: 167–84.

Children Now. (2007). *Big Media, Little Kids 2: Examining the Influence of Duopolies on Children's Television Programming.*

Chmielewiski, Dawn C. (2002, May 2). "SonicBlue Ordered to Track Digital Video Recorder Users." *Mercury News.*

Chocano, Carina. (2003, August 8). "Queer Eye for the Straight Guy." *Entertainment Weekly.*

Chong, Alberto and Eliana La Ferrara. (2009). *Television and Divorce: Evidence from Brazilian Novelas.* Inter-American Development Bank/Banco Interamericano de Desarrollo Research Department/Departamento de Investigación Working Paper 651.

Chris, Cynthia. (2006). *Watching Wildlife*. Minneapolis: University of Minnesota Press.

Chrisafis, Angelique. (2009, January 5). "Strikes Planned as French Public Sector Broadcasters Ditch Advertising." *Guardian*.

Christenson, Peter and Maria Ivancin. (2006, October). *The "Reality" of Health: Reality Television and the Public Health*. Henry J. Kaiser Foundation.

Christophers, Brett. (2009). *Envisioning Media Power: On Capital and Geographies of Television*. Lanham: Lexington Books.

Claeys, Urbain and Herman van Pelt. (1986). "Introduction: Sport and the Mass Media: Like Bacon and Eggs." *International Review for the Sociology of Sport* 21, nos. 2–3: 95–101.

Clark, Nick. (2008, December 23). "Last Rites for Christmas TV?" *Independent*.

Clarke, Alan and John Clarke. (1982). "'Highlights and Action Replays' – Ideology, Sport and the Media." *Sport, Culture and Ideology*. Ed. Jennifer Hargreaves. London: Routledge and Kegan Paul, 62–87.

Clarkson, Jay. (2005). "Contesting Masculinity's Makeover: *Queer Eye*, Consumer Masculinity, and 'Straight-Acting' Gays." *Journal of Communication Inquiry* 29, no. 3: 235–55.

Classen, Steven D. (2004). *Watching Jim Crow: The Struggles Over Mississippi TV, 1955–1969*. Durham: Duke University Press.

Clifford, Reginald. (2005). "Engaging the Audience: The Social Imaginary of the *Novela*." *Television & New Media* 6, no. 4: 360–9.

Cohan, Steven. (2007). "Queer Eye for the Straight Guise: Camp, Postfeminism, and the Fab Five's Makeovers of Masculinity." *Interrogating Postfeminism: Gender and the Politics of Popular Culture*. Eds. Yvonne Tasker and Diane Negra. Durham: Duke University Press, 176–200.

Cohan, Steven. (2008). *CSI: Crime Scene Investigation*. Houndmills: BFI/Palgrave Macmillan.

Cohen, Stanley and Jock Young, eds. (1973). *The Manufacture of News: Social Problems, Deviance and the Mass Media*. London: Constable.

Coleman, Robin Means, ed. (2002). *Say it Loud! African-American Audiences, Media, and Identity*. New York: Routledge.

Collins, Richard. (1990). *Culture, Communication, and National Identity: The Case of Canadian Television*. Toronto: University of Toronto Press.

Collins, Richard. (1998). *From Satellite to Single Market: New Communication Technology and European Public Service Television*. London: Routledge.

Collins, Richard, Nicholas Garnham, and Gareth Locksley. (1988). *The Economics of Television: The UK Case*. London: Sage.

Collins, Scott. (2008, June 16). "Where TV and the Web Converge, There is Hulu." *Los Angeles Times*.

Collins, Scott. (2009, January 11). "Television is Starting to Look Beyond the 18- to 49-Year Old Demographic." *Los Angeles Times*.

Colombo, Fausto, ed. (2004). *TV and Interactivity in Europe: Mythologies, Theoretical Perspectives, Real Experiences*. Milan: Vita e Pensiero.

Colvin, Geoff. (2007, January 23). "TV is Dying? Long Live TV!" *Fortune*.

Cometta, Louise K. (2005, March 21). "Red Sox Get 'Queer Eye' Makeover." *ESPN.com*.

Common Sense Media. (2009, January). *Broadcast Dysfunction: Sex, Violence, Alcohol, and the NFL*.

Comstock, George and Erica Scharrer. (1999). *Television: What's On, Who's Watching, and What it Means*. San Diego: Academic Press.

Conner, Teri L. and Ronald W. Williams. (2004). "Identification of Possible Sources of Particulate Matter in the Personal Cloud Using SEM/EDX." *Atmospheric Environment* 38: 5305–10.

Conroy, Stephen. (2008). "Foreword." *ABC and SBS: Towards a Digital Future*. Department of Broadband, Communications and the Digital Economy. Australian Government, 1–2.

Consoli, John. (2008, December 30). "TV Retains Marketing Dollars in Hard Times." *New York Times*.

Cook, Jim, ed. (1982). *Television Sitcom*. London: British Film Institute.

Cooke, Lez. (2003). *British Television Drama: A History*. London: British Film Institute.

Cooper, Cynthia A. (1996). *Violence on Television: Congressional Inquiry, Public Criticism and Industry Response – A Policy Analysis*. Lanham: University Press of America.

Corner, John, ed. (1991). *Popular Television in Britain: Studies in Cultural History*. London: British Film Institute.

Corner, John. (1999). *Critical Ideas in Television Studies*. Oxford: Clarendon Press.

Corner, John and Sylvia Harvey, eds. (1996). *Television Times: A Reader*. London: Arnold.

Corris, Peter. (2009). *Deep Water*. Sydney: Allen & Unwin.

Cosell, Howard with Peter Bonventre. (1986). *I Never Played the Game*. Boston: GK Hall.

Creeber, Glen. (1997). *Dennis Potter: Between Two Worlds: A Critical Reassessment*. Houndmills: Palgrave Macmillan.

Creeber, Glen. (2006). *Tele-visions: An Introduction to Television Studies*. Houndmills: Palgrave.

Creeber, Glen, ed., assoc. eds. Toby Miller and John Tulloch. (2001). *The Television Genre Book*. London: British Film Institute.

Cristiani, Mathilde and Jean-Louis Missika. (2007, April 12). "Médias, loisirs." *L'Atelier*.

Crosbie, Tracey. (2008). "Household Energy Consumption and Consumer Electronics: The Case of Television." *Energy Policy* 36, no. 6: 2191–9.

Cunningham, Stuart. (2008). *In the Vernacular: A Generation of Australian Culture and Controversy*. St. Lucia: University of Queensland Press.

Cunningham, Stuart and John Sinclair, eds. (2001). *Floating Lives: The Media and Asian Diasporas*. Lanham: Rowman & Littlefield.

Cunningham, Stuart, Elizabeth Jacka, and John Sinclair, eds. (1996). *New Patterns in Global Television: Peripheral Vision*. Oxford: Oxford University Press.

Curran, James, Michael Gurevitch, and Janet Woollacott, eds. (1977). *Mass Communication and Society*. London: Edward Arnold.

Curti, Lidia. (1988). "Genre and Gender." *Cultural Studies* 2, no. 2: 152–67.

Curtin, Michael. (1995). *Redeeming the Wasteland: Television Documentary and Cold War Politics*. New Brunswick: Rutgers University Press.

Curtin, Michael. (2007). *Playing to the World's Biggest Audience: The Globalization of Chinese Film and TV*. Berkeley: University of California Press.

D'Acci, Julie. (1994). *Defining Women: Television and the Case of Cagney & Lacey*. Chapel Hill: University of North Carolina Press.

Dahlgren, Peter. (1995). *Television and the Public Sphere: Citizenship, Democracy and the Media*. London: Sage.

Danziger, Kurt. (1998). *Constructing the Subject: Historical Origins of Psychological Research*. Cambridge: Cambridge University Press.

Daum, Meghan. (2007, September 16). "Turn On, Tune In, Show Off." *West Magazine*: 17.

"Dave Collins, Creator of 'Queer Eye for the Straight Guy,' to Star in New Ad Campaign for Open." (2004, February 23). *AmericanExpress.com*.

Davies, Máire Messenger. (2001). *"Dear BBC": Children, Television Storytelling and the Public Sphere*. Cambridge: Cambridge University Press.

Davin, Solange and Rhona Jackson, eds. (2008). *Television and Criticism*. Bristol: Intellect.

Davis, Glyn and Kay Dickinson, eds. (2004). *Teen TV: Genre, Consumption, Identity*. London: British Film Institute.

Davis, Glyn and Gary Needham, eds. (2009). *Queer TV: Theories, Histories, Politics*. London: Routledge.

Dawson, Donna. (2009). "Psychologist's Choice." *SKY TV*.

Daza Hernández, Gladys. (1989). *TV.cultura: Los jóvenes en el proceso de enculturación*. Bogotá: Nueva América.

de Leeuw, Sonja, with Alexander Dhoest, Juan Francisco Gutiérrez Lozano, François Heinderyckx, Anu Koivunen, and Jamie Medhurst. (2008). "TV Nations or Global Medium? European Television Between National Institution and Window on the World." *A European Television History*. Eds. Jonathan Bignell and Andreas Fickers. Malden: Wiley-Blackwell, 127–53.

de Moraes, Lisa. (2008, December 30). "At NBC, There is No Script for Success." *Washington Post*: C1.

De Moragas Spa, Miquel and Carmelo Gaitaonandia, eds. (1995). *Decentralisation in the Global Era: Television in Regions, Nationalities and Small Countries of the European Union*. Luton: University of Luton Press.

De Moragas Spa, Miquel, Carmelo Gaitaonandia, and Bernat Lopez, eds.

(1999). *TV on Your Doorstep: Decentralisation Experiences in the Euorpean Union.* Luton: University of Luton Press.

de Pedro, Jesús Prieto. (1999). "Democracy and Cultural Difference in the Spanish Constitution of 1978." *Democracy and Ethnography: Constructing Identities in Multicultural Liberal States.* Eds. Carol J. Greenhouse with Roshanak Kheshti. Albany: State University of New York Press, 61–80.

De Silva, J.P. (2000). *La televisión ha muerto: La nueva producción audiovisual en la era de Internet: La tercera revolución industrial.* Barcelona: Editorial Gedisa.

DeBord, Matthew. (2009, April 16). "YouTube Creates Channel for Movies, TV Shows." *The Wrap.*

Deery, June. (2006). "Interior Design: Commodifying Self and Place in *Extreme Makeover, Extreme Makeover: Home Edition,* and *The Swan.*" *The Great American Makeover: Television, History, Nation.* Ed. Dana Heller. New York: Palgrave Macmillan, 159–73.

DeJesus, Erin. (2008, February/March). "The Gayest Moments in TV History." *Metrosource*: 42–7.

del Pino, Cristina and Fernando Olivares. (2006). *Brand Placement: Integración de marcas en la ficción audiovisual.* Barcelona: Gedisa.

DeLillo, Don. (1986). *White Noise.* London: Picador.

DeLillo, Don. (1987). *End Zone.* Harmondsworth: Penguin Books.

DeLillo, Don. (1994). *Great Jones Street.* New York: Penguin Books.

della Cava, Marco R. (2003, April 2). "Iraq Gets Sympathetic Press Around the World." *USA Today*: 1D.

Deloitte Media & Entertainment. (2007). *Are You Ready for the Future of Media? Highlights from Deloitte's 2007* State of the Media Democracy *Survey.*

Deloitte Touche Tohmatsu Global Technology, Media & Telecommunications Industry Group. (2005). *Television Networks in the 21st Century: Growing Critical Mass in a Fragmenting World.*

DeLorme, Denise E. and Leonard N. Reid. (1999). "Moviegoers' Experiences and Interpretations of Brands in Films Revisited." *Journal of Advertising* 28, no. 2: 71–90.

Department of Broadband, Communications and the Digital Economy. (2008). *ABC and SBS: Towards a Digital Future.* Australian Government.

Desmarais, Sarah L., Heather L. Price, and J. Don Read. (2008). "'Objection, Your Honor! Television is Not the Relevant Authority.' Crime Drama Portrayals of Eyewitness Issues." *Psychology, Crime & Law* 14, no. 3: 225–43.

"Deutsche Welle to Launch Second Asian Channel." (2009, January 7). *Indiantelevision.com.*

Di Mattia, Joanna L. (2007). "The Gentle Art of Manscaping: Lessons in Hetero-Masculinity from the Queer Eye Guys." *Makeover Television: Realities Remodelled.* Ed. Dana Heller. London: IB Tauris, 133–49.

Dines, Gail and Jean M. Humez, eds. (1995). *Gender, Race and Class in Media: A Text-Reader.* Thousand Oaks: Sage Publications.

Dixon, Wheeler Winston, ed. (2004). *Film and Television After 9/11*. Carbondale: Southern Illinois University Press.

Dobuzinskis, Alex. (2009, February 19). "Hollywood Struggles to Find Wealth on the Web." *Reuters*.

Doherty, Thomas. (2008, April 18). "Celluloid Under Siege: The Future of Film Studies After the Digital Deluge." *Chronicle of Higher Education*.

Donohue, Steve. (2009, March 18). "YouTube Still Trying to Monetize Content." *Contentinople.com*.

Dorfman, Ariel and Armand Mattelart. (2000). *Para leer al pato Donald: Comunicación de masa y colonialismo*. Mexico City: Siglo Veintiuno Editores.

Dornfeld, Barry. (1998). *Producing Public Television, Producing Public Culture*. Princeton: Princeton University Press.

Dossi, Joel. (2005, January 3). "The Rise and Fall of *Queer Eye for the Straight Guy*." *AfterElton.com*.

Doughty, Steve. (2009, February 3). "Computers and TV Blamed for Teenage Violence and Casual Sex." *Daily Mail*.

Douglas, Susan J. (2009). "My Media Studies: Thoughts from Susan J. Douglas." *Television & New Media* 10, no. 1: 49–51.

Dow, Bonnie J. (1996). *Prime-Time Feminism: Television, Media Culture and the Women's Movement Since 1970*. Philadelphia: University of Pennsylvania Press.

Dowmunt, Tony, ed. (1993). *Channels of Resistance: Global Television and Local Empowerment*. London: British Film Institute and Channel Four.

Downey, Kevin. (2007a, February 8). "TV Viewing is Up, Despite Online Video." *Media Life*.

Downey, Kevin. (2007b, March 5). "In Their TV Tastes, the Rich are Different." *Media Life*.

Downey, Kevin. (2007c, September 3). "Commercial Zapping Doesn't Matter." *Broadcasting & Cable*.

Downing, John. (2007). "Terrorism, Torture, and Television: *24* in its Context." *Democratic Communiqué* 21, no. 2: 62–82.

Downing, John and Charles Husband. (2005). *Representing "Race": Racisms, Ethnicities and Media*. London: Sage.

Downing, John D.H. (1996). *Internationalizing Media Theory: Transition, Power, Culture: Reflections on Media in Russia, Poland and Hungary 1980–95*. London: Sage Publications.

"Downloading TV Programs, Watching Video and Making Online Phone Calls Represent Biggest One-Year Internet Activity Increase." (2008, November 20). Mediamark Research & Intelligence.

"Downloading TV and Watching Video Online Biggest Gainers in 2008." (2009, January 8). Center for Media Research.

Drummond, Phillip and Richard Paterson, eds. (1985). *Television in Transition*. London: British Film Institute.

Drummond, Phillip and Richard Paterson, eds. (1988). *Television and its Audience*. London: British Film Institute.

Drummond, Phillip, Richard Paterson, and Janet Willis, eds. (1993). *National Identity and Europe: The Television Revolution*. London: British Film Institute.

Dumenco, Simon. (2003, August 11). "The Buysexual Agenda." *New York Magazine*.

Duncan, Andy. (2009, January 16). "Britain's Media Needs Radical Change to Stay on Top." *Daily Telegraph*.

Dunleavy, Trisha. (2005). *Ourselves in Primetime: A History of New Zealand Television Drama*. Auckland: Auckland University Press.

Dyer, Richard, Christine Geraghty, Marion Jordan, Terry Lovell, Richard Paterson, and John Stewart. (1980). *Coronation Street*. London: British Film Institute.

Dyke, Greg. (2005, May 16). "Greg Dyke on Broadcasting." *Independent*.

Dyke, Greg. (2009, April 8). "Grade's ITV is in a Classic Lose–Lose Situation." *Times*.

Dylan, Bob. (2004). *Chronicles: Volume One*. New York: Simon & Schuster.

Earls, Mark. (2003). "Advertising to the Herd: How Understanding Our True Nature Challenges the Ways We Think about Advertising and Market Research." *International Journal of Market Research* 45, no. 3: 311–37.

Eco, Umberto. (1972). "Towards a Semiotic Inquiry into the Television Message." Trans. Paola Splendore. *Working Papers in Cultural Studies* 3: 103–21.

Eco, Umberto. (1983). "Stefano Rosso. A Correspondence with Umberto Eco Genoa–Bologna–Binghamton–Bloomington August–September, 1982, March–April, 1983." Trans. Carolyn Springer. *boundary 2* 12, no. 1: 1–13.

Eco, Umberto. (1987). *Travels in Hyperreality*. Trans. William Weaver. London: Picador.

Eco, Umberto and Deborah Solomon. (2007, November 25). "Media Studies." *New York Times*.

Edgar, David. (2000). "Playing Shops, Shopping Plays: The Effect of the Internal Market on Television Drama." *British Television Drama: Past, Present and Future*. Eds. Jonathan Bignell, Stephen Lacey, and Madeleine Macmurraugh-Kavanagh. Houndmills: Palgrave, 73–7.

Edgecliff-Johnson, Andrew. (2007, October 30). "Targeted Television Ads Three Years Away." *Financial Times*.

Edgerton, Gary R. (2007). *The Columbia History of American Television*. New York: Columbia University Press.

Edgerton, Gary R. and Jeffrey P. Jones, eds. (2008). *The Essential HBO Reader*. Lexington: University Press of Kentucky.

Edgerton, Gary and David Ostroff. (1985). "Sports Telecasting." *TV Genres: A Handbook and Reference Guide*. Ed. Brian G. Rose. Westport: Greenwood Press, 257–86.

Edgerton, Gary R. and Brian G. Rose, eds. (2005). *Thinking Outside the Box: A Contemporary Television Genre Reader*. Lexington: University Press of Kentucky.

Eggerton, John. (2008, December 22). "More Than a 'Toaster with Pictures'." *Broadcasting & Cable*.

Einstein, Mara. (2002). "Disney/ABC's Yellow Campaign: 'TV, So Good, They Named a Frozen Meal After It'." *Television Studies*. Ed. Toby Miller. London: British Film Institute, 39.

El-Nawawy, Mohammed and Adel Iskandar. (2002). *Al-Jazeera: How the Free Arab News Network Scooped the World and Changed the Middle East*. Boulder: Westview Press.

El Shal, Ensirah. (1994). *Satellite Television Channels in the Third World*. Cairo: Dar Al-Fikr.

Elasmar, Michael G., ed. (2003). *The Impact of International Television: A Paradigm Shift*. Mahwah: Lawrence Erlbaum Associates.

Elliott, Philip. (1979). *The Making of a Television Series: A Case Study in the Sociology of Culture*. London: Constable.

Ellis, John. (2000). *Seeing Things: Television in the Age of Uncertainty*. London: IB Tauris.

Ellis, John. (2005, August 18). "Media Studies. Discuss." *BBC News*.

Ellis, John. (2007). *TV FAQ*. London: IB Tauris.

ESPN International. (2009). *ESPN International Fact Sheet*.

Euroconsult. (2008). *Satellite TV Platforms World Survey & Prospects to 2017*. Paris.

European Union. (2007, May 24). *Presenting the New Audiovisual Media Services Without Frontiers Directive: Frequently Asked Questions*. MEMO/07/206.

Evangelista, Benny. (2002, June 4). "SonicBlue Ruling Reversed; Judge Says Order for Data Invalid." *San Francisco Chronicle*: B7.

Evusa, Juliet. (2008). "Children's Television in Kenya: The Need for a Comprehensive Media Policy Regulating Children's Content." *African Media, African Children*. Eds. Norma Pecora, Enyonam Osei-Hwere, and Ulla Carlsson. Gothenburg: NORDICOM, 207–18.

FAIR. (2003a, March 14). "Do Media Know That War Kills?"

FAIR. (2003b, March 18). "In Iraq Crisis, Networks Are Megaphones for Official Views."

FAIR. (2005, April 21). "*Time* Covers Coulter."

Federal Communications Commission. (2007). *Report in the Matter of Violent Television Programming and its Impact on Children*. MB Docket No. 04–261.

Federal Trade Commission. (2000). *Marketing Violent Entertainment to Children: A Review of Self-Regulation and Industry Practices in the Motion Picture, Music Recording & Electronic Game Industries*.

Feng, Charles G.C., T.Y. Lau, David J. Atkin, and Carolyn A. Lin. (2008). "Exploring the Evolution of Digital Television in China: An Interplay

Between Economic and Political Interests." *Telematics and Informatics* (doi:10.1016/j.tele.2008.05.002).

Feuer, Jane. (1995). *Seeing Through the Eighties: Television and Reaganism*. Durham: Duke University Press.

Feuer, Jane, Paul Kerr, and Tise Vahimagi, eds. (1984). *MTM: "Quality" Television*. London: British Film Institute.

Fine, Jon. (2009, April 30). "Why TV Advertising Isn't Dead Yet." *Business Week*.

Fisherkeller, JoEllen. (2002). *Growing Up with Television: Everyday Learning Among Young Adolescents*. Philadelphia: Temple University Press.

Fiske, John. (1987). *Television Culture*. London: Routledge.

Fiske, John and John Hartley. (1980). *Reading Television*. London: Methuen.

Fitzsimmons, Caitlin. (2009, January 20). "Recession Could be 'Good News' for TV, Suggests Deloitte Report." *Guardian*.

Flaherty, Mike. (2008, December 10). "Turner Unveils Television Statistics." *Variety*.

Flanders, Laura. (2001, November 9). "Media Criticism in Mono." *WorkingForChange*.

Fleming, Ian. (1964). *You Only Live Twice*. New York: New American Library.

Fleming, Ian. (1984). *From Russia, With Love*. New York: Berkley Books.

Fleury-Vilatte, Béatrice with Pierre Abramovici. (2000). *La mémoire télévisuelle de la guerre d'Algérie (1962–1992)*. Bry-sur-Marne: Institut National de l'Audiovisuel.

Flumenbaum, David. (2009, March 3). "Why Much of Asia Didn't Hear Sean Penn's 'Homo-Loving' Speech." *Huffington Post*.

Fly, James Lawrence. (1942). "Preface I." *4000 Years of Television: The Story of Seeing at a Distance*. Richard Whittaker Hubbell. New York: GP Putnam's Sons, xi.

Foucault, Michel. (2001). *Dits et Écrits 1954–1988. II: 1967–1988*. Eds. Daniel Defert and François Ewald with Jacques Lagrange. Paris: Quarto Gallimard.

Fowler, Mark S. (1981). "*Reason* Interview: Mark S. Fowler." *Reason.com* (Reason.com/9812/interviews.shtml).

Fowles, Jib. (1999). *The Case for Television Violence*. Thousand Oaks: Sage Publications.

Fox, Adam. (2003, May 23). "Talking About My Generation." *Guardian*.

Fox, Elizabeth. (1997). *Latin American Broadcasting: From Tango to Telenovela*. London: John Libbey.

"Fox Soccer Channel Becomes an Official Nielsen[-]Rated Network Starting October 1." (2008, September 15). *Foxsports.com*.

Fraiman, Susan. (2006). "Shelter Writing: Desperate Housekeeping from *Crusoe* to *Queer Eye*." *New Literary History* 37, no. 2: 341–59.

Franchi, Eric. (2009, March 9). "Live Streaming Continues Momentum with March Madness." *VideoInsider*.

Franklin, Bob, ed. (2001). *British Television Policy: A Reader*. London: Routledge.

Freedman, Des. (2008). *The Politics of Media Policy*. Cambridge: Polity Press.

Freeman, Nick. (1999). "See Europe with ITC: Stock Footage and the Construction of Geographical Identity." *Alien Identities: Exploring Difference in Film and Fiction*. Eds. Deborah Cartmell, I.Q. Hunter, Heidi Kaye, and Imelda Whelehan. London: Pluto Press, 49–65.

French, David and Michael Richards, eds. (2000). *Television in Contemporary Asia*. New Delhi: Sage Publications.

Friedman, James, ed. (2002). *Reality Squared: Televisual Discourse on the Real*. New Brunswick: Rutgers University Press.

Friedman, Wayne. (2008a, April 21). "Study: TV Doesn't Deliver Bang for Carmakers' Buck." *MediaPost*.

Friedman, Wayne. (2008b, October 17). "NBC's All-Encompassing TAMI Measurement." *MediaPost's TV Watch*.

Friedman, Wayne. (2008c, November 17). "TV's New Metrics." *MediaPost's TV Watch*.

Friedman, Wayne. (2008d, November 26). "Digital Lessons TV Should Learn from Music Companies." *MediaPost's TV Watch*.

Friedman, Wayne. (2008e, December 18). "Ipsos: Streaming Video Gaining Ground." *MediaDailyNews*.

Friedman, Wayne. (2009a, January 2). "Full Frontal Television." *MediaPost's TV Watch*.

Friedman, Wayne. (2009b, January 13). "Critics Tour: Fox Favors Limited TV Ad Inventory." *MediaDailyNews*.

Friedman, Wayne. (2009c, January 28). "NATPE Executives Call for Risk-Taking with 'Laser Focus'." *MediaPost's TV Watch*.

Friedman, Wayne. (2009d, February 9). "Pepsi Product Placement Deal Goes Inside Out." *MediaPost's TVWatch*.

Friedman, Wayne. (2009e, February 12). "Net Gains: Nielsen Sizes Up TV Hits Online." *MediaDailyNews*.

Friedman, Wayne. (2009f, March 19). "NBC's Zucker: Digital TV Dollars Improved, but Still a Tiny Base." *TVWatch*.

Friedman, Wayne. (2009g, March 20). "Fallen 'Idol': Employees Sue Show." *MediaDailyNews*.

Friedman, Wayne. (2009h, April 21). "Study: Teens Love Live TV." *MediaDailyNews*.

Fry, Katherine G. (2003). *Constructing the Heartland: Television News and Natural Disaster*. Cresskill: Hampton Press.

Fuenzalida, Valerio. (2000). *La télévision pública en América Latina: Reforma o privatización*. Mexico City: Fondo de Cultura Económica.

Fung, Anthony. (2008). *Global Capital, Local Culture: Transnational Media Corporations in China*. New York: Peter Lang.

Galli, Cecilia. (2005, November 7). "Contra la tele basura." *Ciudad*.

Galperin, Hernan. (2004). *New Television, Old Politics: The Transition to Digital TV in the United States and Britain*. Cambridge: Cambridge University Press.

"Games Will 'Eclipse' Other Media." (2009, January 9). *BBC News*.

Gandy, Oscar H. (1998). *Communication and Race: A Structural Perspective*. London: Arnold; Oxford: Oxford University Press.

Gans, Herbert. (1979). *Deciding What's News*. New York: Pantheon.

García-Canclíni, Néstor. (2001). *Consumers and Citizens: Multicultural Conflicts in the Process of Globalization*. Trans. George Yúdice. Minneapolis: University of Minnesota Press.

Garfinkel, Harold. (1992). *Studies in Ethnomethodology*. Cambridge: Polity Press.

Garnham, Nicholas. (1987). "Concepts of Culture: Public Policy and the Cultural Industries." *Cultural Studies* 1, no. 1: 23–37.

Garrahan, Matthew and Paul Taylor. (2009, January 9). "Flat-Panel HDTV Makers Home in on Internet." *Financial Times*: 14.

Gauntlett, David. (1995). *Moving Experiences: Understanding Television's Influences and Effects*. London: John Libbey.

Geraghty, Christine and David Lusted, eds. (1998). *The Television Studies Book*. London: Arnold.

Gerges, Fawaz A. (2003). "Islam and Muslims in the Mind of America." *Annals of the American Academy of Political and Social Science* 588: 73–89.

Gernsback, Hugo. (1909). "Television and the Telephot." *Modern Electrics*.

Getino, Octavio. (1998). *Cine y televisión en América Latina*. Buenos Aires: Lom.

Geurens, Jean-Pierre. (1989). "The Brainbusters: The Upside Down World of Television Wrestling." *Spectator* 9, no. 2: 56–67.

Gibson, Owen. (2008, August 25). "All That Glitters is Not Gold." *Guardian*.

Gibson, Owen. (2009a, January 1). "ITV and Setanta Hope the Magic of the Cup Will Conjure Viewers." *Guardian*.

Gibson, Owen. (2009b, January 22). "Where Will the Big Bucks Go When the Bubble Bursts?" *Guardian*.

Gibson, Owen. (2009c, March 3). "Setanta and ITV to Renegotiate Sports Rights Deals." *Guardian*.

Giddings, Robert and Keith Selby. (2001). *The Classic Serial on Television and Radio*. Houndmills: Palgrave.

Gillespie, Marie. (1995). *Television, Ethnicity and Cultural Change*. London: Routledge.

Giltz, Michael. (2003, September 2). "Queer Eye Confidential." *LookSmart*.

Ginsburg, Faye D., Lila Abu-Lughod, and Brian Larkin, eds. (2002). *Media Worlds: Anthropology on New Terrain*. Berkeley: University of California Press.

Giordano, Eduardo Luchini and Carlos Zeller Orellana. (1999). *Políticas de televisión*. Barcelona: Icaria Editorial.

Gitlin, Todd. (1983). *Inside Prime Time*. New York: Pantheon.

Glaister, Dan. (2009, March 3). "Jack Bauer Saves the World Again: *24* Goes Carbon Neutral." *Guardian*.

Glenn, Ian. (2008). "Cryptic Rhetoric: The ANC and Anti-Americanization." *Safundi: The Journal of South African and American Studies* 9, no. 1: 69–79.

Goddard, Peter, John Corner, and Kay Richardson. (2007). *Public Issue Television: World in Action, 1963–98*. Manchester: Manchester University Press.

Goetzl, David. (2008, December 30). "ESPN: 'Monday Night Football' Top '08 Cable Series." *MediaDailyNews*.

Goetzl, David. (2009, January 12). "Showtime Campaigns for 'Tara' Cross-Platform." *MediaDailyNews*.

Gold, Glen David. (2001). *Carter Beats the Devil: A Novel*. New York: Hyperion.

Golding, Peter and Graham Murdock, eds. (1997). *The Political Economy of the Media*. London: Edward Elgar.

Goldstein, Jeffrey H. and Brenda J. Bredemeier. (1977). "Socialization: Some Basic Issues." *Journal of Communication* 26, no. 3: 154–9.

Goldstein, Richard. (2003, July 23–29). "What Queer Eye?" *Village Voice*.

Gomery, Douglas. (2008). *A History of Broadcasting in the United States*. Malden: Blackwell.

Gomery, Douglas and Luke Hockley, eds. (2006). *Television Industries*. London: British Film Institute.

Gonsalves, Antone. (2008, December 31). "The Internet's Cool, but TV Remains Ad King." *InformationWeek.com*.

Goode, Ian. (2007). "*CSI: Crime Scene Investigation*: Quality, the Fifth Channel and 'America's Finest'." *Quality TV: Contemporary American Television and Beyond*. Eds. Janet McCabe and Kim Akass. London: IB Tauris, 118–28.

Goodwin, Andrew. (1992). *Dancing in the Distraction Factory: Music Television and Popular Culture*. Minneapolis: University of Minnesota Press.

Goodwin, Andrew and Garry Whannel, eds. (1990). *Understanding Television*. London: Routledge.

Goodwin, Christopher. (2009, January 18). "Latino TV Station Tops US Ratings." *Observer*.

Goonasekera, Anura and Paul S.N. Lee, eds. (1998). *TV Without Borders: Asia Speaks Out*. Singapore: Asian Media Information and Communication Centre.

Gopnik, Adam. (1994). "Read All About It." *New Yorker* 70, no. 41: 84–102.

Gottlieb, Nat. (2006, June 27). "MORE HATS IN THE RING: OLN to Launch Series with ex-HBO Exec's Help." *TigerBoxing.com* (tigerboxing.com/articles/index.php?aid=1001235653).

Götz, M., O. Hoffmann, H.-B. Brosius, C. Carter, K. Chan, St. H. Donald, J. Fisherkeller, M. Frenette, T. Kolbjørnsen, D. Lemish, K. Lustyik, D.C. McMillin, J.H. Walma van der Molen, N. Pecora, J. Prinsloo, M. Pestaj, P. Ramos Rivero, A.-H. Mereilles Reis, F. Saeys, S. Scherr, and H. Zang. (2008). "Gender in Children's Television Worldwide." *Televizion* 21: 4–9.

Gough, Paul. (2008, December 30). "In '08, Big Headlines for Everybody." *Hollywood Reporter*.

Gough, Paul J. (2009, February 12). "Fox Cutting Costs on Road to Daytona 500." *Hollywood Reporter*.

Graf, Philip. (2008). "Foreword." *Lifeblood of Democracy? Learning About Broadcast News*. Cary Bazalgette, John Harland, and Christine James. BFI Research Report for Ofcom, 1.

Graham & Associates. (1999). *Building a Global Audience: British Television in Overseas Markets*. London: Department for Culture, Media and Sport. Broadcasting Policy Division.

Graham, David. (2000, December). "A Declaration of Independence." *Economic Affairs*: 7–12.

Grand Rapids Institute for Information Democracy. (2005). *Violence, Soldier Deaths and Omissions*.

Gray, Ann. (1992). *Video Playtime: The Gendering of a Leisure Technology*. London: Routledge.

Gray, Herman. (1995). *Watching Race: Television and the Struggle for "Blackness"*. Minneapolis: University of Minnesota Press.

Gray, Jonathan. (2008). *Television Entertainment*. New York: Routledge.

Gray, Jonathan, Jeffrey P. Jones, and Ethan Thompson, eds. (2009). *Satire TV: Politics and Comedy in the Post-Network Era*. New York: New York University Press.

Gray, Laura Craig. (2009, February 18). "Media Revolution: Tomorrow's TV." *BBC News*.

Green, Philip. (2005). *Primetime Politics: The Truth About Conservative Lies, Corporate Control, and Television Culture*. Lanham: Rowman & Littlefield.

Greenberg, David. (2003, March 16). "We Don't Even Agree on What's Newsworthy." *Washington Post*: B1.

Greenwald, Arthur. (2009, March 2). "KVVU Rewards Build Ratings, Revenue." *TVNewsday*.

Gregory, Steven. (2007). *The Devil Behind the Mirror: Globalization and Politics in the Dominican Republic*. Berkeley: University of California Press.

Grindstaff, Laura and Joseph Turow. (2006). "Video Cultures: Television Sociology in the 'New TV' Age." *Annual Review of Sociology* 32: 103–25.

Gripsrud, Jostein. (1995). *The "Dynasty" Years: Hollywood Television and Critical Media Studies*. London: Routledge.

Gripsrud, Jostein, ed. (1999). *Television and Common Knowledge*. London: Routledge.

Grossberg, Lawrence, Ellen Wartella, D. Charles Whitney, and J. McGregor Wise. (2005). *Media Making: Mass Media in a Popular Culture*, 2nd edn. Thousand Oaks: Sage Publications.

Grossman, Elizabeth. (2006). *High Tech Trash: Digital Devices, Hidden Toxics, and Human Health*. Washington, DC: Island Press.

Gueorguieva, Vassia. (2007). "Voters, MySpace, and YouTube: The Impact of Alternative Communication Channels on the 2006 Election Cycle and Beyond." *Social Science Computer Review* 26, no. 3: 288–300.

Gunaratne, Shelton A., ed. (2000). *Handbook of the Media in Asia*. New Delhi: Sage Publications.

Guo, Zhenzhi. (1991). *Zhongguo Dianshi Shi*. Beijing: Renmin University Press.

Gurevitch, Michael, Tony Bennett, James Curran, and Janet Woollacott, eds. (1982). *Culture, Society and the Media*. London: Methuen.

Gwenllian-Jones, Sara and Roberta E. Pearson, eds. (2004). *Cult Television*. Minneapolis: University of Minnesota Press.

Hale, Mike. (2008, December 29). "NBC Bridges Series Gaps with Online Minidramas." *New York Times*.

Hall, Stuart. (1980). "Encoding/Decoding." *Culture, Media, Language*. Eds. Stuart Hall, Dorothy Hobson, Andrew Lowe, and Paul Willis. London: Hutchinson, 128–39.

Hall, Stuart and Paddy Whannel. (1964). *The Popular Arts*. London: Hutchinson.

Hallenberger, Gerd and Joachim Kaps. (1991). *Hatten Sie's Gewusst? Die Quizsendungen und Game Shows des deutschen Fernsehens*. Marburg: Jones Verlag.

Hallin, Daniel C. (1989). *The "Uncensored War": The Media and Vietnam*. Berkeley: University of California Press.

Hallin, Daniel C. (1993). *We Keep America on Top of the World: Television Journalism and the Public Sphere*. London: Routledge.

Hamamoto, Darrell Y. (1991). *Nervous Laughter: Television Situation Comedy and Liberal Democratic Ideology*. New York: Praeger.

Hamamoto, Darrell Y. (1994). *Monitored Peril: Asian Americans and the Politics of TV Representation*. Minneapolis: University of Minnesota Press.

Hampp, Andrew. (2008, December 23). "ESPN Rolls Out Interactive Features." *Advertising Age*.

Hanewinkel, Reiner and Gudrun Wiborg. (2008). "Smoking in a Popular German Television Crime Series 1985–2004." *Preventive Medicine* 46, no. 6: 596–8.

Haralovich, Mary Beth and Lauren Rabinovitz, eds. (1999). *Television, History, and American Culture: Feminist Critical Essays*. Durham: Duke University Press.

Harmond, Richard. (1979). "Sugar Daddy or Ogre? The Impact of Commercial Television on Professional Sports." *Screen and Society: The Impact Upon Aspects of Contemporary Civilization*. Ed. Frank J. Coppa. Chicago: Nelson-Hall, 81–108.

Hart, Kylo-Patrick R. (2004). "We're Here, We're Queer – And We're Better Than You: The Representational Superiority of Gay Men to Heterosexuals on *Queer Eye for the Straight Guy*." *Journal of Men's Studies* 12.

Hart, Peter. (2009a, April). "Fear & Favor 2008." *Extra!*: 10–12.

Hart, Peter. (2009b, April). "Speaking Up." *Extra!*: 11.

Hartley, John. (1987). "Invisible Fictions: Television Audiences, Paedocracy, Pleasure." *Textual Practice* 1, no. 2: 121–38.

Hartley, John. (1992). *The Politics of Pictures: The Creation of the Public in the Age of Popular Media*. London: Routledge.

Hartley, John. (1999). *Uses of Television*. London: Routledge.

Hartley, John. (2005). "Is Screen Studies a Load of Old Cobblers? And If So, is That Good?" *Cinema Journal* 45, no. 1: 101–6.

Hartley, John. (2008). *Television Truths*. Malden: Blackwell.

Hartley, John and Alan McKee. (2000). *The Indigenous Public Sphere: The Reporting and Perception of Indigenous Issues in the Australian Media, 1994–1997*. Oxford: Oxford University Press.

Hasebrink, Uwe and Anja Herzog. (2007). "Austria." *Broadcasters and Citizens in Europe: Trends in Media Accountability and Viewer Participation*. Eds. Paolo Baldi and Uwe Hasebrink. Bristol: Intellect.

Hassan, Salah S., Stephen Craft, and Wael Kortam. (2003). "Understanding the New Bases for Global Market Segmentation." *Journal of Consumer Marketing* 20, no. 5: 446–62.

Hastings, Michael. (2003, February 26). "Billboard Ban." *Newsweek*.

Havens, Timothy. (2005). "Globalization and the Generic Transformation of Telenovelas." *Thinking Outside the Box: A Contemporary Television Genre Reader*. Eds. Gary R. Edgerton and Brian G. Rose. Lexington: University Press of Kentucky, 271–92.

Havens, Timothy. (2006). *Global Television Marketplace*. London: British Film Institute.

Hay, James, Lawrence Grossberg, and Ellen Wartella, eds. (1996). *The Audience and its Landscape*. Boulder: Westview Press.

Head, Sydney W., ed. (1994). *Broadcasting in Africa*. Philadelphia: Temple University Press.

Heilemann, John. (1994). "Feeling for the Future: A Survey of Television." *Economist* 330, no. 7850: Survey 1–18.

Hein, Kenneth. (2009, February 25). "Study: TV Ads More Effective Than Ever." *AdWeek*.

Heller, Dana, ed. (2006a). *The Great American Makeover: Television, History, Nation*. New York: Palgrave Macmillan.

Heller, Dana. (2006b). "Before: 'Things Just Keep Getting Better ...'." *The Great American Makeover: Television, History, Nation*. Ed. Dana Heller. New York: Palgrave Macmillan, 1–7.

"Hello, Girls." (2009, March 14). *Economist*: 69.

Helm, Burt. (2007, September 24). "Cable Takes a Rating Hit." *Business Week*.

Hendershot, Heather. (1998). *Saturday Morning Censors: Television Regulation Before the V-Chip*. Durham: Duke University Press.

Henderson, Lesley. (2007). *Social Issues in Television Fiction*. Edinburgh: Edinburgh University Press.

Herman, K. (2000). "Screen Test." *Chain Leader* 5, no. 2: 48.

Herold, Marc W. (2001). "Who Will Count the Dead?" *Media File* 21, no. 1.

Herscovici, Alain. (1999). "Globalización, sistema de redes y estructuración del espacio: Un análisis económico." *Globalización y monopolies en la comunicación en América Latina.* Eds. Guillermo Mastrini and César Bolaño. Buenos Aires: Editorial Biblios, 49–60.

Herskovitz, Marshall. (2007, November 7). "Are the Suits Ruining TV?" *Los Angeles Times:* A21.

Hesmondhalgh, David and Jason Toynbee, eds. (2008). *The Media and Social Theory.* London: Routledge.

Heuring, David. (1988). "Live Sports Broadcasts Require Quick Eyes." *American Cinematographer* 69, no. 10: 86–94.

Heyes, Cressida J. (2007). "Cosmetic Surgery and the Televisual Makeover: A Foucauldian Feminist Reading." *Feminist Media Studies* 7, no. 1: 17–32.

Hibberd, Matthew. (2007). "Conflicts of Interest and Media Pluralism in Italian Broadcasting." *West European Politics* 30, no. 4: 881–902.

Hickethier, Knut. (2008). "Early TV: Imagining and Realising Television." *A European Television History.* Eds. Jonathan Bignell and Andreas Fickers. Malden: Wiley-Blackwell, 55–78.

Hiestand, Michael. (2005, November 28). "Colts–Steelers Likely to be Last Good 'MNF' Game." *USA Today:* 2C.

Higgins, John M. (2006, January 9). "CBS: In the Money." *Broadcasting & Cable.*

Higgins, John M. and Jim Benson. (2005, July 18). "Reality Check." *Broadcasting & Cable.*

Hill, Annette. (2005). *Reality TV: Audiences and Popular Factual Television.* London: Routledge.

Hilliard, Robert L. and Michael C. Keith. (1999). *The Hidden Screen: Low-Power Television in America.* Armonk: ME Sharpe.

Hilmes, Michele. (2005). "The Bad Object: Television in the American Academy." *Cinema Journal* 45, no. 1: 111–17.

Hilmes, Michele, ed. (2007). *NBC: America's Network.* Berkeley: University of California Press.

Hilmes, Michele, ed., assoc. ed. Jason Jacobs (2003). *The Television History Book.* London: British Film Institute.

Himmelstein, Hal. (1984). *Television Myth and the American Mind.* New York: Praeger.

Hirschorn, Michael. (2009, March). "The Future is Cheese." *Atlantic Monthly.*

Hitchcock, John R. (1991). *Sportscasting.* Boston: Focal Press.

Hjarvard, Stig. (2001). *News in a Globalized Society.* Göteborg: NORDICOM.

Hobsbawm, Eric. (1998). "The Nation and Globalization." *Constellations* 5, no. 1: 1–9.

Hobson, Dorothy. (1982). *Crossroads: The Drama of a Soap Opera.* London: Methuen.

Hobson, Dorothy. (2003). *Soap Opera.* Cambridge: Polity Press.

Hodge, Bob and David Tripp. (1986). *Children and Television*. Cambridge: Polity Press.

Hodge, Robert. (1990). *Literature as Discourse: Textual Strategies in English and History*. Cambridge: Polity Press.

Hodges, Lucy. (2009, January 8). "Popular Culture: Why Chinese Students are Getting Creative." *Independent*.

Hogan, Phil. (2004, February 1). "Television Studies." *Observer*.

"Hollywood 2.0." (1997). *Wired* 5, no. 11: 200–15.

Holmes, Su. (2008). *Entertaining Television: The BBC and Popular Television Culture in the 1950s*. Manchester: Manchester University Press.

Holmwood, Leigh. (2008, August 15). "Don't Steal TV Formats, ABC is Warned." *Guardian*.

Holtz, Andrew. (2008, September 25). "Evidence-Based Television." *Oncology Times*: 22.

Hood, Stuart. (1980). *On Television*. London: Pluto Press.

Hood, Stuart, ed. (1994). *Behind the Screens: The Structure of British Television in the Nineties*. London: Lawrence and Wishart.

Horkheimer, Max. (1996). *Critique of Instrumental Reason: Lectures and Essays Since the End of World War II*. Trans. Matthew J. O'Connell *et al*. [unnamed]. New York: Continuum.

Horrocks, Roger and Nick Perry, eds. (2004). *Television in New Zealand: Programming the Nation*. Auckland: Oxford University Press.

Horton, D. and R. Wohl. (1956). "Mass Communication and Para-Social Interaction: Observations on Intimacy at a Distance." *Psychiatry* 19, no. 3: 215–29.

"How Not to Annoy Your Customers." (2008, January 5). *Economist*: 54.

Howard, Steve. (2008). "Children and Media in Muslim Africa: Senegal, Sudan, Nigeria." *African Media, African Children*. Eds. Norma Pecora, Enyonam Osei-Hwere, and Ulla Carlsson. Gothenburg: NORDICOM, 55–67.

Hoynes, William. (1994). *Public Television for Sale: Media, the Market, and the Public Sphere*. Boulder: Westview Press.

Hubbell, Richard Whittaker. (1942). *4000 Years of Television: The Story of Seeing at a Distance*. New York: GP Putnam's Sons.

Huff, Richard. (2003, March 24). "Blitz of War Coverage on Nightly News." *Daily News*.

"Hulu Who?" (2009, February 7). *Economist*: 59.

Hundt, Reed E. and Gregory L. Rosston. (2006). "Communications Policy for 2006 and Beyond." *Federal Communications Law Journal* 58, no. 1: 1–34.

Hung, Wu. (2008). "Television in Contemporary Chinese Art." *October* 125: 65–90.

Hunt, Darnell M. (1997). *Screening the Los Angeles "Riots": Race, Seeing, and Resistance*. Cambridge: Cambridge University Press.

Hunter, Ian. (1988). "Providence and Profit: Speculations in the Genre Market." *Southern Review* 22, no. 3: 211–23.

Hutton, Peter. (2009, January 13). "2009 Promises to be More About Consolidation in Challenging Economic Ties." *Indiantelevision.com.*

Iannucci, Armando. (2008). *Alternative McTaggart Lecture*, Edinburgh Television Festival.

IBM Business Consulting Services. (2006). *The End of Television as We Know It: A Future Industry Perspective.*

"In Focus: Writing for the American Screen." (2006). *Cinema Journal* 45, no. 2: 85–107.

Inglis, K.S. assisted by Jan Brazier. (1983). *This is the ABC: The Australian Broadcasting Commission 1932–1983.* Melbourne: Melbourne University Press.

"Internet Radio and TV Increasingly Popular in Germany." (2009, March 4). *Just4Business.*

"IPL Loses Sponsor as Big TV Pulls Out." (2009, February 13). *Indiantelevision.com.*

Iribarren, María. (2005, November 7). "La mala TV." *Ciudad.*

Irwin, William, Mark T. Conard, and Aeon J. Skoble, eds. (2001). The Simpsons and Philosophy. Chicago: Open Court.

Ishikawa, Sakae, ed. (1996). *Quality Assessment of Television.* Luton: University of Luton Press.

Ito, Masami. (1978). *Broadcasting in Japan.* London: Routledge and Kegan Paul.

Jacks, Nilda and Ana Carolina Escosteguy. (2005). *Comunicação e Recepção.* São Paolo: Hackers.

Jacobs, Jason. (2000). *The Intimate Screen: Early British Television Drama.* Oxford: Oxford University Press.

Jacobs, Jason. (2003). *Body Trauma TV: The New Hospital Dramas.* London: British Film Institute.

James, Meg. (2007, August 27). "Nielsen Ends Separate Latino TV Survey." *Los Angeles Times*: C1, C4.

James, Meg. (2009a, January 23). "Univision, Televisa Settle High-Stakes Lawsuit." *Los Angeles Times.*

James, Meg. (2009b, February 18). "Expectations are Low for CBS' Earnings." *Los Angeles Times.*

Jancovich, Mark and James Lyons, eds. (2003). *Quality Popular Television: Cult TV, the Industry and Fans.* London: British Film Institute.

Jarvis, Robert M. and Paul R. Joseph, eds. (1998). *Prime Time Law: Fictional Television as Legal Narrative.* Durham: Carolina Academic Press.

Jasperson, Amy E. and Mansour O. El-Kikhia. (2003). "CNN and al Jazeera's Media Coverage of America's War in Afghanistan." *Framing Terrorism: The News Media, the Government, and the Public.* Eds. Pippa Norris, Montague Kern, and Marion Just. New York: Routledge, 113–32.

Jayaraman, K. (2009, January 17). "Cable TV Sector Sees Rapid Consolidation and New Competition in 2008." *Indiantelevision.com.*

Jeffery, Nicole. (1989, March 31). "Channel Rebuked for Letter to Voters." *Australian*: 26.

Jenkins, Henry. (1992). *Textual Poachers: Television Fans & Participatory Culture*. New York: Routledge.

Jensen, Elizabeth. (2003, March 18). "Network's War Strategy: Enlist Armies of Experts." *Los Angeles Times*.

Jhally, Sut and Justin Lewis. (1992). *Enlightened Racism: The Cosby Show, Audiences, and the Myth of the American Dream*. Boulder: Westview Press.

"Job 1 at Viacom: Fix MTV's Image." (2009, February 12). *Marketwatch*.

Johnson, Catherine and Rob Turnock, eds. (2005). *ITV Cultures: Independent Television Over Fifty Years*. Maidenhead: Open University Press.

Johnson, Victoria E. (2008). *Heartland TV: Prime Time Television and the Struggle for U.S. Identity*. New York: New York University Press.

Jones, Jeffrey P. (2005). *Entertaining Politics: New Political Television and Civic Culture*. Lanham: Rowman & Littlefield.

Jones, Richard and Arthur Bangert. (2006). "The 'CSI' Effect: Changing the Face of Science." *Science Scope* 30, no. 3: 38–42.

Jowett, Lorna. (2005). *Sex and the Slayer: A Gender Studies Primer for the Buffy Fan*. Middletown: Wesleyan University Press.

Juluri, Vamsee. (2003). *Becoming a Global Audience: Longing and Belonging in Indian Music Television*. New York: Peter Lang.

Kackman, Michael. (2005). *Citizen Spy: Television, Espionage, and Cold War Culture*. Minneapolis: University of Minnesota Press.

Kamalipour, Yahya R., ed. (1999). *Images of the U.S. Around the World: A Multicultural Perspective*. Albany: State University of New York Press.

Kamalipour, Yahya R. and Hamid Mowlana, eds. (1994). *The Mass Media in the Middle East: A Comprehensive Handbook*. Westport: Greenwood Press.

Kamat, Rajesh. (2009, January 12). "From Matinee to Prime Time." *Indiantelevision.com*.

Kapatamoyo, Musonda. (2008). "Children's Television in Zambia: Local vs. Imported." *African Media, African Children*. Eds. Norma Pecora, Enyonam Osei-Hwere, and Ulla Carlsson. Gothenburg: NORDICOM, 219–30.

Kapko, Matt. (2008, April 19). "Push for Mobile TV." *RCR Wireless News*.

Kaplan, E. Ann, ed. (1983). *Regarding Television: Critical Approaches – An Anthology*. Frederick: University Publications of America.

Katigbak M.S., A.T. Church, and T.X. Akamine. (1996). "Cross-Cultural Generalizability of Personality Dimensions: Relating Indigenous and Imported Dimensions in Two Cultures." *Journal of Personality and Social Psychology* 70: 99–114.

Katz, Elihu. (1990). "A propos des médias et de leurs effets." *Technologies et Symboliques de la Communication*. Eds. L. Sfez and G. Coutlée. Grenoble: Presses Universitaires de Grenoble.

Kaufman, Leslie. (2009, March 2). "Car Crashes to Please Mother Nature." *New York Times*.

Kavka, Misha. (2008). *Reality Television, Affect and Intimacy: Reality Matters*. Houndmills: Palgrave.

Keane, Michael, Anthony Fung, and Albert Moran. (2007). *New Television, Globalisation, and the East Asian Cultural Imagination*. Hong Kong: Hong Kong University Press.

Kellner, Douglas. (1982). "Television, Mythology and Ritual." *Praxis* 6: 133–55.

Kellner, Douglas. (1990). *Television and the Crisis of Democracy*. Boulder: Westview Press.

Kellner, Douglas. (1992). *The Persian Gulf TV War*. Boulder: Westview Press.

Kellner, Douglas. (2003). *From 9/11 to Terror War: The Dangers of the Bush Legacy*. Lanham: Rowman & Littlefield.

Kellner, Douglas. (2004). "Media Propaganda and Spectacle in the War on Iraq: A Critique of U.S. Broadcasting Networks." *Cultural Studies Critical Methodologies* 4, no. 3: 329–38.

Kenyon, Andrew, ed. (2007). *TV Futures: Digital Television Policy in Australia*. Melbourne: Melbourne University Press.

Kersta, Noran E. (1942). "Television – An Agency for Preparedness." *Electronics* 15, no. 3: 26–9, 116–24.

"Kids Motivated by TV and Print to Visit Web." (2009, January 1). Center for Media Research.

Kiesling, B.C. (1937). *Talking Pictures: How They are Made, How to Appreciate Them*. Richmond: Johnson Publishing.

Kilborn, Richard and John Corner. (1997). *An Introduction to Television Documentary*. Manchester: Manchester University Press.

King, Barry. (1987). "The Star and the Commodity: Notes Towards a Performance Theory of Stardom." *Cultural Studies* 1, no. 2: 145–61.

Kissinger, Henry. (1999, October 12). "Globalization and World Order." Independent Newspapers Annual Lecture, Trinity College Dublin.

Kitley, Philip. (2001). *Television, Nation, and Culture in Indonesia*. Athens: Ohio University Center for International Studies.

Kittross, John Michael. (1999). "A History of the BEA." *Feedback* 40, no. 2.

Klady, L. (1998, October 19–25). "More B.O. Oracles Take Up Trackin'." *Variety*: 9.

Kline, Stephen. (2003). "Media Effects: Redux or Reductive?" *Particip@tions: International Journal of Audience Research* 1, no. 1.

Kluge, Alexander. (1981–2). "On Film and the Public Sphere." Trans. Thomas Y. Levin and Miriam B. Hansen. *New German Critique* 24–5: 221–37.

"'Knowledge Divide' Must be Narrowed Through Education – UNESCO." (2005, November 3). *UN News Service*.

Kompare, Derek. (2005). *Rerun Nation: How Repeats Invented American Television*. New York: Routledge.

Kraidy, Marwan M. (2005). *Hybridity, or the Cultural Logic of Globalization*. Philadelphia: Temple University Press.

Kraidy, Marwan M. (2007). "Reality Television, Politics, and Democratization in the Arab World." *Negotiating Democracy: Media Transformations in Emerging*

Democracies. Eds. Isaac A. Blankson and Patrick D. Murphy. Albany: State University of New York Press, 179–98.

Kraidy, Marwan M. (2009). "My (Global) Media Studies." *Television & New Media* 10, no. 1: 88–90.

Krieg, Peter. "Docs Go Digital." *Dox* 11 (1997): 12–13.

Kruitbosch, Gijs and Frank Nack. (2008). "Broadcast Yourself on YouTube – Really?" *Human Centered Computing '08 – Association for Computing Machinery*.

Kunkel, Dale, Keren Eyal, Erica Biely, and Edward Donnerstein. (2005). *Sex on TV 2005: A Kaiser Family Foundation Report*. Menlo Park: Henry J. Kaiser Family Foundation.

Kushner, David. (2007, September 20). "TV Enters the Blog World." *Rolling Stone*: 48.

La Ferrara, Eliana, Alberto Chong, and Suzanne Duryea. (2008). *Soap Operas and Fertility: Evidence from Brazil*. Bureau for Research and Economic Analysis of Development Working Paper 172.

"La televisión y el futuro del cine." (2008). *La Tempestad* 59: 67.

Lacarrieu, Mónica. (2000). "Construcción de imaginarios locales e identidades culturales en la mundializcación." Paper presented to the Instituto d'Estudis Catalans.

Lacroix, Celeste and Robert Westerfelhaus. (2005). "From the Closet to the Loft: Liminal License and Socio-Sexual Separation in *Queer Eye for the Straight Guy*." *Qualitative Research Reports in Communication* 6, no. 1: 11–19.

Lafayette, Jon. (2008, December 22). "TV Networks Resist Discount Requests from Advertisers." *AdvertisingAge*.

Lange, André. (2003). "Histoire de la télévision." (histv2.free.fr).

Langer, John. (1998). *Tabloid Television: Popular Journalism and the "Other News."* London: Routledge.

Lasagni, Cristina and Giuseppe Richeri. (1986). *L'altro mondo quotidiano: Tele-novelas TV brasiliana e dintorni*. Rome: Edizioni RAI.

Lasch, Christopher. (1979). *The Culture of Narcissism: American Life in an Age of Diminishing Expectations*. New York: Warner Books.

Latour, Bruno. (1993). *We Have Never Been Modern*. Trans. Catherine Porter. Cambridge: Harvard University Press.

Lavery, David. (2004). "Twin Peaks." *Fifty Key Television Programmes*. Ed. Glen Creeber. London: Arnold, 222–6.

Lavine, Elana and Lisa Parks, eds. (2007). *Undead TV: Essays on* Buffy the Vampire Slayer. Durham: Duke University Press.

Le Bon, Gustave. (1899). *Psychologie des Foules*. Paris: Alcan.

Learmonth, Michael. (2009a, February 17). "Can Hulu Hold Off TV.com?" *AdvertisingAge*.

Learmonth, Michael. (2009b, April 16). "YouTube to Roll Out Film-, TV-Friendly Portal." *AdvertisingAge*.

Lee, Mike. (2007, June 19). "Our Electronic Waste is Piling Up Overseas." *San Diego Union-Tribune*: A1.

Lee, Sherry. (2002, May 12). "Ghosts in the MACHINES." *South China Morning Post Magazine.*

Leets, Laura, Gavin de Becker, and Howard Giles. (1995). "Fans: Exploring Expressed Motivations for Contacting Celebrities." *Journal of Language and Social Psychology* 14, nos. 1–2: 102–23.

Lembo, Ron. (2000). *Thinking Through Television*. Cambridge: Cambridge University Press.

Lemish, Dafna. (2007). *Children and Television: A Global Perspective*. Malden: Blackwell.

Lemmonier, Jonathan. (2008, February 20). "Marketers Losing Confidence in TV." *Advertising Age.*

Lent, John A. (1990). *Mass Communications in the Caribbean*. Ames: Iowa State University Press.

Lever, Janet and Stanton Wheeler. (1993). "Mass Media and the Experience of Sport." *Communication Research* 20, no. 1: 125–43.

Leverette, Marc, Brian L. Ott, and Cara Louise Buckley, eds. (2008). *It's not TV: Watching HBO in the Post-Television Era*. New York: Routledge.

Levine, Elana. (2007). *Wallowing in Sex: The New Sexual Culture of 1970s American Television*. Durham: Duke University Press.

Lewis, Gerry. (2001, February 26–March 4). "Think Local When Going Global." *Variety*: 7.

Lewis, Justin. (1991). *The Ideological Octopus: An Exploration of Television & Its Audience*. New York: Routledge.

Lewis, Justin. (2009). "What's the Point of Media Studies?" *Television & New Media* 10, no. 1: 91–3.

Lewis, Justin, Sanna Inthorn, and Karin Wahl-Jorgensen. (2005). *Citizens or Consumers? What the Media Tell Us About Political Participation*. Maidenhead: Open University Press.

Lewis, Justin, Terry Threadgold, Rod Brookes, Nick Mosdell, Kirsten Brander, Sadie Clifford, Ehab Bessaiso, and Zahera Harb. (2004). *Too Close for Comfort? The Role of Embedded Reporting During the 2003 Iraq War: Summary Report*. British Broadcasting Corporation.

Lewis, Leo. (2009, January 2). "Nintendo to Take on Broadcasters with Wii TV." *The Times.*

Lewis, Lisa. (1990). *Gender Politics and MTV: Voicing the Difference*. Philadelphia: Temple University Press.

Lightfoot, Liz. (2005, September 8). "Students Mark Down Media and Tourism Degrees." *Daily Telegraph.*

"Lighting Assignment of Olympic Proportions." (1988, September 20). *Australian*: 50–1, 58.

Lindelof, Damon. (2007, November 11). "Mourning TV." *New York Times.*

Lipczynska, Sonya. (2007). "Website Review." *Journal of Mental Health* 16, no. 4: 545–8.

"Listen to the Music." (2008, November 22). *Economist*: 78.

Lithwick, Dahlia. (2008, July 26). "The Bauer of Suggestion." *Slate*.

Livingstone, Sonia and Peter Lunt. (1994). *Talk on Television: Audience Participation and Public Debate*. London: Routledge.

Loechner, Jack. (2007, September 5). "Multi-Tasking Sports Fans See More Ads." *MediaPost*.

Lotz, Amanda D. (2006). *Redesigning Women: Television After the Network Era*. Urbana: University of Illinois Press.

Lotz, Amanda D. (2008). *The Television Will Be Revolutionized*. New York: New York University Press.

Love, Maryann Cusimano. (2003). "Global Media and Foreign Policy." *Media Power, Media Politics*. Ed. Mark J. Rozell. Lanham: Rowman & Littlefield, 235–64.

Low, Valentine. (2009, January 14). "Last British Television Factory Closes." *The Times*.

Lowry, Brian. (2009, January 16). "TV Movies Get New Lease on Life." *Variety*.

Lozano, Juan Francisco Gutiérrez. (2005). *La television en el recuerdo: La recepción de un mundo en blanco y negro en Andalucía*. Málaga: Servicio de Publicaciones Universidad de Málaga/Radio y Televisión de Andalucia.

Lund, Anker Brink and Christian Edelvold Berg. (2009). "Denmark, Sweden and Norway: Television Diversity by Duopolistic Competition and Co-Regulation." *International Communication Gazette* 71, nos. 1–2: 19–37.

Lury, Karen. (2005). *Interpreting Television*. London: Hodder Arnold.

Ma, Eric Kit-wai. (1999). *Culture, Politics, and Television in Hong Kong*. London: Routledge.

McArthur, Colin. (1978). *Television and History*. London: British Film Institute.

MacCabe, Colin. (2008). "An Interview with Stuart Hall, December 2007." *Critical Quarterly* 50, nos. 1–2: 12–42.

McCabe, Janet and Kim Akass, eds. (2007). *Quality TV: Contemporary American Television and Beyond*. London: IB Tauris.

McCarthy, Anna. (2001). *Ambient Television: Visual Culture and Public Space*. Durham: Duke University Press.

McCarthy, Michael. (2004, May 18). "Violence in Iraq Puts Advertisers on Edge." *USA Today*: 2B.

McChesney, Robert W. (2007). *Communication Revolution: Critical Junctures and the Future of Media*. New York: New Press.

McChesney, Robert W. (2009). "My Media Studies: Thoughts from Robert W. McChesney." *Television & New Media* 10, no. 1: 108–9.

McDermott, John. (1969). "A Special Supplement: Technology: The Opiate of the Intellectuals." *New York Review of Books* 13, no. 2.

McDonald, Ian R. and Regina G. Lawrence. (2004). "Filling the 24 × 7 News Hole." *American Behavioral Scientist* 48, no. 3: 327–40.

McDonald, Kevin M. (1999). "How Would You Like Your Television: With or Without Borders and With or Without Culture – A New Approach to Media Regulation in the European Union." *Fordham International Law Journal* 22: 1991–2023.

McGee, Micki. (2005). *Self-Help, Inc.: Makeover Culture in American Life.* New York: Oxford University Press.

McGuigan, Jim. (1996). *Culture and the Public Sphere.* London: Routledge.

Machado, Arlindo. (2003). *A Televisão levada a sério,* 3rd edn. São Paolo: Editora Senac.

McIlwain, Charlton D. (2005). *When Death Goes Pop: Death, Media & the Remaking of Community.* New York: Peter Lang.

McInerney, Jay. (1987). *Ransom.* London: Flamingo.

MacKay, Charles. (n.d.). *Extraordinary Popular Delusions & the Madness of Crowds.* New York: Three Rivers Press.

McKay, Jim. (1991). *No Pain, No Gain? Sport and Australian Culture.* New York: Prentice Hall.

McKay, Jim and Debbie Huber. (1992). "Anchoring Media Images of Technology and Sport." *Women's Studies International Forum* 15, no. 2: 205–18.

McKay, Jim and David Kirk. (1992). "Ronald McDonald Meets Baron de Coubertin: Prime Time Sport and Commodification." *Australian Council on Health, Physical Education and Recreation National Journal* 136: 10–13.

McKee, Alan. (2001). *Australian Television: A Genealogy of Great Moments.* Melbourne: Oxford University Press.

McLean, Gareth. (2009, January 5). "It's Crunch Time: Drama or Reality." *Guardian.*

McLuhan, Marshall. (1974). *Understanding Media: The Extensions of Man.* Aylesbury: Abacus.

McMahon, Jennifer L. (2008). "*24* and the Existential Man of Revolt." *The Philosophy of TV Noir.* Eds. Steven M. Sanders and Aeon J. Skoble. Lexington: University Press of Kentucky, 115–29.

MacMillan, Douglas. (2009, January 11). "Yahoo!'s Next Frontier: Internet TV." *Business Week.*

McNamara, Mary. (2007, August 28). "Film Loses its Feminine Touch." *Los Angeles Times*: E1, E9.

McPherson, Tara. (2008). "'The End of TV As We Know It': Convergence Anxiety, Generic Innovation, and the Case of *24.*" *The Oxford Handbook of Film and Media Studies.* Ed. Robert Kolker. New York: Oxford University Press, 306–26.

McQuail, Denis. (1997). *Audience Analysis.* London: Sage Publications.

McQueen, David. (1998). *Television: A Media Student's Guide.* London: Arnold.

Madianou, Mirca. (2005). *Mediating the Nation: News, Audiences and the Politics of Identity*. London: UCL Press.

Maggio, Frank. (2008, December 12). "The Forest from the TVs." *MediaPost's TVBoard*.

Mair, George. (1988). *Inside HBO: The Billion Dollar War Between HBO, Hollywood, and the Home Video Revolution*. New York: Dodd, Mead.

"Majority of Americans Believe Television Programming is Getting Worse, Yet They're Watching More Than Ever." (2007, September 13). AOL Television and Associated Press.

Malik, Sarita. (2001). *Representing Black Britain: Black and Asian Images on Television*. London: Sage Publications.

Mangan, Lucy. (2008, December 24). "Tinsel and Telly." *Guardian*.

Mankekar, Purnima. (1999). *Screening Culture, Viewing Politics: An Ethnography of Television, Womanhood, and Nation in Postcolonial India*. Durham: Duke University Press.

Manning, Elizabeth. (2006). "Local Content Policy in the Australian Television Industry." *International Journal of Economic Policy Studies* 1, no. 2: 25–43.

Marc, David. (1989). *Comic Visions: Television Comedy and American Culture*. Winchester: Unwin Hyman.

Marcus, Caroline. (2008, November 2). "The Future of TV is Online." *Sydney Morning Herald*.

Marling, Karal Ann. (1994). *As Seen on TV: The Visual Culture of Everyday Life in the 1950s*. Cambridge: Harvard University Press.

Martin, Nicole. (2007, August 29). "TV is Dying, Says Google Expert." *Daily Telegraph*.

Martín-Barbero, Jesús. (2003). "Proyectos de Modernidad en América Latina." *Metapolítica* 29: 35–51.

Martín-Barbero, Jesús and Germán Rey. (1999). *Los ejercicios del ver: Hegemonía audiovisual y ficción televisiva*. Barcelona: Gedisa Editorial.

Masterman, Len, ed. (1984). *Television Mythologies: Stars, Shows and Signs*. London: Comedia.

Mattelart, Armand. (1976). *Multinationales et systèmes de communication*. Paris: Anthropos.

Mattelart, Armand. (1980). *Mass Media, Ideologies and the Revolutionary Movement*. Trans. Malcolm Joad. Brighton: Harvester Press/Atlantic Highlands: Humanities Press.

Mattelart, Armand and Michèle Mattelart. (1990). *The Carnival of Images: Brazilian Television Fiction*. Trans. David Buxton. New York: Bergin and Garvey.

Mattelart, Michèle. (1986). *Women, Media and Crisis: Femininity and Disorder*. London: Comedia.

Mattelart, Michèle (1988). "Can Industrial Culture Be a Culture of Difference? A Reflection on France's Confrontation with the U.S. Model of Serialized Cultural Production." Trans. Stanley Gray and Nelly Mitchell. *Marxism and the Interpretation of Culture.* Eds. Lawrence Grossberg and Cary Nelson. Urbana: University of Illinois Press, 429–44.

Mattos, Sérgio. (2002). *Historía da televisão brasileira: Uma visão econômica, social e política*, 2nd edn. Petrópolis: Editora Vozes.

Maxwell, Richard. (1995). *The Spectacle of Democracy: Spanish Television, Nationalism, and Political Transition.* Minneapolis: University of Minnesota Press.

Maxwell, Richard. (1996). "Out of Kindness and Into Difference: The Value of Global Market Research." *Media, Culture & Society* 18, no. 2: 105–26.

Maxwell, Richard. (2000). "Picturing the Audience." *Television & New Media* 1, no. 2: 135–57.

Maxwell, Richard. (2002, December 20). "Citizens, You are What you Buy." *Times Higher Education Supplement.*

May, Mark A. and Frank K. Shuttleworth. (1933). *The Social Conduct and Attitudes of Movie Fans.* New York: Macmillan.

Mayer, Vicki. (2003). *Producing Dreams, Consuming Youth: Mexican Americans and Mass Media.* New Brunswick: Rutgers University Press.

Mazziotti, Nora. (1996). *La industria de la telenovela: La producción de ficción en América latina.* Buenos Aires: Paidós.

"Media Jobs? Depressing." (2008, December 29). *AdvertisingAge.*

Mediamark Research & Intelligence (2008, December 16). *Kids Intelligence.*

Meehan, Eileen R. (2002). "Gendering the Commodity Audience: Critical Media Research, Feminism, and Political Economy." *Sex & Money: Feminism and Political Economy in the Media.* Eds. Eileen R. Meehan and Ellen Riordan. Minneapolis: University of Minnesota Press, 209–22.

Meehan, Eileen R. (2005). *Why TV is Not Our Fault: Television Programming, Viewers, and Who's Really in Control.* Lanham: Rowman & Littlefield.

Meehan, Eileen R. and Ellen Riordan, eds. (2002). *Sex & Money: Feminism and Political Economy in the Media.* Minneapolis: University of Minnesota Press.

Mehta, Nalin. (2007). "The Great Indian Willow Trick: Cricket, Nationalism and India's TV News Revolution, 1998–2005." *International Journal of the History of Sport* 24, no. 9: 1187–99.

Meier, Klaus V. (1984). "Much Ado About Nothing: The Television Broadcast Packaging of Team Sport Championship Games." *Sociology of Sport Journal* 1, no. 3: 263–79.

Melkote, Srinivas R., Peter Shields, and Binod C. Agrawal, eds. (1998). *International Satellite Broadcasting in South Asia: Political, Economic and Cultural Implications.* Lanham: University Press of America.

Mellencamp, Patricia, ed. (1990). *Logics of Television: Essays in Cultural Criticism.* Bloomington: Indiana University Press.

Mendes de Almeida, Candido José, and Maria Elisa de Araújo, eds. (1995). *As perspectivas da televisão Brasiliera au vivo.* Rio de Janeiro: Imago.

Mermigas, Diane. (2008, December 29). "Hulu CEO: More Global Moves Planned for '09." *Media PostNews Online Media Daily.*

Mickiewicz, Ellen. (1999). *Changing Channels: Television and the Struggle for Power in Russia*, rev. edn. Durham: Duke University Press.

Microsoft. (2009, April). *Europe Logs On: European Internet Trends of Today and Tomorrow*.

Miklos, David. (2008). "El império en peligro." *La Tempestad* 59: 78–9.

Miller, Jeffrey S. (2000). *Something Completely Different: British Television and American Culture*. Minneapolis: University of Minnesota Press.

Miller, Leslie, Kelly Biddle, and Charlie Walter. (2008). "Combining the Best of Television, Forensic Science, and Multimedia Pedagogy: Creating a *CSI* Website." *Proceedings of World Conference on Educational Multimedia, Hypermedia and Telecommunications 2008*. Chesapeake: AACE, 766–70.

Miller, Martin. (2007, February 14). "'24' and 'Lost' Get Symposium on Torture." *Seattle Times*.

Miller, Toby. (1997). *The Avengers*. London: British Film Institute.

Miller, Toby. (1999). "Television and Citizenship: A New International Division of Cultural Labor?" *Communication, Citizenship, and Social Policy: Rethinking the Limits of the Welfare State*. Eds. Andrew Calabrese and Jean-Claude Burgelman. Lanham: Rowman & Littlefield, 279–92.

Miller, Toby. (2001a). *SportSex*. Philadelphia: Temple University Press.

Miller, Toby. (2001b). "The Action Series." *The Television Genre Book*. Ed. Glen Creeber, Assoc. Eds. Toby Miller and John Tulloch. London: British Film Institute, 17–21.

Miller, Toby, ed. (2002). *Television Studies*. London: British Film Institute.

Miller, Toby. (2003a). *SpyScreen: Espionage on Film and TV from the 1930s to the 1960s*. Oxford: Oxford University Press.

Miller, Toby, ed. (2003b). *Television: Critical Concepts in Media and Cultural Studies* (5 vols.). London: Routledge.

Miller, Toby. (2005). "Hollywood, Cultural Policy Citadel." *Understanding Film: Marxist Perspectives*. Ed. Mike Wayne. London: Pluto Press, 182–93.

Miller, Toby. (2006). "US Journalism: Servant of the Nation, Scourge of the Truth?" *Conflict, Terrorism and the Media in Asia*. Ed. Benjamin Cole. London: Routledge, 5–22.

Miller, Toby. (2007). *Cultural Citizenship: Cosmopolitanism, Consumerism, and Television in a Neoliberal Age*. Philadelphia: Temple University Press.

Miller, Toby. (2008). *Makeover Nation: The United States of Reinvention*. Columbus: Ohio State University Press.

Miller, Toby, Nitin Govil, John McMurria, and Ting Wang. (2005). *Global Hollywood 2*. London: British Film Institute.

Miller, Toby, David Rowe, Jim McKay, and Geoffrey Lawrence. (2001). *Globalization and Sport: Playing the World*. London: Sage.

Miller, Toby, David Rowe, Jim McKay, and Geoffrey Lawrence. (2003). "The Over-Production of US Sports and the New International Division of Cultural Labor." *International Review for the Sociology of Sport* 38, no. 4: 427–40.

Millerson, Gerald. (1990). *The Technique of Television Production*, 12th edn. London: Focal Press.

Mills, C. Wright. (1970). *Power, Politics and People: The Collected Essays of C. Wright Mills*. Ed. Irving Louis Horowitz. New York: Oxford University Press.

Minogue, Kenneth. (1994, November 25). "Philosophy." *Times Literary Supplement*: 27–8.

Minow, Newton. (1971). "The Broadcasters are Public Trustees." *Radio & Television: Readings in the Mass Media*. Eds. Allen Kirschener and Linda Kirschener. New York: Odyssey Press, 207–17.

Minow, Newton N. (2001, May 9). "Television, More Vast than Ever, Turns Toxic." *USA Today*: 15A.

Minow, Newton N. and Fred H. Cate. (2003). "Revisiting the Vast Wasteland." *Federal Communications Law Journal* 55: 407–40.

Missika, Jean-Louis. (2006). *La fin de la télévision*. Paris: Seuil.

Mitell, Jason. (2004). *Genre and Television: From Cop Shows to Cartoons in American Culture*. New York: Routledge.

Modleski, Tania. (1984). *Loving with a Vengeance: Mass-Produced Fantasies for Women*. New York: Methuen.

Mooney, Chris. (2005). *The Republican War on Science*. New York: Basic Books.

Moorti, Sujata. (2001). *The Color of Rape: Gender and Race in Television's Public Spheres*. Albany: State University of New York Press.

Moorti, Sujata. (2007). "Imaginary Homes, Transplanted Traditions: The Transnational Optic and the Production of Tradition in Indian Television." *Journal of Creative Communications* 2, nos. 1–2: 1–21.

Moran, Albert. (1982). *Making a TV Series: The Bellamy Project*. Sydney: Currency Press.

Moran, Albert. (1985). *Images & Industry: Television Drama Production in Australia*. Sydney: Currency Press.

Moran, Albert. (1989). "Crime, Romance, History: Television Drama." *The Australian Screen*. Eds. Albert Moran and Tom O'Regan. Ringwood: Penguin Books, 236–55.

Moran, Albert. (1998). *Copycat TV: Globalisation, Program Formats and Cultural Identity*. Luton: University of Luton Press.

Moran, Albert and Michael Keane, eds. (2004). *Television Across Asia: Television Industries, Programme Formats and Globalization*. London: RoutledgeCurzon.

Moran, Albert with Justin Malbon. (2006). *Understanding the Global TV Format*. Bristol: Intellect.

Morduchowicz, Roxana. (2008). *La generación multimedia: Significados, consumos y prácticas culturales de los jóvenes*. Buenos Aires: Paidós.

Moring, Inka Salovaara. (2009, February 15). Personal communication.

Morley, David. (1980). *The Nationwide Audience*. London: British Film Institute.

Morley, David. (1992). *Television, Audiences and Cultural Studies*. London: Routledge.

Morley, David. (2007). *Media, Modernity and Technology: The Geography of the New*. London: Routledge.

Morris, Barbra and Joel Nydahl. (1985). "Sports Spectacle as Drama: Image, Language and Technology." *Journal of Popular Culture* 18, no. 4: 101–10.

Morris, Eugene. (2007, September 11). "The Evolution of Targeting the Black Audience." *AdvertisingAge*.

Morris, Jeremy. (2007). "Drinking to the Nation: Russian Television Advertising and Cultural Differentiation." *Europe–Asia Studies* 59, no. 8: 1387–403.

Morris, Meaghan. (1990). "The Banality of Cultural Studies." *Logics of Television: Essays in Cultural Criticism*. Ed. Patricia Mellencamp. Bloomington: Indiana University Press, 14–43.

Morrison, David. (1998). *The Search for a Method: Focus Groups and the Development of Mass Communications Research*. Luton: University of Luton Press.

Morrison, Nick. (2008, August 15). "Mediaocre?" *Times Educational Supplement*: 8.

Morse, Margaret. (1983). "Sport on Television: Replay and Display." *Regarding Television*. Ed. E. Ann Kaplan. Los Angeles: AFI, 44–66.

Mosco, Vincent. (2004). *The Digital Sublime: Myth, Power, and Cyberspace*. Cambridge: MIT Press.

Moses, Asher. (2009, January 9). "TV or Not TV?" *Sydney Morning Herald*.

"Most Media to Suffer Retrenchment in 2009." (2008, December 30). Center for Media Research.

Motion Picture Association of America. (2007). *U.S. Entertainment Industry: 2006 Market Statistics*.

Mowlana, Hamid. (2000). "The Renewal of the Global Media Debate: Implications for the Relationship Between the West and the Islamic World." *Islam and the West in the Mass Media: Fragmenting Images in a Globalizing World*. Ed. Kai Hafez. Cresskill: Hampton Press, 105–18.

Mulgan, Geoff, ed. (1990). *The Question of Quality*. London: British Film Institute.

Mullen, Megan. (2003). *The Rise of Cable Programming in the United States: Revolution or Evolution?* Austin: University of Texas Press.

Mullen, Megan. (2008). *Television in the Multichannel Age: A Brief History of Cable Television*. Malden: Blackwell.

Munson, Wayne. (1993). *All Talk: The Talkshow in Media Culture*. Philadelphia: Temple University Press.

Murdoch, Rupert. (1989, March 25). "Freedom in Broadcasting." MacTaggart Lecture. Edinburgh Television Festival.

Murray, Susan. (2005). *Hitch Your Antenna to the Stars: Early Television and Broadcast Stardom*. New York: Routledge.

Murrow, Edward R. (1958, October 15). Speech to the Radio–Television News Directors Association, Chicago.

"My Media Studies." (2009). *Television & New Media* 10, no. 1.

Nadel, Alan. (2005). *Television in Black-and-White America: Race and National Identity*. Lawrence: University Press of Kansas.

Nader, Laura. (1972). "Up the Anthropologist – Perspectives Gained from Studying Up." *Reinventing Anthropology*. Ed. Dell H. Hymes. New York: Pantheon Books, 284–311.

Naficy, Hamid. (1993). *The Making of Exile Cultures: Iranian Television in Los Angeles*. Minneapolis: University of Minnesota Press.

National Association of Hispanic Journalists. (2006). *Network Brownout Report: The Portrayal of Latinos and Latino Issues on Network Television News, 2005*.

National Grid. (2006). *The Power Behind the World Cup!*

Navar, Murgesh. (2008, June 30). "The New TV Ecosystem." *Media Post's Video Insider*.

Neale, Steve and Frank Krutnik. (1990). *Popular Film and Television Comedy*. London: Routledge.

Neff, Jack. (2009, February 23). "Guess Which Medium is as Effective as Ever: TV." *AdvertisingAge*.

Negri, Antonio. (2007). *goodbye mister socialism*. Paris: Seuil.

Negrine, Ralph and Stylianos Papathanassopoulos. (1990). *The Internationalisation of Television*. London: Pinter Publishers.

Nelson, Joyce. (1992). *The Perfect Machine: Television and the Bomb*. Philadelphia: New Society.

Nelson, Robin. (1997). *TV Drama in Transition*. Houndmills: Macmillan.

Newcomb, Horace. (1974). *TV: The Most Popular Art*. Garden City: Anchor Press/Doubleday.

Newcomb, Horace. (1986). "American Television Criticism, 1970–1985." *Critical Studies in Mass Communication* 3, no. 2: 217–28.

Newcomb, Horace, ed. (1997). *Encyclopedia of Television*. Chicago: Fitzroy-Dearborn.

Newcomb, Horace, ed. (2000a). *Television: The Critical View*, 6th edn. New York: Oxford University Press.

Newcomb, Horace. (2000b). "Preface to the Sixth Edition." *Television: The Critical View*, 6th edn. New York: Oxford University Press, xi–xii.

Newcomb, Horace. (2005). "Studying Television: Same Questions, Different Contexts." *Cinema Journal* 45, no. 1: 107–11.

Newcomb, Horace. (2009). "My Media Studies = My TV ..." *Television & New Media* 10, no. 1: 117–18.

Newcomb, Horace and Robert S. Alley. (1983). *The Producer's Medium: Conversations with Creators of American TV*. New York: Oxford University Press.

Newcomb, Horace and Paul M. Hirsch. (1983). "Television as a Cultural Forum: Implications for Research." *Quarterly Review of Film Studies* 8, no. 3: 45–55.

Nielsen. (2008). *Nielsen's Three Screen Report: Television, Internet and Mobile in the U.S.*

"Nielsen Media Research Reports Television's Popularity is Still Growing." (2006, September 21). Nielsen Media Research.

"Nielsen Reports Growth of 4.4% in Asian and 4.3% in Hispanic U.S. Households for 2008–2009 Television Season." (2008, August 28). Nielsen Media Research.

"Nielsen Reports TV, Internet and Mobile Usage Among Americans." (2008, July 8). Nielsen Media Research.

Nigro, Patricia. (2008, October 29). "La televisión no está difunta." *Página 12*.

Noam, Eli and Joel C. Millonzi, eds. (1993). *The International Market in Film and Television Programs*. Norwood: Ablex.

Nordyke, Kimberly. (2008, December 23). "USA Returns as King of Cable." *Hollywood Reporter*.

Noriega, Chon A. (2000). *Shot in America*. Minneapolis: University of Minnesota Press.

Nutter, Chris. (2004). "Circling the Square." *Gay & Lesbian Review Worldwide* 11, no. 6: 19–22.

O'Day, Marc. (2001). "Of Leather Suits and Kinky Boots: *The Avengers*, Style and Popular Culture." *Action TV: Tough-Guys, Smooth Operators and Foxy Chicks*. Eds. Bill Osgerby and Anna Gough-Yates. London: Routledge, 221–35.

O'Donnell, Hugh. (1999). *Good Times, Bad Times: Soap Operas and Society in Western Europe*. London: Leicester University Press.

O'Donnell, Victoria. (2007). *Television Criticism*. Los Angeles: Sage Publications.

Ofcom. (2007). *Public Service Broadcasting: Annual Report 2007.*

Ofcom. (2008a). *Code on Sports and Other Listed and Designated Events.*

Ofcom. (2008b). *Review of Ofcom's Media Literacy Programme 2004–08.*

Ofcom. (2008c, December 24). *Audience Complaints.*

Ofcom. (2009). *Putting Viewers First: Ofcom's Second Public Service Broadcasting Review.*

Ofcom and Human Capital. (2006). *Premier League Football.*

Olivesi, Stephane. (1998). *Histoire politique de la télévision*. Paris: Harmattan.

O'Malley, Gavin. (2009, February 17). "CBS' TV.com Sees Rise in Viewership." *MediaDailyNews*.

Onwumechili, Chuka. (2007). "Nigeria: Equivocating While Opening the Broadcast Liberalization Gates." *Negotiating Democracy: Media Transformations in Emerging Democracies*. Eds. Isaac A. Blankson and Patrick D. Murphy. Albany: State University of New York Press, 123–42.

Open Society Institute EU Monitoring and Advocacy Program, Network Media Program. (2005). *Television Across Europe: Regulation, Policy and Independence*. Budapest: Open Society Institute.

O'Regan, Tom. (1993). *Australian Television Culture*. Sydney: Allen & Unwin.

Oren, Tasha G. (2004). *Demon in the Box: Jews, Arabs, Politics, and Culture in the Making of Israeli Television*. New Brunswick: Rutgers University Press.

Organisation for Economic Co-operation and Development. (2007). *OECD Communication Outlook 2007*. Paris.

Orwell, George. (1977). *1984: A Novel*. New York: Signet.

Osei-Hwere, Enyonam and Norma Pecora. (2008). "Children's Media in Sub-Saharan Africa." *African Media, African Children*. Eds. Norma Pecora, Enyonam Osei-Hwere, and Ulla Carlsson. Gothenburg: NORDICOM. 15–27.

Osei-Hwere, Patrick V. (2008). "Children's Television Programs in Ghana: The Challenges of Local Production." *African Media, African Children*. Eds. Norma Pecora, Enyonam Osei-Hwere, and Ulla Carlsson. Gothenburg: NORDI-COM, 179–92.

Osgerby, Bill and Anna Gough-Yates, eds. (2001). *Action TV: Tough Guys, Smooth Operators and Foxy Chicks*. London: Routledge.

Ott, Brian L. (2007). *The Small Screen: How Television Equips Us to Live in the Information Age*. Malden: Blackwell.

Ouellette, Laurie. (2002). *Viewers Like You? How Public TV Failed the People*. New York: Columbia University Press.

Ouellette, Laurie and James Hay. (2008). *Better Living Through Reality TV: Television and Post-Welfare Citizenship*. Malden: Blackwell.

Ouellette, Laurie and Susan Murray. (2008). "Introduction." *Reality TV: Remaking Television Culture*, 2nd edn. Eds. Susan Murray and Laurie Ouellette. New York: New York University Press, 1–20.

Ourand, John. (2006, October 9). "On-Demand Demand: Dedicated HBO Sports Category Scoring with Viewers, Network Says." *SportsBusiness Journal*: 13.

"Overview of Passenger Vehicles Advertising on TV During 2008." (2009, March 3). *AdEx India Analysis*.

Owen, Bruce M. (2000). *The Internet Challenge to Television*. Cambridge: Harvard University Press.

Ozersky, Josh. (2003). *Archie Bunker's America: TV in an Era of Change, 1968–1978*. Carbondale: Southern Illinois University Press.

Pace, Stefano. (2008). "YouTube: An Opportunity for Consumer Narrative Analysis?" *Qualitative Market Research: An International Journal* 11, no. 2: 213–26.

Padovani, Cinzia. (2005). *A Fatal Attraction: Public Television and Politics in Italy*. Lanham: Rowman & Littlefield.

Paley, Williams S. (1942). "Preface II." *4000 Years of Television: The Story of Seeing at a Distance*. Richard Whittaker Hubbell. New York: GP Putnam's Sons, xii–xiii.

Palmer, Gareth, ed. (2008). *Exposing Lifestyle Television: The Big Reveal*. Aldershot: Ashgate.

Papathanassopoulos, Stylianos. (2002). *European Television in the Digital Age: Issues, Dynamics and Realities*. Cambridge: Polity Press.

Parente, Donald. (1977). "The Interdependence of Sports and Television." *Journal of Communication* 26, no. 3: 128–32.

Parkin, Frank. (1971). *Class Inequality and Political Order.* London: MacGibbon & Kee.

Parks, Lisa. (2005). *Cultures in Orbit: Satellites and the Televisual.* Durham: Duke University Press.

Parks, Lisa and Shanti Kumar, eds. (2003). *Planet TV: A Global Television Reader.* New York: New York University Press.

Paton, Graeme. (2007a, May 7). "Media Studies Wastes Good Brains, Says Sugar." *Daily Telegraph.*

Paton, Graeme. (2007b, August 15). "Growth in A-Level Students Fuelled by Rise of 'Trendy' Subjects." *Daily Telegraph.*

Paton, Graeme. (2008, November 25). "Media Studies Degrees 'Require Less Work'." *Daily Telegraph.*

Pattenden, Miles. (2008). "The Canonisation of Clare of Assisi and Early Franciscan History." *Journal of Ecclesiastical History* 59: 208–26.

Pavelchak, Mark A., John H. Antil, and James M. Munch. (1988). "The Super Bowl: An Investigation into the Relationship Among Program Context, Emotional Experience, and Ad Recall." *Journal of Consumer Research* 15, no. 3: 360–7.

Peacock, Steven. (2007). *Reading 24: TV Against the Clock.* London: IB Tauris.

Peck, Janice. (1993). *The Gods of Televangelism: The Crisis of Meaning and the Appeal of Religious Television.* Cresskill: Hampton Press.

Peck, Janice. (2008). *The Age of Oprah: Cultural Icon for the Neoliberal Era.* Boulder: Paradigm Publishers.

Penley, Constance. (1997). *NASA/TREK: Popular Science and Sex in America.* New York: Verso.

Peters, Roy. (1976). *Television Coverage of Sport.* Birmingham: Centre for Contemporary Cultural Studies.

Pew Research Center. (2005). *Trends 2005.*

Pew Research Center for the People & the Press. (2005). *The Internet and Campaign 2004.*

Pew Research Center for the People & the Press. (2008). *Internet Overtakes Newspapers as News Source.*

Philo, Greg, ed. (1999). *Message Received: Glasgow Media Group Research 1993–1998.* London: Longman.

Pickard, Anna. (2008, December 17). "TV Drama – A Precise Science." *Guardian.*

Pilger, John. (2003, April 6). "We See Too Much. We Know Too Much. That's Our Best Defense." *Independent.*

Pius XII. (1957). *Miranda Prorsus: Encyclical Letter of His Holiness Pius XII by Divine Providence Pope.*

Polan, Dana. (2006). "Foucault TV." *Flow* 4, no. 7.

Polan, Dana. (2009). *The Sopranos.* Durham: Duke University Press.

Poole, Mike. (1984). "The Cult of the Generalist: British TV Criticism, 1936–83." *Screen* 25, nos. 4–5: 41–61.

Porto, Mauro. (2007). "TV News and Political Change in Brazil: The Impact of Democratization on TV Globo's Journalism." *Journalism: Theory, Practice and Criticism* 8, no. 4: 363–84.

Postman, Neil. (1987). *Amusing Ourselves to Death: Public Discourse in the Age of Show Business*. London: Methuen.

Postrel, Virginia. (1999, August 2). "The Pleasures of Persuasion." *Wall Street Journal*.

Powdermaker, Hortense. (1950). *Hollywood: The Dream Factory: An Anthropologist Looks at the Movie-Makers*. Boston: Little, Brown and Company.

Powell, Lisa M., Glen Szczypka, Frank J. Chaloupka, and Carol L. Braunschweig. (2007). "Nutritional Content of Television Food Advertisements Seen by Children and Adolescents in the United States." *Pediatrics* 120, no. 3: 576–83.

"Precious Little Time." (2008, December 24). Center for Media Research.

Press, Andrea L. (1991). *Women Watching Television: Gender, Class, and Generation in the American Television Experience*. Philadelphia: University of Pennsylvania Press.

Press, Andrea L. and Elizabeth R. Cole. (1999). *Speaking of Abortion: Television and Authority in the Lives of Women*. Chicago: University of Chicago Press.

Preston, Mark. (2007, October 15). "Political Television Advertising to Reach $3 Billion." *CNN.com*.

Price, Monroe E. (1996). *Television, the Public Sphere, and National Identity*. New York: Oxford University Press.

Priest, Patricia Joyner. (1995). *Public Intimacies: Talk Show Participants and Tell-All TV*. Cresskill: Hampton Press.

Probyn, Elspeth. (2008). "Troubling Safe Choices: Girls, Friendship, Constraint, and Freedom." *South Atlantic Quarterly* 107, no. 2: 231–49.

Projanksy, Sarah. (2001). *Watching Rape: Film and Television in Postfeminist Culture*. New York: New York University Press

Project for Excellence in Journalism. (2005). *The State of the News Media: An Annual Report on American Journalism*.

Protzel, Javier. (2005). "Changing Political Cultures and Media Under Globalism in Latin America." *Democratizing Global Media: One World, Many Struggles*. Eds. Robert A. Hackett and Yuezhi Zhao. Lanham: Rowman & Littlefield, 101–20.

Pullen, Christopher. (2007). *Documenting Gay Men: Identity and Performance in Reality Television and Documentary Film*. Jefferson: McFarland.

Putnam, Robert D. (2000). *Bowling Alone: The Collapse and Revival of American Community*. New York: Simon & Schuster.

Puzzanghera, Jim. (2007, May 24). "High-Tech TV Upgrades Will Create Low-Tech Trash." *Los Angeles Times*: C1, C6.

Quality Assurance Agency for Higher Education. (2002). *Communication, Media, Film and Cultural Studies*. Gloucester: Quality Assurance Agency for Higher Education.

Quality Assurance Agency for Higher Education. (2007). *Communication, Media, Film and Cultural Studies*. Gloucester: Quality Assurance Agency for Higher Education.

Rajagopal, Arvind. (2001). *Politics After Television: Hindu Nationalism and the Reshaping of the Public in India*. Cambridge: Cambridge University Press.

Rajagopal, Arvind. (2002, 5 January). "Violence of Commodity Aesthetics." *Economic and Political Weekly*.

Rantanen, Terhi. (2002). *The Global and the National: Media and Communications in Post-Communist Russia*. Lanham: Rowman & Littlefield.

Rash, John. (2009, February 23). "Oscar Night Ratings Improved, but Far from Golden." *AdvertisingAge*.

Rawnsley, Gary D. and Ming-Yeh T. Rawnsley. (2001). *Critical Security, Democratisation and Television in Taiwan*. Aldershot: Ashgate.

Redden, Guy. (2007). "Makeover Morality and Consumer Culture." *Makeover Television: Realities Remodelled*. Ed. Dana Heller. London: IB Tauris, 150–64.

Redmon Wright, Robin. (2007). "*The Avengers*, Public Pedagogy, and the Development of British Women's Consciousness." *New Directions for Adult and Continuing Education* 115: 63–72.

Reeves, Jimmie L. and Richard Campbell. (1994). *Cracked Coverage: Television News, The Anti-Cocaine Crusade, and the Reagan Legacy*. Durham: Duke University Press.

Rendall, Steve and Daniel Butterworth. (2004, May/June). "How Public is Public Radio?" *EXTRA!*: 16–19.

"ReplayTV Users' Lawsuit is Dismissed." (2004, January 13). *Los Angeles Times*: C2.

"The Revolution That Wasn't." (2009, April 25). *Economist*: 68, 70.

Reygadas, Luis. (2002). *Ensamblando Culturas: Diversidad y conflicto en la globalización de la industria*. Barcelona: Gedisa.

Reynolds, Mike. (2008, December 24). "Nielsen Log: Football, Holiday Fare Rule." *Multichannel News*.

Reynolds, Mike. (2009, February 11). "CNN, MTV Among Top 10 Most Social Brands: Vitrue Study." *Multichannel News*.

Rich, Vera. (2003). "The Price of Return." *Index on Censorship* 32, no. 3: 82–6.

Richards, Ed. (2009, January 21). "A Vision for a Digital Age." *Guardian*.

Richardson, Damone and Maria C. Figueroa. (2005). *Basic Cable Television Industry Research and Corporate Profiles*. Industrial & Labor Relations, Cornell University for the Writers Guild of America, East.

Richardson, Kay and Ulrike Meinhof. (1999). *Worlds in Common: Television Discourse in a Changing Europe*. London: Routledge.

Richmond, Will. (2009, January 27). "New Research from Starz on Media Consumption Behaviors." *VideoNuze*.

Richtel, Matt. (2009, February 16). "TV, the Internet's Final Frontier." *International Herald Tribune*.

Riegert, Kristina. (1998). *"Nationalising" Foreign Conflict: Foreign Policy Orientation as a Factor in Television News Reporting*. Edsbruk: Akademitryck.

Riegert, Kristina, ed. (2007). *Politicotainment: Television's Take on the Real*. New York: Peter Lang.

Riegert, Kristina. (2008, December 23). Personal communication.

Riggs, Karen E. (1998). *Mature Audiences: Television in the Lives of Elders*. New Brunswick: Rutgers University Press.

Rincón & Associates. (2004). *Latino Television Study*. National Latino Media Coalition.

Rintels, Jonathan. (2006). *Big Chill: How the FCC's Indecency Decisions Stifle Free Expression, Threaten Quality Television and Harm America's Children*.

Rivero, Yediy M. (2005). *Tuning Out Blackness: Race & Nation in the History of Puerto Rican Television*. Durham: Duke University Press.

Rivero, Yediy. (2008). "A Señora Drinks Café with a Fea in Bogota, the New Hip TV Production Place in Latin America." *Flow* 9, no. 4.

Rizkallah, Elias G. and Nabil Y. Razzouk. (2006). "TV Viewing Motivations of Arab American Households in the US: An Empirical Perspective." *International Business & Economics Research Journal* 5, no. 1: 65–74.

Roberts, Graham and Philip Taylor, eds. (2001). *The Historian, Television and Television History*. Luton: University of Luton Press.

Robinson, James. (2009, January 18). "TV Waits to See a Preview of its New World." *Guardian*.

Robinson, John P. and Steven Martin. (2008). "What Happy People Do?" *Social Indicators Research* 89, no. 3: 565–71.

Robinson, Thomas N., Dina L.G. Borzekowski, Donna M. Matheson, and Helena C. Kraemer. (2007). "Effects of Fast Food Branding on Young Children's Taste Preferences." *Archives of Pediatric and Adolescent Medicine* 161, no. 8: 792–6.

Rocchio, Christopher and Steve Rogers. (2007, January 12). "Bravo Announces 'Queer Eye' to End, Final Episodes to Air This Summer." *Realitytvworld.com*.

Rockwell, Rick. (2007). "Vestiges of Authoritarianism: Monopoly Broadcasting in Central America." *Negotiating Democracy: Media Transformations in Emerging Democracies*. Eds. Isaac A. Blankson and Patrick D. Murphy. Albany: State University of New York Press, 35–50.

Rodriguez, América. (1999). *Making Latino News: Race, Language, Class*. Thousand Oaks: Sage Publications.

Rogers, Steve. (2003, November 20). "New 'Queer Eye' Episode Kicks Off New Episodes Run with Strong Ratings." *Realitytvworld.com*.

Romano, Carlin. (2006, July 28). "What We Have Here is … the International Communication Association." *Chronicle of Higher Education*.

Rose, Brian G., ed. (1985). *TV Genres: A Handbook and Reference Guide*. Westport: Greenwood.

Rose, Marla Matzer. (2001). "Television Industry Profile." *Business.com*.

Rosen, Robert. (1997). "Teaching Film in a Company Town: An Agenda for Discussion in the Digital Age." *Metro* 112: 55–9.

Ross, Andrew. (2009). "The Political Economy of Amateurism." *Television & New Media* 10, no. 1: 136–7.

Ross, Sharon Marie. (2008). *Beyond the Box: Television and the Internet*. Malden: Blackwell.

Roth, Lorna. (2005). *Something New in the Air: The Story of First Peoples Television in Canada*. Montreal: McGill-Queens University Press.

Roth, Philip. (2002). *The Dying Animal*. New York: Vintage International.

Rothenbuhler, Eric W. (1988). "The Living Room Celebration of the Olympic Games." *Journal of Communication* 38, no. 4: 61–81.

Rothenbuhler, Eric W. (1989). "Values and Symbols in Orientations to the Olympics." *Critical Studies in Mass Communication* 6, no. 2: 138–57.

Rowe, David. (1991). "Sport and the Media." *Metro Magazine* 86: 41–7.

Russell, Ben. (2006, November 1). "Flat Screen Televisions 'Will Add to Global Warming'." *Independent*.

Said, Edward. (2003). "Blind Imperial Arrogance: Vile Stereotyping Of Arabs By The U.S. Ensures Years Of Turmoil." *Los Angeles Times* July 20.

Sakr, Naomi. (2001). *Satellite Realms: Transnational Television, Globalization & the Middle East*. London: IB Tauris.

Sakr, Naomi. (2007). *Arab Television Today*. London: IB Tauris.

Sammond, Nicholas, ed. (2005). *Steel Chair to the Heap: The Pleasure and Pain of Professional Wrestling*. Durham: Duke University Press.

Sample, Ian. (2009, March 3). "Children Who Spend Hours in Front of TV are Prone to Asthma." *Guardian*.

"Samsung Holds Lead in Global Television Market in Q2 2007, Says iSuppli." (2007, September 25). *Tekrati.com*.

Sanders, Marlene and Marcia Rock. (1994). *Waiting for Prime Time: The Women of Television News*. Champaign: University of Illinois Press.

Sarat, Austin. (2001). *When the State Kills: Capital Punishment and the American Condition*. Princeton: Princeton University Press.

Sarnoff, David. (1942). "Preface III." *4000 Years of Television: The Story of Seeing at a Distance*. Richard Whittaker Hubbell. New York: GP Putnam's Sons, xiii–xiv.

Sarnoff, David. (2004). "Our Next Frontier … Transoceanic TV." *Mass Communication and American Social Thought: Key Texts, 1919–1968*. Eds. John Durham Peters and Peter Simonson. Lanham: Rowman & Littlefield, 309–10.

"Saturday Morning Network News Shows Growth." (2009, February 12). *TVNEWSER*.

Savorelli, Antonio. (2008). *Oltre la Sitcom: Inagine sulle nuove forme comiche della televisione Americana*. Rome: Franco Angeli.

Sawyer, Terry. (2003, July 22). "Blind Leading the Bland." *PopMatters.com*.

Scardino, Albert. (2005, March 9). "Sun Sets on US Broadcast Golden Age." *Guardian*.

Schechner, Sam and Rebecca Dana. (2009, February 10). "Local TV Stations Face a Fuzzy Future." *Wall Street Journal*.

Schiller, Herbert I. (1969). *Mass Communications and American Empire*. Boston: Beacon Press.

Schiller, Herbert I. (1973). *The Mind Managers*. Boston: Beacon Press.

Schiller, Herbert I. (1976). *Communication and Cultural Domination*. New York: International Arts and Sciences Press.

Schiller, Herbert I. (1989). *Culture, Inc.: The Corporate Takeover of Public Expression*. New York: Oxford University Press.

Schiller, Herbert I. (1991). "Not Yet the Post-Imperialist Era." *Critical Studies in Mass Communication* 8, no. 1: 13–28.

Schlesinger, Philip, Graham Murdock, and Philip Elliott. (1983). *Televising "Terrorism": Political Violence in Popular Culture*. London: Comedia.

Schneider, Cynthia and Brian Wallis, eds. (1988). *Global Television*. New York: Wedge Press/Cambridge: MIT Press.

Schramm, Wilbur. (1973). "Communication Research in the United States." *The Voice of America Forum Lectures 1962: Mass Communication*, 1–9.

Schramm, Wilbur, Jack Lyle, and Edwin B. Parker. (1961). *Television in the Lives of Our Children*. Stanford: Stanford University Press.

"Screen Test." (2007, September 8). *Economist*: 69.

Schudson, Michael and Susan E. Tifft. (2005). "American Journalism in Historical Perspective." *The Press*. Eds. Geneva Overholser and Kathleen Hall Jamieson. Oxford: Oxford University Press, 17–47.

Schwartz, H.M. and Aida Hozic. (2001). "Who Needs the New Economy?" *Salon.com*.

Schwartz, Peter J. (2008, December 17). "On Sports Broadcasting." *Forbes.com*.

Sconce, Jeffrey. (2004). "What If? Charting Television's New Textual Boundaries." *Television After TV: Essays on a Medium in Transition*. Eds. Lynn Spigel and Jan Olsson. Durham: Duke University Press, 93–112.

Scriven, Michael and Monia Lecompte, eds. (1999). *Television Broadcasting in Contemporary France and Britain*. Oxford: Berghahn.

Seiter, Ellen. (1999). *Television and New Media Audiences*. Oxford: Clarendon Press.

Seiter, Ellen, Hans Borchers, Gabriele Kreutzner, and Eva-Marie Wrath, eds. (1989). *Remote Control: Television, Audiences and Cultural Power*. London: Routledge.

Selby, Keith and Ron Cowdery. (1995). *How to Study Television*. London: Macmillan.

Selznick, Barbara J. (2008). *Global Television: Co-producing Culture*. Philadelphia: Temple University Press.

Semati, Mehdi. (2007). "Media, the State, and the Prodemocracy Movement in

Iran." *Negotiating Democracy: Media Transformations in Emerging Democracies*. Eds. Isaac A. Blankson and Patrick D. Murphy. Albany: State University of New York Press, 143–60.

Semuels, Alana. (2009, February 13). "Alcohol, Sex Ads Get Prime TV Time." *Los Angeles Times*.

Sender, Katherine. (2006). "Queens for a Day: *Queer Eye for the Straight Guy* and the Neoliberal Project." *Critical Studies in Media Communication* 23, no. 2: 131–51.

Settel, Irving and William Laas. (1969). *A Pictorial History of Television*. New York: Grosset and Dunlap.

Setzer, Florence and Jonathan Levy. (1991). *Broadcast Television in a Multichannel Marketplace*. Washington: Federal Communications Commission Office of Plans and Policy Working Paper 26.

Shabi, Rachel. (2002, November 30). "The E-Waste Land." *Guardian*.

Shade, Leslie Regan and Nikki Porter. (2008). "Empire and Sweatshop Girl-hoods: The Two Faces of the Global Culture Industry." *Feminist Interventions in International Communication: Minding the Gap*. Eds. Katharine Sarikakis and Leslie Regan Shade. Lanham: Rowman & Littlefield, 241–56.

Shanahan, James and Michael Morgan. (1999). *Television and its Viewers: Cultivation Theory and Research*. Cambridge: Cambridge University Press.

Sharkey, Jacqueline E. (2003, May). "The Television War." *American Journalism Review*.

Sharrock, Wes and Wil Coleman. (1999). "Seeking and Finding Society in the Text." *Media Studies: Ethnomethodological Approaches*. Ed. Paul L. Jalbert. Lanham: University Press of America, 1–30.

Shattuc, Jane M. (1997). *The Talking Cure: TV Talk Shows and Women*. New York: Routledge.

Shields, Mike. (2009, January 8). "Nielsen: Mobile Video Usage Small, but Growing." *MediaWeek.com*.

Shim, Doobo and Dal Yong Jin. (2007). "Transformations and Development of the Korean Broadcasting Media." *Negotiating Democracy: Media Transformations in Emerging Democracies*. Eds. Isaac A. Blankson and Patrick D. Murphy. Albany: State University of New York Press, 161–76.

Shiva, Vandana. (2002). *Water Wars: Privatization, Pollution, and Profit*. Boston: South End Press.

Shubik. Irene. (2000). "Television Drama Series: A Producer's View." *British Television Drama: Past, Present and Future*. Eds. Jonathan Bignell, Stephen Lacey, and Madeleine Macmurraugh-Kavanagh. Houndmills: Palgrave, 42–7.

Silber, John R. (1968). "Television: A Personal View." *The Meaning of Commercial Television: The Texas–Stanford Seminar*. Ed. Stanley T. Donner. Austin: University of Texas Press, 113–39.

Silj, Alessandro, ed. (1988). *East of Dallas: The European Challenge to American Television*. London: British Film Institute.

Silj, Alessandro, ed. (1992). *The New Television in Europe*. London: John Libbey.

Silverstone, Roger. (1985). *Framing Science: The Making of a TV Documentary*. London: British Film Institute.

Simon, Ron. (2005). "The Changing Definition of Reality Television." *Thinking Outside the Box: A Contemporary Television Genre Reader*. Eds. Gary R. Edgerton and Brian G. Rose. Lexington: University Press of Kentucky, 179–200.

Simons, Margaret. (2008, October 23). "Movement at Last on Media Policy." *Creative Economy*.

Simpson, Mark. (2004, June 27). "Forget New Man." *Observer*.

Sinclair, John. (1982). "From 'Modernization' to Cultural Dependence: Mass Communication Studies and the Third World." *Media Information Australia* 23: 5–11.

Sinclair, John. (1999). *Latin American Television: A Global View*. Oxford: Oxford University Press.

Sinclair, John, ed., Graeme Turner, assoc. ed. (2004). *Contemporary World Television*. London: British Film Institute.

Singer, Dorothy G. and Jerome L. Singer. (2001). "Introduction: Why a Handbook on Children and the Media?" *Handbook of Children and the Media*. Eds. Dorothy G. Singer and Jerome L. Singer. Thousand Oaks: Sage Publications, xi–xvii.

Skidmore, Thomas E., ed. (1993). *Television, Politics, and the Transition to Democracy in Latin America*. Washington, DC: Woodrow Wilson Center Press.

Skinner, David. (2003, August 14). "Queer Like Us." *Weekly Standard*.

Slabbert, Sarah, Iske van der Berg, and Rosalie Finlayson. (2007). "Jam or Cheese? The Challenges of a National Broadcaster in a Multilingual Context." *Language Matters* 38, no. 2: 332–56.

Slade, Christina. (2002). *The Real Thing: Doing Philosophy with Media*. New York: Peter Lang.

Slade, Christina and Annabel Beckenham. (2005). "Introduction: Telenovelas and Soap Operas: Negotiating Reality." *Television & New Media* 6, no. 4: 337–41.

Sleznick, Barbara J. (2008). *Global Television: Co-Producing Culture*. Philadelphia: Temple University Press.

Smith, Anthony, ed. (1998). *International History of Television*, 2nd edn. Oxford: Oxford University Press.

Smith, Greg M. (2007). *Beautiful TV: The Art and Argument of* Ally McBeal. Austin: University of Texas Press.

Smith, Matthew J. and Andrew F. Wood, eds. (2003). Survivor *Lessons: Essays on Communication and Reality Television*. Jefferson: McFarland & Company.

Smith-Shomade, Beretta E. (2008). *Pimpin' Ain't Easy: Selling Black Entertainment Television*. New York: Routledge.

Smythe, Dallas. (1954). "Reality as Presented by Television." *Public Opinion Quarterly* 18, no. 2: 143–56.

Smythe, Dallas. (1981). *Dependency Road: Communications, Capital, Consciousness, and Canada.* Norwood: Ablex.

Smythe, Dallas. (2004). "The Consumer's Stake in Radio and Television." *Mass Communication and American Social Thought: Key Texts, 1919–1968.* Eds. John Durham Peters and Peter Simonson. Lanham: Rowman & Littlefield, 318–28.

"Sony to Launch Power-Saving TVs." (2009, January 19). Jiji Press.

Spangler, Todd. (2009, February 19). "ESPN, Discovery are Top 'Must-Keep' Cable Nets: Survey." *Multichannel News.*

Sparks, Robert. (1992). "'Delivering the Male': Sports, Canadian Television, and the Making of TSN." *Canadian Journal of Communication* 17, no. 1: 319–42.

Speranza, Graciela. (2008). "Retrato de familia." *La Tempestad* 59: 72–3.

Spigel, Lynn. (1992). *Make Room for TV: Television and the Family Ideal in Postwar America.* Chicago: University of Chicago Press.

Spigel, Lynn. (2001). *Welcome to the Dreamhouse: Popular Media and Postwar Suburbs.* Durham: Duke University Press.

Spigel, Lynn. (2005a). "Our TV Heritage: Television, the Archive, and the Reasons for Preservation." *A Companion to Television.* Ed. Janet Wasko. Malden: Blackwell. 67–99.

Spigel, Lynn. (2005b). "TV's Next Season?" *Cinema Journal* 45, no. 1: 83–90.

Spigel, Lynn. (2008). *TV by Design: Modern Art and the Rise of Network Television.* Chicago: University of Chicago Press.

Spigel, Lynn and Michael Curtin, eds. (1997). *The Revolution Wasn't Televised: Sixties Television and Social Conflict.* New York: Routledge.

Spigel, Lynn and Denise Mann, eds. (1992). *Private Screenings: Television and the Female Consumer.* Minneapolis: University of Minnesota Press.

Spigel, Lynn and Jan Olsson, eds. (2004). *Television After TV: Essays on a Medium in Transition.* Durham: Duke University Press.

Sreberny, Annabelle. (2008). "The Analytic Challenges of Studying the Middle East and its Evolving Media Environment." *Middle East Journal of Culture and Communication* 1, no. 1: 8–23.

Sreberny, Annabelle and Chris Paterson. (2004). "Introduction: Shouting from the Rooftops: Reflections on International News in the 21st Century." *International News in the 21st Century.* Eds. Chris Paterson and Annabelle Sreberny. London: John Libbey, 3–27.

Sreberny-Mohammadi, Annabelle and Ali Mohammadi. (1994). *Small Media, Big Revolution: Communication, Culture, and the Iranian Revolution.* Minneapolis: University of Minnesota Press.

Stabile, Carol A. and Mark Harrison, eds. (2003). *Prime Time Animation: Television Animation and American Culture.* London: Routledge.

Staiger, Janet. (2005). *Media Reception Studies.* New York: New York University Press.

Standage, Tom. (2006, October 12). "Your Television is Ringing." *Economist.*

Stasi, Linda. (2009, January 26). "'Trust' Issues." *New York Post.*

Steemers, Jeanette. (2004). *Selling Television: British Television in the Global Marketplace.* London: British Film Institute.

Steinberg, Brian. (2009a, February 20). "Is CBS's 'Harper's Island' a New Broadcast Model?" *AdvertisingAge.*

Steinberg, Brian. (2009b, April 13). "Top-Tier Cable Networks Set to Take on Broadcast." *AdvertisingAge.*

Stelter, Brian. (2008, March 27). "A Showtime Experiment: Giving Away Content." *New York Times.*

Stempel, Tom. (1992). *Storytellers to the Nation: A History of American Television Writing.* New York: Continuum.

Stoddart, Brian. (1986). *Saturday Afternoon Fever: Sport in the Australian Culture.* Sydney: Angus and Robertson.

Stokes, Jane. (2000). *On Screen Rivals: Cinema and Television in the United States and Britain.* New York: St. Martin's Press.

Straubhaar, Joseph. (2007). *World Television: From Global to Local.* Thousand Oaks: Sage.

Streeter, Thomas. (1996). *Selling the Air: A Critique of the Policy of Commercial Broadcasting in the United States.* Chicago: University of Chicago Press.

Stutzman, Ellen. (2008, November 3). "Hello Cable." *POV.*

"Subscription Television Sets New Records in Summer 2008." (2008, February 12). ASTRA.

"Subscription TV Goes Over the Top in 2009." (2009, January 12). ASTRA.

Surgeon General's Scientific Advisory Committee on Television and Social Behavior. (1971). *Television and Growing Up: The Impact of Televised Violence.* Report to the Surgeon General, U.S. Public Health Service. Washington, DC: U.S. Government Printing Service.

Sussman, Gerald and John A. Lent, eds. (1998). *Global Productions: Labor in the Making of the "Information Society."* Cresskill: Hampton Press.

Swearingen, Jake and Jeni Chapman. (2008, June 20). "Is DVR the Difference Between U.S. and U.K. TV Markets?" *BNET.COM.*

Sweney, Mark. (2008, December 24). "Pull Out of Project Kangaroo, Broadcasters Told." *Guardian.*

Sydney-Smith, Susan. (2002). *Beyond Dixon of Dock Green: Early British Police Series.* London: IB Tauris.

Szalai, Georg. (2008, December 30). "Who Will the Financial Crisis Hit Next?" *Hollywood Reporter.*

Tancer, Bill. (2009, February 10). "With Hulu, Older Audiences Lead the Way." *Wall Street Journal.*

Tatz, Colin. (1986). "The Corruption of Sport." *Power Play: Essays in the Sociology of Australian Sport.* Eds. Geoffrey Lawrence and David Rowe. Sydney: Hale and Ironmonger, 46–63.

Taylor, Ella. (1989). *Prime-Time Families: Television Culture in Post-War America.* Berkeley: University of California Press.

Taylor, Laurie. (2006). "Culture's Revenge: Laurie Taylor Interviews Stuart Hall." *New Humanist* 121, no. 2.

Teinowitz, Ira. (2008, July 23). "Olympic Deal Sealed: Obama Makes $5 Million Buy." *AdvertisingAge.*

Television Business International. (2008, October/November). *Programme Prices Guide.*

"Television in an Era of Fundamental Change: An Assessment Drawn from the Inaugural Peabody/Loveless Seminar, University of Georgia." (2007).

"Tell Your Local NBC Affiliate You Want to See *Queer Eye for the Straight Guy.*" (2003, August 7). *GLAAD.org.*

Telotte, J.P., ed. (2008). *The Essential Science Fiction Reader.* Lexington: University Press of Kentucky.

Thiel, Simon. (2009, January 14). "ESPN Said to Plan Bid for English Premier League Soccer Rights." *Bloomberg.*

Thomas, Amos Owen. (2001). *Transnational Media and Contoured Markets: Redefining Asian Television and Advertising.* London: Sage Publications.

Thomas, Amos Owen. (2005). *Imagi-Nations and Borderless Television: Media, Culture and Politics Across Asia.* New Delhi: Sage Publications.

Thomasch, Paul. (2009, February 20). "As Advertisers Scrap Deals, TV Faces Cold Spring." *Reuters.*

Thompson, E.P. (1959). "A Psessay in Ephology." *New Reasoner* 10: 1–8.

Thompson, Kristin. (2003). *Storytelling in Film and Television.* Cambridge: Harvard University Press.

Thompson, Mark. (2006, March 22). "BBC 2.0: Why On Demand Changes Everything." Royal Television Society Baird Lecture.

Thompson, Mark. (2009, January 12). "Broadcasting Must Restructure to Survive." *Financial Times*: 11.

Thornham, Sue and Tony Purvis. (2005). *Television Drama: Theories and Identities.* Houndmills: Palgrave Macmillan.

Thornton, Kirby. (2009, March 9). "An Analysis of Playback Viewing of Fall '08 Prime-Time Premieres." *TVBoard.*

Thumin, Janet. (2004). *Inventing Television Culture: Men, Women and the Box.* Oxford: Oxford University Press.

Thussu, Daya Kishan. (2004). "Media Plenty and the Poverty of News." *International News in the 21st Century.* Eds. Chris Paterson and Annabelle Sreberny. London: John Libbey, 47–61.

Thussu, Daya Kishan. (2007). "The 'Murdochization' of News? The Case of Star TV in India." *Media, Culture & Society* 29, no. 4: 593–611.

Timberg, Bernard M. with Robert J. Erler. (2002). *Television Talk: A History of the TV Talk Show.* Austin: University of Texas Press.

TNS Media Intelligence. (2007). *An Analysis of 2007 and 2008 Political, Issue and Advocacy Advertising*.

Torres, César Albarrán. (2008). "Ahí, donde nadie se salva." *La Tempestad* 59: 80–1.

Torres, Sasha, ed. (1998). *Living Color: Race and Television in the United States*. Durham: Duke University Press.

Torres, Sasha. (2003). *Black White and in Color: Television and Black Civil Rights*. Princeton: Princeton University Press.

Toto, Dominic. (2000, August). "Job Growth in Television: Cable Versus Broadcast, 1958–99." *Monthly Labor Review:* 3–14.

Toussaint, Florence. (2007). "La televisión cultural Mexicana." *Flow* 5, no. 14.

Tracey, Michael. (1998). *The Decline and Fall of Public Service Broadcasting*. Oxford: Oxford University Press.

"Tragedy or Farce?" (2009, January 10). *Economist:* 47.

Traugott, Michael W. and Ted Brader. (2003). "Explaining 9/11." *Framing Terrorism: The News Media, the Government, and the Public*. Eds. Pippa Norris, Montague Kern, and Marion Just. New York: Routledge, 183–201.

Tricot, Agnès. (2000). "Screens Without Frontiers": Project to Establish a Database for Television Programs for Use of the Public Television Channels of Developing Countries. UNESCO/URTI.

Tuchman, Gaye. (1979). "Women's Depiction by the Mass Media." *Signs: Journal of Women in Culture and Society* 4, no. 3: 528–42.

Tuchman, Gaye, Arlene Kaplan Daniels, and James Benet, eds. (1978). *Hearth and Home: Images of Women in the Mass Media*. New York: Oxford University Press.

Tudor, Andrew. (1992). "Them and Us: Story and Stereotype in TV World Cup Coverage." *European Journal of Communication* 7, no. 3: 391–413.

Tueth, Michael V. (2005). *Laughter in the Living Room: Television Comedy and the American Home Audience*. New York: Peter Lang.

Tufte, Thomas. (2000). *Living with the Rubbish Queen: Telenovelas, Culture and Modernity in Brazil*. Luton: University of Luton Press.

Tuggle, C.A., Suzanne Huffman, and Dana Rosengard. (2007). "A Descriptive Analysis of NBC's Coverage of the 2004 Summer Olympics." *Journal of Sports Media* 2, no. 1: 54–75.

Tulloch, John. (1990). *Television Drama: Agency, Audience and Myth*. London: Routledge.

Tulloch, John. (2000). *Watching Audiences: Cultural Theories and Methods*. London: Arnold.

Tulloch, John and Manuel Alvarado. (1983). *Doctor Who: The Unfolding Text*. New York: St Martin's Press.

Tulloch, John and Albert Moran. (1986). *A Country Practice: "Quality" Soap*. Sydney: Currency Press.

Tulloch, John and Graeme Turner, eds. (1989). *Australian Television: Programs, Pleasures and Politics*. Sydney: Allen & Unwin.

Tunstall, Jeremy. (1993). *Television Producers*. London: Routledge.

Turner, Graeme. (2005). *Ending the Affair: The Decline of Current Affairs in Australia*. Sydney: University of New South Wales Press.

Turner, Graeme. (2007, May 30). "Another Way of Looking at It." *Australian*.

Turner, Graeme and Stuart Cunningham, eds. (2000). *The Australian TV Book*. Sydney: Allen & Unwin.

Turner, Graeme and Jinna Tay, eds. (2009). *Television Studies After TV: Understanding Television in the Post-Broadcast Era*. London: Routledge.

Turnock, Rob with Alexander Hecht, Dana Mustata, Mari Pajala, and Alison Preston. (2008). "European Television Events and Euro-Visions: Tensions Between the Ordinary and the Extraordinary." *A European Television History*. Eds. Jonathan Bignell and Andreas Fickers. Malden: Wiley-Blackwell, 184–214.

Turow, Joseph. (1989). *Playing Doctor: Television, Storytelling and Medical Power*. Oxford: Oxford University Press.

Turow, Joseph. (2004). "'The Answer is Always in the Body': Forensic Pathology in US Crime Programmes." *The Lancet* 364 Suppl. 1: s54–s55.

Turow, Joseph and Rachel Gans-Boriskin. (2007). "From Expert in Action to Existential Angst: A Half Century of Television Doctors." *Medicine's Moving Pictures: Medicine, Health, and Bodies in American Film and Television*. Eds. Leslie J. Reagan, Nancy Tomes, and Paula A. Treichler. Rochester: University of Rochester Press, 263–81.

Turse, Nick. (2008). *The Complex: How the Military Invades Our Everyday Lives*. New York: Metropolitan Books.

"TV Advertising Worse Than Expected, But Increasing Share." (2009, April 14). *Television Business International*.

Tyndall Report. (2003). *On Aftermath of September 11* (tyndallreport.com/0911. php3).

Umstead, R. Thomas. (2006, March 6). "HBO Plans Knockout Year." *Multichannel News*: 30.

United States Atomic Energy Commission. (1954). *In the Matter of J. Robert Oppenheimer*. Transcript of Hearing Before Personnel Security Board.

Uricchio, William. (2008). "Television's First Seventy-Five Years: The Interpretive Flexibility of a Medium in Transition." *The Oxford Handbook of Film and Media Studies*. Ed. Robert Kolker. New York: Oxford University Press, 286–305.

Vachss, Andrew. (2006). *Mask Market*. New York: Vintage Crime/Black Lizard.

Vachss, Andrew. (2008). *Another Life*. New York: Pantheon.

Valls-Fernández, Federico and José Manuel Martínez-Vicente. (2007). "Gender Stereotypes in Spanish Television Commercials." *Sex Roles* 56, nos. 9–10: 691–9.

van Vuuren, Daan. (2004). "Radio and Television Audiences in South Africa: 1994–2002." *Communicatio* 30, no. 2: 1–23.

Vande Berg, Leah R., Lawrence A. Wenner, and Bruce E. Gronbeck. (1998). *Critical Approaches to Television.* Boston: Houghton Mifflin.

vanden Heuvel, Katrina. (2008, July 21–28). "Just Democracy." *The Nation:* 31–40.

Varela, Mirta. (2005). *La televisión Criolla: Desde sus inicios hasta la llegada del hombre a la luna, 1951–1969.* Buenos Aires: EUDEBA.

Varela, Mirta and Alejandro Grimson. (1999). *Audiencias, cultura y poder: Estudios sobre la televisión.* Buenos Aires: EUDEBA.

Vascellaro, Jessica E., Elizabeth Holmes, and Sarah McBride. (2009, April 17). "Video Sites Duke it Out for Content." *Wall Street Journal.*

Venegas, Cristina. (2008). "Dreaming with Open Eyes: Latin American Media in the Digital Age." *The Oxford Handbook of Film and Media Studies.* Ed. Robert Kolker. New York: Oxford University Press, 447–83.

Verón, Eliseo. (2008, September 28). "Réquiem para una televisión difunta." *Perfil.*

Vilches, Lorenzo. (2009). *Meracdos globales, historias nacionales.* Barcelona: Gedisa.

Vincent, Norah. (2000, February 2–8). "Lear, Seinfeld, and the Dumbing Down of the Academy." *Village Voice.*

Vizeu, Alfredo. (2005). *O lado oculto do telejornalismo.* Florianópolis: Calandra.

Vizeu, Alfredo, ed. (2008). *A Sociedade do Telejornalismo.* Petrópolis: Vozes.

Vizeu, Alfredo, F. Porcello, and C. Ladeira Mota, eds. (2006). *Telejornalismo: A nova praça pública.* Florianópolis: Editora Insular.

Vogel, Kenneth P. (2009, April 12). "Avalanche! Agenda Fuels Ad Landslide." *Politico.com.*

Wallace, David Foster. (1997). *A Supposedly Fun Thing I'll Never Do Again.* New York: Little Brown and Company.

Wallerstein, Immanuel. (1989). "Culture as the Ideological Battleground of the Modern World-System." *Hitotsubashi Journal of Social Studies* 21, no. 1: 5–22.

Wandera, Gilbert. (2008, December 7). "Pay TV Battle Turns Hot." *Eastern Standard.*

Wanta, Wayne and Dawn Leggett. (1988). "'Hitting Paydirt': Capacity Theory and Sports Announcers' Use of Clichés." *Journal of Communication* 38, no. 4: 82–9.

Wasko, Janet. (1994). *Hollywood in the Information Age: Beyond the Silver Screen.* Cambridge: Polity Press.

Wasko, Janet. (2005a). "Introduction." *A Companion to Television.* Ed. Janet Wasko. Malden: Blackwell, 1–12.

Wasko, Janet, ed. (2005b). *A Companion to Television.* Malden: Blackwell.

Wasko, Janet, Vincent Mosco, and Manjunath Pendakur, eds. (1993). *Illuminating the Blindspots: Essays Honoring Dallas W. Smythe.* Norwood: Ablex.

Watson, Mary Ann. (2008). *Defining Visions: Television and the American Experience in the 20th Century*, 2nd edn. Malden: Blackwell.

Wayne, Mike, ed. (1998). *Dissident Voices: The Politics of Television and Cultural Change.* London: Pluto Press.

Wedell, George and Bryan Luckham. (2001). *Television at the Crossroads*. Houndmills: Palgrave.

Weinstein, David. (2004). *The Forgotten Network: DuMont and the Birth of American Television*. Philadelphia: Temple University Press.

Weiss, David. (2005). "Constructing the Queer 'I': Performativity, Citationality, and Desire in *Queer Eye for the Straight Guy*." *Popular Communication* 3, no. 2: 73–95.

Wells, Matt. (2003, July 14). "Channel Five Programming Stripped Bare of Pornography." *Guardian*.

Wenner, Lawrence A. (2004). "On the Ethics of Product Placement in Media Entertainment." *Journal of Promotion Management* 10, nos. 1–2: 101–33.

Wentz, Laurel. (2009, February 12). "Univision: YouTube's Most Pirated Broadcast TV Network." *AdvertisingAge*.

West, Patrick. (2008). "Abject Jurisdictions: *CSI: Miami*, Globalisation and the *Body Politic*." *Critical Studies in Television* 3, no. 1: 60–75.

Westerfelhaus, Robert and Celeste Lacroix. (2006). "Seeing "Straight" Through *Queer Eye*: Exposing the Strategic Rhetoric of Heteronormativity in a Mediated Ritual of Gay Rebellion." *Critical Studies in Media Communication* 23, no. 5: 426–44.

Whannel, Gary. (1985). "Television Spectacle and the Internationalization of Sport." *Journal of Communication Inquiry* 9, no. 2: 54–74.

Whannel, Gary. (1992). *Fields in Vision: Television Sport and Cultural Transformation*. London: Routledge.

"What Impact Does Broadband Have on TV Viewing?" (2008, December 23). *VideoNuze.com*.

Wheatley, Helen, ed. (2007). *Re-Viewing Television History*. London: IB Tauris.

White, E.B. (1997). *One Man's Meat*. Gardiner: Tilbury House.

Whiten, Jon. (2005, March/April). "'The World Little Noted': CBS Scandal Eclipses Missing WMDs." *Extra!*: 7.

Whittam Smith, Andreas. (2008, February 25). "Media Studies is no Preparation for Journalism." *Independent*.

Wieten, Jan, Graham Murdock, and Peter Dahlgren, eds. (2000). *Television Across Europe: A Comparative Introduction*. London: Sage Publications.

Williams, Raymond. (1966). *Communications*. Harmondsworth: Penguin.

Williams, Raymond. (1978). *Television: Technology and Cultural Form*. Glasgow: Fontana/Collins.

Williams, Raymond. (1983). *Keywords: A Vocabulary of Culture and Society*, rev. edn. New York: Oxford University Press.

Windschuttle, Keith. (2006, June 17). "Communication Breakdown." *Australian*.

Winocur, Rosalía. (2002). *Ciudadanos Mediáticos: La construcción de lo publico en la radio*. Barcelona: Editorial Gedisa.

Wolton, Dominique. (1990). *Éloge du grand public: Une théorie critique de la télévision*. Paris: Flammarion.

"Women's Favorites on TV." (2009, February 18). Center for Media Research.

Wong, Kokkeong. (2001). *Media and Culture in Singapore: A Theory of Controlled Commodification*. Cresskill: Hampton Press.

Wood, Helen. (2009). *Talking with Television: Women, Talk Shows and Modern Self-Reflexivity*. Urbana: University of Illinois Press.

Woodhead, Chris. (2009, March 8). "Dive for Cover if You See 'Studies': It Means Bogus." *Times*: 9.

"World Television Market." (2009, January 14). *IDATE NEWS* 452.

Writers Guild of America. (2008). *Who We Are: The Marketplace for Writing*.

Yang, Hyeseung, Srividya Ramasubramaniam, and Mary Beth Oliver. (2008). "Cultivation Effects on Quality of Life Indicators: Exploring the Effects of American Television Consumption on Feelings of Relative Deprivation in South Korea and India." *Journal of Broadcasting & Electronic Media* 52, no. 2: 247–67.

Yehya, Naief. (2008). "Herejía y extrañeza." *La Tempestad* 59: 68–9.

Young, Sally. (2008, December 17). "The Bad News." *Inside Story*.

Zhao, Yuezhi. (2008). *Communication in China: Political Economy, Power, and Conflict*. Lanham: Rowman & Littlefield.

Zogby International. (2004). *Impressions of America 2004: How Arabs View America, How Arabs Learn About America: A Six-Nation Survey Commissioned by the Arab American Institute*.

Zook, Kristal Brent. (1999). *Color by Fox: The Fox Network and the Revolution in Black Television*. New York: Oxford University Press.

INDEX